Forbes **ASAP**®

BIG ISSUES™

Forbes **ASAP** ®

BIG ISSUES ™

*The Examined Life
in the Digital Age*

FOREWORD BY PETER JENNINGS
FROM THE EDITORS OF *FORBES ASAP*

John Wiley & Sons, Inc.
New York · Chichester · Weinheim · Brisbane · Singapore · Toronto

Published by John Wiley & Sons, Inc.
Published simultaneously in Canada.

This publication is designed to provide accurate and authoritative information in regard to the subject matter covered. It is sold with the understanding that the publisher is not engaged in rendering professional services. If professional advice or other expert assistance is required, the services of a competent professional person should be sought.

Library of Congress Cataloging-in-Publication Data:

Forbes ASAP big issues : the examined life in the digital age / from the editors of Forbes ASAP ; foreword by Peter Jennings.
    p. cm.
   Includes bibliographical references and index.
   ISBN 0-471-41491-3 (cloth : alk. paper)
    1. Information society.   2. Information society—Forecasting.   3. Information superhighway.   I. Title: Big issues.   II. Forbes ASAP.

HM851 .F67 2001
303.48′33—dc21

                                                       2001026130

Printed in the United States of America
10 9   8   7   6   5   4   3   2

CONTENTS

FOREWORD

Peter Jennings

I WAS PACING at a safe distance from my computer the other day, trying to focus on what to say about such a unique body of work. I had reread many of the articles in the *Forbes ASAP Big Issue* series and was finding it hard to express what the digital revolution means to me: how enthusiastic I am, how defensive I am, and whether I am really able to cope with all that is happening.

As a journalist I am constantly dazzled by the speed with which I can reach out for information and amazed that often when I do, I lose valuable editing time for my daily news broadcast, because I inevitably venture off into Web site after Web site for the sheer joy of learning something I didn't know seconds before. I am an indiscriminate grazer, a trait that drives my more disciplined colleagues crazy.

I have tried to comprehend the new language of the digital revolution, but I throw up my hands when trying to wade through a piece on "efficiency enhancement in the supply-chain management." I know that I should be able to grasp the inner workings of modular and molecular corporations, but I haven't got the patience. And I am, like David Brooks, terrified that some technological breakthrough is going to make cell phone use possible during airplane flights.

I have struggled for years to overcome the psychological burden of being a high school dropout, but nothing has made me feel quite so ignorant as my inability to grasp the technical discussions of the technological titans who seem so at home with a language that is utterly foreign to me. My son is studying Greek. A woman I once tried to impress told me that had I studied Greek I would have found everything else, including her, less intimidating. Another lost opportunity.

So I sometimes think that the *Forbes ASAP Big Issue* series, which was created in early 1996, was designed specifically with me in mind. Mike Malone and Rich Karlgaard started with an idea—a passion, really. First they wrote down the names of all the people they admired most (I was not on the list) and wrote them letters asking how their lives had been affected by the digital revolution. After they had stared at the fax machine for a couple of weeks, wondering whether they were crazy, it finally sputtered to life, and they could hardly believe their eyes: Stephen Ambrose, Robert Conquest, Bill Gates, Andy Grove, John Keegan, Simon Schama, and on and on. All these people actually wanted to write something. And then the crowning touch: an acceptance from Tom Wolfe that was nearly thrown out with a pile of press releases. The resulting essay was the widely celebrated "Sorry, but Your Soul Just Died," one of Tom's few published works between *The Bonfire of the Vanities* and *A Man in Full*.

That first *Big Issue* was a smash. Certainly no one in the tech or business press had seen anything like it. I was one of many in the mainstream press who was intrigued. After all, here was a literary magazine (which actually made money) that had one after another thoughtful essay by a leading thinker or writer or historian or corporate CEO addressing powerful topics with which millions of us were grappling.

Like many of them I was aware that the brave new world of the Knowledge Age was precipitating a cultural crisis. Computer games were replacing reading. Anonymous chat rooms were replacing family and friendship. The Internet world was undermining public discourse.

And God knows we are anesthetizing ourselves with trivia. James Billington, the Librarian of Congress, suggested in *Civilization* magazine that the unifying fear among people who thought about this was that the digital revolution would ultimately lead to the dissolution of the American community.

The editors of the *Big Issues* thought about this, too. Among their most commendable qualities has been their refusal to be cheerleaders for the revolution. What you have here in this collection is a great conversation about the metaphysical subjects of Living in the Digital Age, Work, Time, Convergence, and Truth. The editors have taken a step back from the Internet evangelists and have encouraged real-life commentary. One essay after the other is not merely smart, but intelligent. No one has done a better job of putting Web euphoria into context. For the editors it must sometimes seem like trying to grasp mercury, but so is life. George Gilder reflects that the Web, as seen from space, is a swirling sphere of light. For some of us it is a swirling sphere of contradictions and confusions that often amount to digibabble.

In many ways, the *Big Issue* each year is the most eclectic magazine I know. It is provocative and exciting. I realize repeatedly how many times I have been obliged to think again about a premise or theory that I had either taken for granted, or, more likely, was ignorant of in the first place.

Gore Vidal wrote in the Work issue that while technology has made work so much easier for writers and journalists who want to stay up to date, the deep, complex issues are still deep and complex. The Time issue came along just as many of us were feeling overwhelmed and unable to cope with a world moving at a speed that millions of us had never imagined. I work today at a pace that I couldn't have imagined several years ago. I have less time to think than at any other point in my career.

That acceleration ultimately means I have less time to contemplate and plan projects that might make *World News Tonight* distinctive in a media universe with so many options. Michael Lewis writes that he can still remember when time was too abundant to seem valuable. No kidding!

I remember having the time as a foreign correspondent to know a country before writing a piece on what was happening there. Today the cable news reporter is hardly off the plane before the home office wants him to plug in and start talking. I don't envy him. The March of Time, as Ralph Nader writes here, has been replaced by the blitz of time. Regis McKenna hits the nail on the head when he says that we are trying so hard to keep up with the bombardment of new facts and new developments that we are cutting into our time to listen to the past, much less make a judicious reckoning of its significance. I lived for many years in the Middle East, where the truth had as many interpretations as there were borders and villages and families and sects. The issue titled "What is True?" proved again that the editors never shrink from scope. I laughed when I heard that Richard Ford had called in to say, sure, he'd write a piece, but what did the editors mean?

In the digital age nothing is more challenging for an editor than coming to grips with a question that is lingering at the corners of our minds, yet has not been fully verbalized. I recognize that the Net is a complex set of social arrangements on a global scale. I understand now that the Net, as Don Tapscott writes, is attaining ubiquity because of its mobility and functionality and general robustness. But of all the essays here, Tom Wolfe's "Digibabble, Fairy Dust, and the Human Ant Hill" is a classic reminder—emblematic of this book—that the mind is and always will be the last great, unconquerable frontier.

ACKNOWLEDGMENTS

WE ARE ESPECIALLY GRATEFUL to all the *Forbes ASAP* staffers—editors, researchers, art directors, fact checkers, production staff, interns, and proofreaders—who helped create, word by word and image by image, each of the five *Big Issues*. Special thanks go to *Forbes* Publisher and *ASAP* founder Rich Karlgaard and *ASAP* Editor Michael S. Malone for conjuring up the idea of the *Big Issue* six years ago, to Executive Editor Karen Southwick and Projects Editor Rodes Fishburne for realizing that the essays could be collected in this book, and to John Wiley & Sons' Senior Editor Matthew Holt for making it happen.

Suzie Amer
Martin Aronson
Geoffrey Baum
Richard Bischoff
Michael Boland
Sarah Bolles
Tony Brandt
Beth Brann
Natalie Cannestra
Edward Clendaniel
Donald Conway
Kip Crosby
Deborah Crowe
Patrick Dillon
Owen Edwards
Donnali Fifield

Rodes Fishburne
Alex Frankel
David H. Freedman
Andrew Freiburghouse
Ewa Gavrielov
George Gilder
Linda Byron Glucksman
Ted Gramkow
Mark Halper
Darren Hanshaw
Jake Harrington
Joanne Hoffman
Daneen Holman
Donna Hunter
Michelle Jeffers
Rich Karlgaard

Dustin Kehoe
Andy Kessler
Karina Kinik
Lisa Alcalay Klug
Jerry Knight
Mark Kuerschner
Scott Lajoie
Tony Lane
Laura A. Locke
Toni Logan
Catherine Lukas
Fred Luminoso
Michael S. Malone
John T. Maybury
Ann McAdam
Ollie McIntyre
Warren McPherson
John Micklewright
Tripp Mikich
Alex Millie
Ana Maria Miranda
Terry Nagel
Richard M. Owens
Peter Pallans
Shelley Pannill
Lee C. Patterson
Gregg Pernick

Eric Pfeiffer
Gary Andrew Poole
Virginia Postrel
Richard Rapaport
David Raymond
Jennifer Rodenbach
John Romeo
Lisa Rosenthal
Cynthia Rubin
Nancy Rutter
Chiori Santiago
Sarah Schafer
David Scheff
Evantheia Schibsted
Kimberly Shapiro
Pat Soberanis
Virginia Sorisio
Karen Southwick
Nancy Steele
Monica Suder
Gary Taubes
Robert Vallem
Leslie Weiss
Clint Willis
Marilyn Wills
Alan Yost
Zachariah Zimmerer

THE IMPLICATIONS OF
THE DIGITAL REVOLUTION

———◦◦◦———

Rodes Fishburne

THE IDEA BEGAN as a pipe dream—a real laugh between an ambitious magazine editor and a veteran freelance writer during late-night brainstorming sessions. It was 1996, and both men sensed that something cataclysmic was under way. Companies such as Intel and Microsoft were growing at unprecedented rates; all sorts of people were making vast fortunes; and the Internet was roaring into view. Technology suddenly seemed to be the American story: a new narrative to be scrutinized, studied, and even in some acute cases worshipped.

Bored by the constraints imposed by traditional business writing, Rich Karlgaard and Michael S. Malone, respectively past and current editors of *Forbes ASAP*, decided to treat the digital revolution as a *cultural* phenomenon, much as philosophy or evolution had been debated in 19th-century Parisian salons. They conceived an expansive, unlikely format: Why not ask the best writers and thinkers—the top authors, scientists, economists, politicians, and religious leaders—to contribute to a special annual issue of *Forbes ASAP*? Both men admired the epic Jubilee issues of *Esquire* magazine in the 1960s, where the likes of Arthur Miller and Emperor Hirohito discussed the issues of the day. In that spirit letters were duly drafted, inviting writers and experts such as Reynolds Price, Bill Gates, Mark Helprin, William F. Buckley, Steven Weinberg, and many others to contribute to an issue devoted to the big topic of the digital revolution.

Karlgaard and Malone figured that they would probably get responses from a prominent CEO or two, and then fill out the ranks by calling in favors from freelance writers. As for the great thinkers and writers—well, the only risk was postage stamps and the time spent crafting personalized letters.

To their friends, colleagues, and even wives, this latest brainstorm gone wild was still little more than a lark . . . right until the acceptances started coming in. Not only did top writers and thinkers want to contribute, but they had controversial and emotionally profound opinions on the new Digital Age as well. In the months that followed, the *Forbes ASAP* staff edited and arranged the essays into a single magazine that was to serve as the bellwether for the era.

But that was only part of the story. The *Big Issue* also became a publishing sensation, thanks in large part to a single essay. To this day, Karlgaard remembers working in his office on a Saturday when he heard the fax machine start whirring away in the next room. Fifty-six pages of double-spaced, typed manuscript poured forth. He recognized the ornate script on the cover sheet: Tom Wolfe. Karlgaard shouted out the news to George Gilder, who was also working that day. Wolfe had contributed an original manuscript for the first *Big Issue*. The resulting article, "Sorry, but Your Soul Just Died," was the most talked-about essay of the year.

The *Big Issue* became an instant institution. Quoted in newspapers, taught in college courses, and the model for books on similar big themes, Karlgaard and Malone's brainstorm had created a forum for ideas that, once arrived, seemed inevitable.

OWEN EDWARDS

Remembrance of Things Fast

OWEN EDWARDS *is a consulting editor for* Forbes ASAP, *a contributing writer for* GQ, *and the founding editor of* Parenting *magazine. He is currently working on his next book, a memoir about life in the Greek Isles.*

As SHE MOVED toward the end of a long life, my mother quietly embarked on a process of de-acquisition. Like the British Empire at the end of *its* long life, she gave away possessions that once had defined her, with an air (I sensed) of relief rather than regret. Things I once couldn't have imagined her parting with—her silver place settings, her Wedgwood china, her jewelry—were dispatched without, it seemed, a second thought. Mom was an equal opportunity giver. My brother and I got some of her treasures, but others went to the woman who cleaned her apartment, some to a niece and nephew so distant I couldn't remember her ever speaking about them. I don't think my mother considered these things as gifts given, but as problems disposed of. "Property is nuisance," said the mathematician Paul Erdos, and I'm sure, in her last year or two, Mother would have agreed. It was as if she had laid out an intercept vector, so that at the moment she and death converged there would be nothing left of her worldly goods but her wedding ring. With the exception of a few odds and ends she couldn't find takers for, she came very close.

When this process first started, or at least when it became apparent to me, I was upset by it. My mother had diminished mentally and physically as she aged, and I suppose I had begun to feel that her true essence somehow remained more in her things than in herself. What I failed to understand was that her "going out of business" giveaway was inseparably tied to the running down of her energy. Like a balloonist throwing ballast over the side, she retained just enough buoyancy to keep herself afloat till the end. Without intending to, my mother had converted naturally to a kind of Zen, striving toward what bodhisattvas call "the being of no being." With unsentimental determination, she contrived to put a perfect finis on the last act of her life, to dematerialize totally, until at last we were left with our memories of her, eighty-eight years' accumulation of photographs, a tiny gold band, and a small container of ashes labeled with the dreary neologism "cremains."

As a compulsive collector, I'm not sure I will ever behave as my mother did. But in the past few years, I've begun to understand her pleasure in the ritual of good riddance. Not too many years ago, my work as a writer was measured out in the palpable material of manuscripts—typed ink on paper, piled up piece by piece until the finished stack was tamped into a neat rectangle (this small act like a finalizing punctuation mark), put in an envelope, taken to the post office, and sent off like a small wrapped present to a magazine or publishing house. In the slow but steady accretion of visible work, I wasn't much different from a bricklayer or a tailor. Admittedly, writing didn't do much for muscle tone, and the sense of accomplishment latent in a couple dozen sheets of paper probably is on a lower order than that in a well-built wall or a hand-sewn suit. But a day's labor left similarly tangible evidence of work done.

The digital revolution has changed the nature of that evidence, and the sources of satisfaction. No more stacks of paper to be squared off with a gratifying thump. Now pages don't pile up, they scroll up and disappear. Files are no longer in plain sight on top of my desk (there to chide me for inattention); they are stored on my computer's hard disk. I still have a small pile of newspaper and magazine clips to be used as reference, but one of these days I'll buy a scanner so that these, too, will vanish from the analog world into the parallel digital universe. There are no envelopes to be sealed anymore, no ritual trips to the post office. All these homey signs of work done have been replaced by a small horizontal box on my monitor that slowly fills in from left to right as articles or chapters travel electronically from my computer to the computers of editors hundreds or thousands of miles away. In most cases, the first time I actually see my words on paper is when I see them in a magazine. Like my mother, but for different reasons and under very different circumstances, I have begun to approach the insubstantiality of a kind of Zen. Digital Zen.

Though the bricklayer in me ought to be dismayed by this, the writer (the more ironical of the two) is delighted. That the only substance of my work is whatever ideas it may contain, that those ideas flow from my head through wires directly to the people who pay for them, seems close to sublime—a frictionless process with nothing solid to slow it down, and little evidence left behind. From paper trail to vapor trail.

I feel lightened by this digital technology: agile, facile, fluid, fast as thought. With only the mildest qualm, I've bought into the fabulous future.

A price must be paid, however, for this lightness afoot. In my case, the cost of digital Zen's fluid speed is a certain loss of contact with my work. Not that I work any less hard. On the contrary, with the process of writing accelerated, I'm filling in the time saved not with quiet contemplation but with more work. Yet the abstraction of my electronic means seems to have caused a disconnect. All the former small acts of production—watching the stack of pages grow, neatening the pile, sealing the envelope, delivering it to the post office—had a way of reaffirming the bond between me and what I'd written, between the bricklayer and his walls. Now, the second that little box on my screen is filled in and the piece has flashed to its destination, I begin to forget what has been dispatched and race on to the next thing to do. There is a quicksilver quality to the once stately process that prevents anything from rubbing off and remaining with me.

As the fluidity of computer technology loosens mnemonic bonds, the insubstantiality of electronic media may be leading to a loss of awareness of reality. If a precomputer writer like me can respond with such pleasure to sloughing off the little chores of dealing with paper, envelopes, stamps, and so forth—chores that put the brakes on headlong, heedless progress—others will respond with a zeal that dismisses anything that doesn't run on light-speed rails. How easy it will be for generations in lifelong contact with digital fun, games, and work (in addition to their continual view of life through the odorless, untactile medium of television) to forget that at some point things still have to be made, that ore must be mined and ships sailed—that the muscle and sweat of hard physical labor precede and undergird the abstract dance that produces intellectual property.

We hardly need to list the consequences of a growing gap between a world where the physical can be entirely denied—where people can meet on the Internet without ever actually encountering each other—and the world where things really happen—dams burst, planes crash, wars break out, ships sink, and failure and frustration are the common currency. Is it the disjuncture between the virtual and actual worlds that causes grieving relatives, grousing reporters, and grandstanding politicians to demand that the bodies of the victims of an air disaster be retrieved *now*, while 120 feet under the sea, navy divers struggle against the inescapable reality of cold and pressure in order to find the dead and decomposing? The digital revolution can't be blamed for every missed connection between the virtual and the real, but it is likely that eventually the speed and ease of electronic work will cause more and more people to forsake—even forget—reality.

Speed kills, it's said, and in this case what it kills is memory. "There is a secret bond between slowness and memory, between speed and forgetting," writes Milan Kundera in the novel *Slowness.* "Consider this utterly commonplace situation: A man is walking down the street. At a certain moment, he tries to recall something, but the recollection escapes him. Automatically, he slows down. Meanwhile, a person who wants to forget a disagreeable incident he has just lived through starts unconsciously to speed up his pace, as if he were trying to distance himself from a thing still too close to him in time.

"In existential mathematics, that experience takes the form of two basic equations: the degree of slowness is directly proportional to the intensity of memory; the degree of speed is directly proportional to the intensity of forgetting."

Some years ago, I managed to spend a few hours a week rowing a single shell. Then, enabled by the tools of the information age to cram more productivity into fewer hours, I increased my working hours (to make more money) and decided that a rowing machine would let me burn calories without the inconvenience of straying too far from my computer. The result was efficient but, in the end, a bland simulation. Then, responding to a sense that all was not entirely well, I joined a rowing club with a boathouse on a lake not far from my house. Now I am on the water most mornings around seven, using a technology that has changed little since Thomas Eakins was painting scullers on the Schuylkill River a century ago. I don't burn any more calories than I do on my home machine, but I watch the gulls and pelicans land and take off, I deal with the wind and the mist, I feel how the long, narrow shell glides over the water when my strokes are good, and, if I make a clumsy mistake, there's always the chance I'll encounter the shocking reality of cold water.

Today, we hear politicians and sociologists warn of the coming division between digital haves and have-nots. I suspect this is simply another of the historic separations that inevitably follow close behind technological change—after all, half the world's population still doesn't have toilets, yet life goes on. The coming division that will really matter to many of us will be between those who have found a way to balance the yin of digital Zen and the yang of substantial reality, and those who haven't. The former will understand the power of the digital advantage, and also the consequences of forgetfulness and disassociation that wait in ambush for those possessed by speed. The latter will grow ever more enamored of disengagement—or resistant to reality with all its messiness and unpredictability—and will become a new kind of cloistered, misanthropic monk, socially maladroit, politically unconcerned. Digital adepts increasingly devoid of analog wisdom. People without memories.

The haves of cybersociety, even those who once knew the satisfaction of watching paper pile up or enjoyed the closure of a trip to the post office, will not reject the power the information age has given them. They're neither Luddites, addled romantics, nor fools. When it makes sense to be virtual, virtual is what they'll be. But they will find ways to reconnect with the substance of the physical world in order to put some friction back into life, to slow things down and give their dazzling speed and enviable fluidity a larger, rational context. Just as the Industrial Revolution spawned William Morris's hand-working Arts and Crafts movement, devoted to countering the effects of mass production, the digital revolution will create a New Reality Movement (for want of a better name), in which a tumble into icy water is always possible. Sanity will demand the slowness of actual things, the shock of surprises, and the natural resistance of physical acts. We may revel justifiably in our growing electronic ability to shed the weight of work as we knew it, but for our own well-being we must rediscover the means to memory.

MARK HELPRIN

—————>•◆•<—————

The Acceleration of Tranquility

MARK HELPRIN *is a contributing editor for the* Wall Street Journal *and a senior fellow at the Claremont Institute. His best-known novels are* Winter's Tale *and* A Soldier of the Great War.

H ISTORY IS IN MOTION, and those moving with it are so caught up that they cannot always see its broad outlines. Like soldiers in battle, they are concerned with objectives rather than principles. Who are these soldiers? They are you. And what are the principles? If you search the past, hindsight makes them easy to see, but in the brightness of the present they are almost invisible. Still, it is possible to catch a fleeting glimpse of them, even if only as alterations in contrast.

In that spirit, consider the two paradigms that follow, not as you would two spirited debaters but rather two paintings hanging at opposite ends of a gallery. You are in the middle, bathed in natural light, forced by history to judge their color and attraction.

I. August 2016, California

You are a director of a firm that supplies algorithms for the detection and restoration of damaged molecular memories in organic computation. Previously you specialized in the repair of cosmic ray degradation of atomic lattices in gallium arsenide nanorobotics, but the greater promise of organic replication and the lure of photon interlinking led you in a new direction.

You raised $2 billion, most of which was devoted to the purchase of computers and laser armature looms for the growth and manipulation of organic components. Though your entire company is housed in a single 40,000-square-foot facility and has only 90 employees, it records assets of $9 billion and annual revenue of $32 billion.

All transactions are accomplished through data links—licensing, sales, billing, remittances, collections, investments. A customer can make a purchase, receive your product, and pay you as fast as he can speak orders to his computer. As your product begins immediately to work for him, the money you've earned begins immediately to work for you, in, perhaps, Czech dormitory bonds that compound interest hourly.

You go to your headquarters mainly for picnics, and otherwise work at home, as does your wife, who is a partner in a law firm in Chicago, where she has never been. In her study and in yours are giant screens that produce three-dimensional images so vivid that they appear to be real. Your best friend has grown rich writing the software that serves as your secretary. The preparation of documents is done by voice in another program, and the secretary concentrates on planning, accounting, arranging your schedule, and screening what used to be called calls but what are now called apparitions.

You instruct the secretary to allow your wife's apparition to override all others. She is at a beach in Indonesia, where you will shortly join her. Recently, you and she have quarreled. In virtual sex, in which you both wear corneal lenses that create a perfect illusion of whomever you might want, she discovered that you were entertaining not a commercial prostitutional apparition but an old girlfriend. Hence her early departure for Indonesia.

But this is August, the season of vacations, and you and she are bound to make up. You are to take a one and one-half hour, suborbital flight to Indonesia, where you will spend several days at the beach in a primitive resort with no screens. Still, you have a backup of email despite a recent tightening of your rejection protocols and a new investment in automated reply software, the chief disadvantage of which is that, when in conversation with other automated reply software, it tends to get overly enthusiastic. You were dismayed lately when you discovered that it and another ARS were building a golf course in Zimbabwe, but there is software for controlling it, and software for controlling the software that controls this, and so on and so forth.

Though seventy-five messages remain, you must catch your plane, so you instruct your screen to send them to your notebook. You'll take levels one and two coded personal apparitions as well, in the air and even on the winding track that leads to the Indonesian resort.

As you wait in San Francisco International Airport (having floated there in the Willie Brown Memorial Blimp), you read in your notebook. There are no bookstores, and there are no books, but in the slim leather-bound portfolio is an uplink that gives you access to everything ever published or logged, and in any format. You can call for a dual-language text of Marcus Aurelius, or the latest paper in Malay on particle acceleration. Your reading can be interrupted by the appearance of a friend in your portfolio, a look at the actual weather in Djakarta, a film clip of Lyndon Johnson's inaugural, or, for that matter, anything, summoned by voice, available instantaneously, and billed to your central account.

"Go to my files," you might say as you sit in the airport, "and get me everything I've said in the last five years about Descartes. I made a remark with a metaphor about the law, coordinates, and virtual prisons. When you get it, put it on the screen in blue. Take a letter to Schultz and file a copy at home and with the office."

But as you issue, you must also receive, and it never stops. Though the screen of your portfolio is electronically textured to feel like paper, and is as buff or white as flax or cotton, you miss the days of faxes, when you could hold the paper in your hands and when things were a little slower, but you can't go back to them, you can't fall behind, you can't pass up an opportunity, and if you don't respond quickly at all times somebody else will beat you to it, even if you have no idea what *it* is.

The world flows at increasingly faster and faster speeds. You must match them. When you were a child, it was not quite that way. But your father and grandfather did not have the power to make things transparent, to be, instantaneously, here or there without constraint. They, unlike you, were the prisoners of mundane tasks. They wrote with pens, they did addition, they waited endlessly for things that come to you instantly, they had far less than do you, and they bowed to necessity, as you do not. You love the pace, the giddy, continual acceleration. Though what is new may not be beautiful, it is marvelously compelling, and your life is lived with the kind of excitement that your forebears knew only in battle and with the ease of which they could only dream.

II. August 1906, Lake Como, Italy

You are an English politician, a member of Parliament suffering patiently between cabinet posts, on holiday in Italy. In the two days it has taken to reach your destination, you have fallen completely out of touch, although you did manage to pick up a day-old Paris newspaper in Turin. The *Times* will be arriving a week late, as will occasional letters from your colleagues and your business agent. Your answers to most of their queries will arrive in London only slightly before you yourself return at the end of the month.

The letters you receive are in ecru and blue envelopes, with crests, stamps reminiscent of the Italian miniaturists, and, sometimes, varicolored wax seals over ribbon. Even before you read them, the sight of the penmanship gives away their authors and may be the cause for comfort, dread, amusement, curiosity, or disgust. And, as you read, following the idiosyncratic, expressive, and imprecise swells and dips like a sailor in a small boat on an agitated sea, the hand of your correspondent reinforces his thoughts, as do the caesuras rhythmically arrayed in conjunction with the need to dip the pen.

Some of your younger colleagues use fountain pens, and this you can detect in lines that do not thin before a pause only to fatten with a new load of ink. Now and then, a letter will arrive, typewritten. This you associate with the telegraph office, official documents, and things that lean in the direction of function far enough to exclude almost completely the presence of grace—not grace in the religious sense, but in the sense of that which is beautiful and balanced.

You will receive an average of one letter every two days, fifteen or sixteen in all, and will write slightly more than that. You are a very busy man for someone on holiday, and wish that you were not. Half the letters will be related to governance, the other half to family and friendship. An important letter, written by the prime minister eight days before its reception, will elicit from you a one-page response composed over a period of an hour and three-quarters and copied twice before it assumes final form, for revision and so you may have a record. You will mail it the next morning when you pass the post office during your walk. The prime minister will receive his answer, if he is in London, two weeks after his query. He will consider you prompt.

During your holiday you will climb hills, visit chapels, attend half a dozen formal dinners, and read many books, several thousand pages all told. If upon reading a classical history you come across a Greek phrase with an unfamiliar word you will have to wait until the library opens, walk there by the lakeside, and consult a Greek lexicon: one and one-half hours. Sitting in your small garden with its view of lake and mountains, you will make notes as you read, and some of these will be incorporated in your letters. Most will languish until your return to London. By the time you look at them in a new season, only a few will seem worthy, and the rest you will gratefully discard.

During August you will hear music seventeen times. Five times it will have been produced by actual musicians, twelve times by a needle tracing the grooves in a cylinder and echoing songs in extremely melancholy imperfection through a flowerlike horn. You will attend the theater once, in Italian, but you will spend many hours reading *Henry V* and *The Tempest* (which you read each summer), and several plays by George Bernard Shaw. In your mind's eye you will see the richest scenes and excitements known to man, and your dreams will echo what you've read, in colors like those of gemstones, but diamond-clear, and with accompaniment in sound as if from a symphony orchestra.

Your shoes are entirely of leather, your clothes cotton, silk, linen, and wool. You and your wife hired a rowboat and went to a distant outcropping of granite and pine. No one could be seen, so you stripped down to the cotton and swam in the cold fresh water. Her frock clung to her in a way that awoke in you extremely strong sexual desire (for someone your age), and though you made no mention of it in the bright sunlight on the ledge above the lake, later that night your memory of her rising from sparkling water into sparkling sunlight made you lively in a way that was much appreciated.

Indeed, your memory has been trained with lifelong diligence. You know tens of thousands of words in your own language, in Latin, Greek, French, and German. You are haunted by declensions, conjugations, rules, exceptions, and passages that linger many years after the fact. Calculations, too, built your character in that you were forced to work elaborate equations in painstaking and edifying sequences. As

in other things, in mathematics you were made to study not only concept but craft. And, yes, in your letter to the prime minister, you repeated—with honorable alteration—a remark you made some time
ago regarding Descartes. At first you could not remember it, but then
you did, because you had to.

Necessity you find to be your greatest ally, an anchor of stability, a
pier off of which, sometimes, you may dive. Discipline and memory
are strengths that in their exercise open up worlds. The lack of certain
things when you want them makes your desire keener and you better
rewarded when eventually you get them.

You cannot imagine a life without deprivations, and without the
compensatory power of the imagination, moving like a linnet with apparent industry and certain grace, to strengthen the spirit in the face
of want. Your son went out to India, and you have neither seen him
nor heard his voice for two years. Thus, you have learned once more
the perfection of letters, and when you see him again, worlds will have
turned, and for the best. It was like that when you were courting your
wife. Sometimes you did not see her for weeks or months. It sharpened your desire and deepened your love.

You have learned to enjoy the attribute of patience in itself, for it
slows time, honors tranquility, and lets you savor a world in which you
are clearly aware that your passage is but a brief candle.

I must confess that I am deeply predisposed in favor of the second
paradigm, and in my view the vast difference between the two is at-
tributable not to some inexplicable superiority of morals, custom, or
culture, but rather to facts and physics, two things that, in judging our
happiness, we tend to ignore in favor of an evaporative tangle of ab-
stractions.

Unlike machines, we are confined to an exceedingly narrow range
of operations. Though we may marvel at the apparent physical diversity of the human race, it is, given its billions of representatives, astonishingly homogeneous. Of these billions, only a handful rise above
seven feet. Not a one is or has been over nine feet. And the exceedingly low standard deviation in form is immense compared to that
which applies to function. There is no escape from the fact that after
a set exposure to radiation; absent a given number of minutes of oxygen; at, above, or below a particular temperature; or subject to a

specific G-force, we will expire. No one will ever run the mile in two minutes, crawl through a Cheerio, or memorize the *Encyclopaedia Britannica*.

Because of our physical constraints we require a specific environment and a harmony in elements that relate to us and of which we are often unaware. The Parthenon is a very pleasing building, and Mozart's Fifth Piano Concerto a very pleasing work, because each makes use of proportions, relations, and variations that go beyond subjective preference, education, and culture into the realm of universal appeal conditioned by universal human requirements and constraints.

A life lived with these understood, even if vaguely, will have the grace that a life lived unaware of them will not. When expanding one's powers, as we are in the midst of now doing by many orders of magnitude in the mastery of information, we must always be aware of our natural limitations, mortal requirements, and humane preferences.

For example, the Englishman at Lake Como, unlike his modern counterpart, is graciously limited in time and space. Because the prime minister is in London or at Biarritz, the prime minister cannot sit down with him and discuss. In fact, during his fictional stay, only one of his colleagues visited, and spent several hours on the terrace with him in the bright but cool sunshine. All others were kept away by the constraints of time and distance.

The man of '16, on the other hand, is no longer separated from anyone. Any of his acquaintances may step into his study at will—possibly twenty, thirty, forty, or fifty a day. If not constantly interrupted, he is at least continually subject to interruption, and thus the threshold of what is urgent drops commensurately. No matter how urgent or pressing a matter, the prime minister *cannot* sit down with the tranquil politician. No matter how petty a matter, a coworker *can* appear to the man of '16 . . . in a trice. Screening devices or not, the modern paradigm is one of time filled to the brim. Potential has always been the overlord of will, and the man of the first paradigm finds himself distracted and drawn in different directions a hundred times a day, whereas the British statesman is prodded from without only once or twice.

Were we gods, we might be able to live well without rest and contemplation, but we are not and we cannot. Whereas our physical capacities are limited, those of the machine are virtually unlimited. As the capabilities of the machine are extended, we can use it—we imagine—to supplement our own in ways that will not strain our humanity. Had we no appetite or sin, this might be true, but our desires tend to lead us to excess, and as the digital revolution has quickly progressed, we have not had time to develop the protocols, manners, discipline, and ethics adequate for protecting us from our newly augmented powers.

The history of this century has been, as much as anything else, the process of encoding information: at first analog, in photographic emulsions, physical and magnetic patterns in needle grooves or on tapes, waves in packets blurted into the atmosphere, or in the action of X-rays recording paths of varying difficulty through tissues of various densities on plates of constant sensitivity. With binary coding, electrons as messengers, and the hard-fought mathematical adaptation necessary for control, we can now do almost everything with information. We may, for example, look through billions of pages in an instant, or process and match data fast enough so that a cruise missile can make a "mental" picture of the terrain it overflies at least as impressive as that of an eagle.

And because potential has always been the overlord of will, and as the means of conveyance hunger for denser floods of data, words have been gradually displaced by images. The capacious, swelling streams of information have brought little change in quality and vast overflows of quantity. In this they are comparable to the ornamental explosions of the baroque, when a corresponding richness of resource found its outlet mainly in decorating the leaner body of a previous age.

All the king's horses and all the king's men of multimedia cannot improve upon a single line of Yeats. One does not need transistors, clean alternating current, spring-loaded keys, and ten-million-hour "programs" for writing a note or a love letter—and yet this is how we are beginning to write notes and love letters, going even to the extreme of doing so on complicated electronic pads that tediously strain to imitate a sheet of paper and fail for want of simplicity.

If by now you think that I am decrying the digital revolution, that I am a sort of Luddite Percy Dovetonsils who would recommend for you and your children the cold water, wood fires, and Latin declensions of my brick-and-iron childhood, you had better think again. For

I understand and have always understood that the heart of Western civilization is not the abdication of powers but rather meeting the challenge of their use. And, of course, it would take a person of less than doltish imagination not to be attracted by the wonders and aware of the benefits of all this.

The British statesman of the second paradigm might well have lost a son or daughter to a disease that could have been detected early and with precision by computerized tomography or any of the other digitally dependent diagnostic techniques of modern medicine. The *Titanic*, six years in the future, might not have gone down—with him aboard, perhaps—had real-time thermal maps of the North Atlantic been available to its captain. And so on: you know the litany if you have read an IBM annual report.

The impossibility of abdication is also due to the necessity of racing with the genie after it has exited the bottle. Although antediluvian nuclear protestors have not, apparently, even a clue, they are on the wrong track. Nuclear weapons are now small enough, reliable enough, simulable enough, and widespread enough to be a rather mundane constant in calculations of the military balance. The guaranteed action and volatility is in command, control, communications, intelligence, and guidance. Digitally dependent advances will enable submunitions scattered in great numbers over a future battlefield to hide, wait, seek, fight, and maneuver. For example, rather than a platoon of tank-killing infantry, a flight of submunitions will someday be dropped or fly with little detection very far behind enemy lines, where it will hide in the treetops or the brush and await patiently for as long as required the approach of an appropriate enemy target, such as a tank, which it will then dutifully pursue, engage, and destroy, its reflexes as fast as light.

With the passage of each day, a first nuclear strike becomes more and more feasible. The possibility of real-time terminal guidance as a gift from satellites to maneuverable reentry vehicles makes any kind of mobile deterrent just a temporary expedient. Even submarines, nuclear stability's ace in the hole, will no longer be secure bastions for nuclear weapons, as thermal and radar imaging from satellites picks up surface perturbations upwelling from their undersea tracks, and as the panoply of antisubmarine warfare is refined, empowered, sensitized, and mounted on ballistic missiles that will be able to reach any area of ocean within minutes.

It is possible that in some war of the not-so-distant future a combatant will electronically seize control of enemy command structures and direct his opponent's arsenal onto his opponent. Eventually, all battles will be entirely computational. The "arms competition" of this sort has already begun. To step out of it at this point would be to lose it, and, with it, everything else.

The attraction is strong, the need is real, the marvels truly marvelous, and there is no going back. The speed with which all is taking place is almost a self-organizing principle. Like many changes in history, it seems to have its own internal logic, and it mainly pulls us after it. Why then do we need an ethos, a set of principles, and an etiquette specifically fashioned for the rest of this revolution that will (I predict) follow with stunning force the mere prologue through which we are now living?

Of course, one always needs ethics, principles, and etiquette, but now more than ever do we need them as we leave the age of brick and iron. For the age of brick and iron, shock as it might have been to Wordsworth, was friendlier to mankind than is the digital age, more appropriate to the natural pace set by the beating of the human heart, more apprehensible in texture to the hand, better suited in color to the eye, and, in view of human frailty, more forgiving in its inertial stillness.

Put quite simply, the life of the British statesman was superior because he was allowed rest and reflection, his contemplation could seek its own level, and his tranquility was unaccelerated. While he was in his time a member of a privileged class unburdened by many practical necessities, today most Americans have similar resources and freedoms, and yet they, like their contemporaries in even the most exalted positions, have chosen a different standard, closer to that of the first paradigm.

The life of the exemplary statesman, then dependent upon a large staff of underpaid servants, and children working in mines and mills (if not in Lancashire, then certainly in India), is now available to almost anyone. Even if in one's working hours one does not sit in the cabinet room at No. 10 Downing Street, one can have a quiet refuge, dignified dress, paper, a fountain pen, books, postage, Mozart with astonishing fidelity and ease, an excellent diet, much time to one's self, the opportunity to travel, a few nice pieces of furniture and decoration, medical care far beyond what the British statesman might have dreamed of, and, yes, a single-malt scotch in a crystal glass, for less than the average middle-class income. If you think not, then add up the prices and see how it is that people with a strong sense of what they want, need, and do not require can live like kings of a sort if they exhibit the appropriate discipline and self-restraint.

Requisite, I believe, for correcting the first paradigm until it approximates the second, and bringing to the second (without jeopardizing it) the excitements and benefits of the first, are the discipline, values, and clarity of vision that tend to flourish as we grapple with necessity and to disappear when by our ingenuity we float free of it.

The law itself can be mobilized to protect the privacy and dignity of the individual according to the original constitutional standard of the founders and what they might expect. Even now, that standard has been violated enough to make inroads on enlightened democracy, which depends first and foremost upon the sanctity of individual rights. As if they could foresee the unforeseeable, the founders laid down principles that have served to prevent the transformation of individual to manipulable quantity, of citizen to subject. It does not matter what convenience is sacrificed in pursuit of this. Convenience is, finally, nothing, and even destructive. The standard must be restored, for it is slipping too fast. Bluntly, there are practices and procedures that legislation must end, and databases now extant that it must destroy, in a deliberate and protective step back. Revolutions and revolutionaries tear down walls. Though some walls are an affront to human dignity, others protect it. I do not want my life history in the hands of either Craig Livingstone or Walt Disney, thank you very much.

Quite apart from the reach of the law is the voluntary reformation of educational practices. Is the reader aware of the immense proportion of this country's academic energies devoted to the study of off-the-shelf software? Terrified lest their children be computer illiterate, lemming parents have pushed the schools into a computer frenzy in which students spend years learning to use Windows and WordPerfect. This is much like *Sesame Street,* which, instead of waiting until a child is five and teaching him to count in an afternoon, devotes thousands of hours drumming it into him during his underdeveloped infancy. But while numbers will remain the same, fifth-graders will, when they get to graduate school, have no contact with Windows 95. The "teaching" of computer in the schools may be likened to a business academy in the 1920s founded for the purpose of teaching the telephone: "When you hear the bell, pick up the receiver, place it thusly near your face, and say 'Hello?'"

Basic computer literacy is a self-taught subject requiring no more than a week. Ordinary literacy, however, requires twenty years or more, and that is only a beginning. And yet the schools are making of these two—unrelated—things a vast and embarrassing spoonerism. In the schools computers should be tools for the study of other subjects, not a subject in themselves. The masters of the digital world will be, not today's students who will have spent their high school years learning Lotus 1-2-3, but those who will guide the future of computation at the molecular and atomic levels where they will find it when they are adults, having devoted hard study to physics, chemistry, and mathematics.

In the same vein, but with almost biblical implications, is the necessity of making certain distinctions. Most multimedia is appalling for several reasons. It endeavors to do the integrative work that used to be the province of the intellect, and that, if it is not in fact accomplished by the intellect, is of absolutely no value. It fails to distinguish between entertainment and education, style and substance, image and fact. It integrates promiscuously, blurring in the addled minds that it addles the differences between things that are different. It removes as far as it possibly can the element of labor from learning, which is comparable, in my view, to making a world without gravity, drinking a milk shake without milk, or living in an iron lung.

Whenever man opens a new window of power he imagines that he can do without the careful separations, distinctions, and determinations mandated by the facts of his existence and his mortal limitations. And whenever he does this he suffers a terrible degradation that casts him back even as he imagines himself hurtling forward.

Put simply, I want the *O.E.D.* on my computer, I want everything in the Library of Congress, I want great search engines, fuzzy logic, and programs that do statistical analysis, but I do not want multiple-choice television programs, and neither should you, for the good of us all. I'm not sure if I want email, but I'm certain that I do not want my contact with my fellow man to proceed mainly through his imagination—no matter how precise—in the fluorescence behind a glass plate. An example I might cite is that if you sail you really need wind and water: the idea and depiction of them are not sufficient. So with human presence: reality and actuality have their attractions and advantages.

In regard to this—the question of man and his image—whereas the Englishman has the exquisite memory of his wife emerging in wet cotton from the cold water of the lake into the Alpine sunshine, and whereas his relations with her must be based on subtlety and restraint, the man of '16 on his way to Indonesia will be able to graft by virtual reality any image he pleases onto the tactile base of his wife's body. This and its variants have been in the dreams of mankind at least since Leda, and Pygmalion, and sex is undoubtedly responsible for much of the momentum of virtual reality.

Many varieties of sensual manipulation will come to pass, and will be promoted as ways to refresh and save marriage, but they will, if they are embraced, entirely destroy marriage. The saving graces and fragile institutions of our humanity depend upon our humanity itself, which in turn depends absolutely upon the rejection and discipline of many of our appetites. We have many a resolution that separates us from the other animals, many a custom, practice, and taboo, and if we do away with these in the pursuit of power or the imitation of time-and-space-flouting divinity, we will become a portion for foxes.

The revolution that you have made is indeed wonderful, powerful, and great, and it has hardly begun. But you have not brought to it the discipline, the anticipation, or the clarity of vision that it, like any vast augmentation in the potential of humankind, demands. You have been too enthusiastic in your welcome of it, and not wary enough. Some of you have become arrogant and careless, and, quite frankly, too many of you at the forefront of this revolution lack any guiding principles whatsoever or even the urge to seek them out. In this, of course, you are not alone. Nor are you the first. But you must. You must fit this revolution to the needs and limitations of man, with his delicacy, dignity, and mortality always in mind. Having accelerated tranquility, you must now find a way to slow it down.

AL GOLDSTEIN

—=≫·◆·≪=—

Cybersex Leaves Me Limp

AL GOLDSTEIN *is best known as the founder and publisher of* Screw *magazine, which he describes as "the most controversial, irreverent pastiche of satire and sex ever placed on newsprint."*

S OMEWHERE IN THE WILDS outside of Las Vegas, they are laying plans for the world's first cyberbrothel. I've seen the type of QuickTime VR effects the place will use. They're like holograms, in that you can view them from all angles. They're like holograms, only they take off their clothes.

A woman I know, "a niece who's not related," as Oscar Levant used to say, thinks this cyberdello is a pretty good idea. She's working at a cathouse outside of Carson City now, but she told me she wants to work at the cyberbrothel just as soon as it's a virtual reality.

"It'll save the wear and tear," she said of her new dream job.

I'm not sure she has a firm grasp of the concept. For one thing, the "work" there will be pretty much a one-shot deal. They'll digitize her voluptuous images, and then she'll be available to anyone who has sweaty palms and the price of admission. I doubt if she'll get royalties.

For another thing, I wonder if the visionary geniuses behind this new venture will want to hire her. She has something of the air of the trailer park about her, and all the bulges and creases attendant upon a woman of thirty-plus years. In the freeze-dried realms of cybertopia, only hard-bodies need apply.

I've just hit sixty, gone gray and gone to Florida, but I've spent a lifetime in the world of commercial sex. I should have known it would come to this. I've watched as the human urge for zipless sex has played itself out in endless variations. A cyberbrothel may be the end of the line.

I stood by and watched when, way back in the seventies, the first VCR machines hit the market. They were clumsy and cost a grand. Who bought them? The raincoat crowd. The startup capital for today's video-store-on-every-corner reality was provided by the hordes of the horny. I wonder if Wayne Huizenga, the former Blockbuster Video guy who would not deign to stock adult titles, knows that if it weren't for the perverts out there, he might still be back where he started, hauling garbage.

As the video revolution unfolded, I stood by and watched as the adult theaters of my go-go years went dark, one by one. Their denizens were all too willing to abandon the embarrassments of the communal porn experience for the private pleasures of living room or den. Times Square missed a step on its hustling gait, on its way to becoming the Mickey Mouse real estate boondoggle of the present day.

I stood by and watched when the phone sex bandwagon careened through the world of adult entertainment. Once again, biology subsidized technology. There was a long stretch of time when the New York telephone monopoly was unable to convince public utility commissioners to let it hike pay-phone rates from a dime to twenty-five cents, primarily because the phone company could make so much coin off phone sex.

Now I'm in the bleachers for the cyberrevolution (I own several computers, but they function mainly as night-lights). I don't see much immediate effect on the old-fashioned, outmoded world of my commercial sex newspaper. My ad pages are holding steady. New York is still Fun City.

If I have any reservations about the brave new world of cybersex, they don't change my strong feelings against censorship of any sort. Government interference with freedom of expression is always wrongheaded and, given the lure of the taboo, usually backfires.

Censors like virtue-man William Bennett and Donna Rice Hughes (that's right—Gary Hart's old lap girl, who has now made it her mission to de-sex the Internet) are busy trying to close the barn door after the horse is off galloping down the road toward the next county.

The amazing wealth of sexual material on the Net is a tribute to human libido, which has all the subtlety of a juggernaut. As for the extremes of this realm—virtual snuff stuff and kiddie porn—I'm bothered by it, but I think I'll let the legions of eager bluenoses attempt to deal with it. They don't need my help.

But I would like to interject a few observations about the bloodlessness of it all. Cyberotica has brought out the cerebral side of sexuality, which up to now has lain unexploited in the human psyche. It's as if we always had this sexual inclination within us, and cybersex allowed it to flower.

The Internet is the ultimate realm of mind-sex. The connection is mind to mind, not body to body. VCRs to phones to computers—the air is getting rarer by the minute.

What strikes me most about technology is how clean it is. It's so antiseptic it squeaks. There is none of the funky-mucky-nasty element of human experience, and as a big fan of that element, I miss it. "Is sex dirty?" asks Woody Allen. "Only if it's done right."

Computers can't do sex right.

I also think that a lot of the cyberaction out there is concerned not with orgasm but with something else—with the thrill of finding sex, trafficking in it, sharing it around the electronic campfire. A lot of the action is in offices, with the boys trading their latest, hottest downloads as if they were baseball cards. The male thrill of the hunt has been severely curtailed in these PC times, but it's still alive on the Net.

I know an animator who has built himself a great search engine, which he uses to browse all the sex-oriented Usenet groups (there are a lot of them). He's got it programmed to download any binary picture it finds. He unleashes the sucker and then heads out for a cappuccino. When he comes back in a couple of hours, he has four or five hundred files waiting for him.

But he doesn't look at them right away. He burns them all onto a CD-ROM, which he then shares with his office mates. This is trophy hunting updated for a new age.

If by "real" we mean visceral, then the reality of sex has been receding from us like the tide of an ocean. People are retreating to their complicated caves. Technology has replaced technique.

It's the end of the world, at least as I know it, as I experienced it in those darkened Times Square porn theaters lo these many years ago. I don't know, and don't want to judge, finally, if what is replacing it is a good thing or a bad thing. So far, cybersex is cybercipher to me.

But as the lady said, it saves the wear and tear.

PAUL ROMER

———✦———

In the Beginning Was the Transistor

PAUL ROMER, *a leading proponent of new growth theory, is one of America's leading economic thinkers. He is a professor at the Graduate School of Business at Stanford University and a senior fellow at the Hoover Institution.*

EVERY CULTURE DEVELOPS its own creation myth. The myth for Silicon Valley starts with the discovery of the transistor. It unfolds according to the irresistible logic of Moore's Law: The size and cost of a transistor are cut in half every eighteen to twenty-four months. Like all myths, this one tells a simple story: "Before transistors, there were few computers. After the transistor was invented, computer power grew rapidly, transforming our lives."

Myths capture elements of truth, but they make sense of events only by hiding many important details. There is more to the computer revolution than the development of smaller and cheaper transistors. For example, why has hard-drive storage capacity increased so rapidly when no transistors appear on the surface of the disk? Forecasts about the long-run effects of the digital revolution hinge on the answer to this question.

The myth correctly identifies the discovery of transistors as the seminal event in the digital revolution. Charles Babbage worked out the basic principles for a general-purpose computer in the 1840s. In the century following Babbage's discovery, people made almost no progress in building a working model. Since the discovery of the transistor, however, computer power has grown exponentially. The contrast could hardly be sharper.

So it's no exaggeration to say that the discovery of the transistor and its subsequent development set the pace for the digital revolution. The myth, however, suggests that the transistor's progress sufficiently explains growth in computing power. This is very misleading. Many supporting technologies needed to be developed to make a working computer. Some of these—magnetic disk drives, fiber-optic data networks, graphical user interfaces—exploited very different technological principles from the ones behind the transistor.

Nevertheless, most commentators focus their story on the transistor, allowing them to create a myth in technological determinism. An innovative new production process is serendipitously discovered, eventually evolving along a predetermined technological trajectory. The emergence of the technology is then used to explain coinciding changes in social, political, and economic life. Thus one reads that the steam engine caused the Industrial Revolution and society's division into workers and capitalists. Now, we hear that the transistor is causing the digital revolution, globalization, and the rise of the knowledge-based economy.

In these accounts, however, the causal arrows run only one way. Once an important new technology is invented, it develops according to its own logic, independent of surrounding events.

As individuals, we often feel powerless to affect the course of technological change. Technological determinism, therefore, appeals to our intuition. When studying markets, in contrast, intuition offers little guidance. People generally believe that an increase in the price of a basic commodity, such as milk, has little effect on the quantity purchased individually. Nevertheless, the evidence is clear. In the aggregate, when price increases, quantity purchased decreases. Incentives have subtle but pervasive effects on human behavior, effects that we may fail to see or understand.

Similarly, when the profit from developing a new type of technology increases, people will respond by developing the technology more rapidly. Example: Scientists understood the principles behind magnetic data storage long before the transistor, but in the early 1900s there was little demand. With the advent of the transistor and subsequent development of the central processing unit (CPU), demand for permanent data storage surged ahead, leading to innovations in this area. Instead of using plastic tape, engineers put the magnetic medium on a moving surface, first on the outside of a cylinder, then on the surface of a disk. Prior to the 1950s, innovations such as these were technologically feasible, but the lack of incentives limited their development.

As the example of hard-disk storage already suggests, cheaper transistors will continue to encourage innovation in complementary technologies. Improvements in one area will raise our impatience with bottlenecks that prevent us from enjoying technological advances in another. Fortunes will be made by people who remove these bottlenecks. Currently, cheaper transistors are the most important force inducing technological change in related fields. As breakthroughs occur, a different engine of growth could evolve. For instance, cheaper transistors have encouraged broadband graphics applications, which in turn have created users impatient with the slow speed of data transmission. As a result, communications technologies are now poised for a big increase in performance.

Forecasts about the digital revolution's future depend on the potential for induced innovation. Sometime in the next two decades, physical barriers will limit our ability to make transistors any smaller. If the determinists are correct, nothing can be done, except to wait for a new source of technological change. If economists are right—if incentives do matter—the digital revolution will continue to spur innovation long after the death of Moore's Law.

Researchers respond not just to rewards, but also to costs. This creates another channel through which digital information technology will encourage technological change. Our physical world presents us with a relatively small number of building blocks—the elements of the periodic table—that can be arranged in an inconceivably large number of ways. Search costs limit our discovery of valuable new arrangements. Over time, we have found some useful combinations. Mix iron and carbon together with small amounts of manganese, chromium, nickel, molybdenum, copper, tungsten, cobalt, or silicon, and you can produce a range of different steel alloys. Arrange silicon, some impurities, and some metals in just the right way, and you get a microprocessor.

But nature shows us that we have a long way to go. By pure trial and error, evolution found a way to mix carbon, oxygen, hydrogen, and a few other elements into the seed for a tree. Think of this seed as the software and hardware for building a solar-powered factory. It sucks raw materials out of the ground and air. Depending on the software coded into its DNA, the tree will convert these raw materials into construction material or fruit. In comparison with the tree, existing software-controlled manufacturing systems don't seem very sophisticated.

Of course, the vast majority of possible arrangements lead to muck. The key to technological change and economic growth is to sort quickly and inexpensively through the possibilities to find valuable formulas.

Fundamentally, this search is an information-processing activity. We can start with established bodies of scientific knowledge and predetermine an arrangement that will do something valuable. Alternatively, we can create many different arrangements and try them out, looking for the ones that are valuable. In the pharmaceutical industry, these techniques are labeled rational design and mass screening. Most search processes involve some combination of the two. Chip design, for example, involves extensive design work in the initial stages and many rounds of trial-and-error screening as the chip moves into production.

From the beginning, everyone expected that computers would aid the process of rational design. For products ranging from airliners to power tools, computer design and simulation methodologies have already reduced product cycles and yielded better products. Surprisingly, computer-automated systems are also making screening more efficient. Using methods such as combinatorial chemistry and automated machinery, we can synthesize and screen large numbers of different compounds quickly and inexpensively.

So even if the rate of technological progress in the computer industry itself comes to a stop, the digital revolution will leave us with valuable information-processing tools for the future. Because searching will be cheaper, market incentives will cause us to search more. Technological change and economic growth will therefore be more rapid.

Myths may be comforting, but science is exciting. According to the myth of determinists, the digital revolution has been one long ride down a technological trajectory leading to smaller transistors. They suggest that we were lucky to stumble onto it. More accurately, the long sweep of human history shows that the more we learned and discovered, the better we got at learning and discovering.

We have had more change and growth in the last one hundred years than in the previous nine hundred. New methods of information processing—spoken language, writing, and printing with movable type—were pivotal developments in the acceleration of growth in knowledge and standards of living. There is every reason to hope that the digital revolution will have this same effect, making growth and technological change in the next century even more impressive than it has been in this one.

Of course, humans could make a mess of things. The Chinese had cast iron fifteen centuries before Westerners did and movable type four hundred years before Gutenberg. Nevertheless, the political and social system in China eventually stifled the incentives for additional discovery, and progress there virtually came to a halt. It is always possible that the same thing could happen for the human race as a whole. Technological determinists would then tell us that the technology did it to us. In truth, for progress to come to an end, we will have to do it to ourselves.

JOE QUEENAN

———◆———

How I Was Flamed by Serb Heat and Survived

J OE Q UEENAN *is a contributing editor for* GQ *and* Movieline. *He is the author of* My Goodness: A Cynic's Shortlived Search for Sainthood *and* Confessions of a Cineplex Heckler: Celluloid Tirades and Escapades.

B ACK IN M AY, I spent three days writing an online novel for Mr. Showbiz, a service launched in 1995 by Microsoft cofounder Paul Allen. *Serb Heat* dealt with a bloodthirsty Bosnian Serb militiaman who reads a *New York Times* article on his laptop and finds out that he has been insulted by a journalist who had a frightening encounter with him several months earlier. Tired of slaughtering innocent women and children, he grabs the next flight to the United States, kills the journalist, then sets out to polish off the only other person who can link him with the crime: a pathetic old folksinger named Ramblin' Pete Maneshewitz.

Serb Heat consisted of twenty-two chapters, each of which was electronically filed as soon as I finished it. My editors at Mr. Showbiz would quickly clean up any spelling mistakes or typos, then post it on the Net, where anyone on the planet could read it. Readers could then send me email telling me precisely what they thought of the work in progress.

For me, this interactive component was by far the most fascinating, yet frightening, feature of what had started out as a good-natured publicity stunt. Traditionally, when you write nasty, hopelessly unfair, generally mean-spirited material—the kind that I write—there is a long gap between the moment the material is actually written and the moment the people you are making fun of get to tell you how much they hate you. In the case of a national magazine, months can go by between the appearance of your article and the publication of the angry letters to the editor by people claiming that they were maligned, libeled, or misquoted.

Even with a newspaper, there is at least a gap of a few days between the publication of the offensive material and the outraged protests of the massacred innocents. Moreover, unless the newspaper or magazine physically forwards the angry letters to the writer, he can blissfully go about his business, confident that only one or two people hated his article, because only one or two angry letters were selected for publication. In fact, there may be thousands of people out there who think he is a scoundrel, an idiot, a leftist, or a tool of Satan. But he'd rather not know.

The Net and, most particularly, email have changed all that. Scant minutes after I had posted the first chapter of *Serb Heat,* which introduced Ratko Krudzik and his murderous comrades, I began to receive hate mail from wronged Serbs all over the world. One man in Mississippi threatened a lawsuit. Another pilloried Mr. Showbiz for publishing "hate literature." A third said that I would never dare write about Africans, Americans, or Irish Catholics the way I had written about his beloved Central European compatriots. A fourth called me a Nazi—a personal first. Though some of the electronic correspondence was supportive, most was not. The vast majority of people who sent emails thought I was the scum of the earth.

Whether or not I am the scum of the earth is a point open to endless discussion. If my wife knew how to compose email, I would have strongly suspected her of being the author of some of the more abusive missives. But my putative scumminess need not concern us here. What interests us here is how I reacted to this electronic onslaught of outrage. Did I do what courageous novelists have done down through the course of history and ignore this torrent of deprecation, confident that I held a loftier moral footing than my correspondents, and thus have the verdict of history on my side? Or did I cave in to the pressure?

I caved. By the time I got around to writing the final chapters, the emails were becoming so nasty, so personal, and so threatening that I decided to turn Ratko Krudzik, a lion of Serbia, into one Tom Burke, Canada's most elusive hit man—and a master of disguise. I did this because I knew that Canadians are the one nationality on the face of the earth that you can make fun of with absolute impunity.

What did I learn from my experience writing an online, inadvertently interactive novel? What I learned is that our new communications technologies, far from making us freer and more courageous, have a terrifying capacity to turn us all into lily-livered mushmouths. Without the interactive element provided by the Net, I would certainly have pulled no punches on the rapacious Bosnian Serbs. But cowed as I was by the volume and ferocity of the email reaching me while I was writing the book, I took the easy way out. Had Salman Rushdie composed his controversial novel *The Satanic Verses* online, he probably would have had the same experience, and probably could have saved himself a lot of trouble by making all the bad guys Canadians the first time a homicidal email reached his desk.

Someone recently asked me if my experiences online had persuaded me that new forms of humor were being generated by our new technologies. The answer is an emphatic *yes*. Anyone planning to write online humor with even the slightest tinge of ethnic satire in the near future had better be prepared for an immediate, massive, and ferocious counterattack by the ethnic group he has selected as his target. This being the case, I think we're going to be seeing an awful lot of humor in the next few years where the butt of the joke is a Canadian.

I don't think we are heading into a great age of comedy.

STEVEN WEINBERG

At Last—What Sort of World Is This?

Winner of a 1979 Nobel Prize in physics, STEVEN WEINBERG *is a theoretical physicist and a professor at the University of Texas at Austin. He is the author of more than 275 scientific articles and eight books, the latest of which is* The Quantum Theory of Fields, Volume III: Supersymmetry.

IT IS POSSIBLE that some readers of this magazine may live to see the end of a historic intellectual search. Philosophers and scientists have dreamed of a unified view of all nature since the scientific revolution of the seventeenth century. Sir Isaac Newton imagined that this unified theory would describe a number of fundamental forces, such as the force of gravitation, that act on particles of matter and produce all the phenomena of heat, light, and chemistry.

Today we have a somewhat more sophisticated theory known as the standard model. Together with general relativity, Einstein's theory of gravitation, it accounts in principle for all the phenomena that Newton hoped to explain. The standard model and general relativity are not the final answer; they have several features that seem quite arbitrary. Moreover, gravitation and the other forces they describe are not unified in a coherent way.

The hope of elementary particle physicists today is to take the next step—and eventually the final step—toward finding a deeper set of physical laws that explain both the standard model and general relativity in a way that is simple, unified, and altogether persuasive. No one can say that this will happen soon, but there is a growing sense that the answer is within our grasp.

This is not the only kind of important science, or even the only kind of important physics. Most scientific research is motivated by practical needs, or by a fascination with strange phenomena, or by our natural wish to know more about ourselves. As I explain in my book *Dreams of a Final Theory,* elementary particle physics is different— its aim is to complete our understanding of the ultimate rules that, at bottom, govern everything.

Sometimes I am brought up short by the realization of how little this is understood by most people, including those who control the funding of scientific research. For about a decade after 1983 I was involved in a campaign to get funding for a large scientific instrument, the Superconducting Super Collider. This machine was intended to accelerate beams of electrically charged particles called protons to unprecedented high energies and allow them to collide head-on, producing matter of a type that has not existed in nature since the first microsecond of the universe. Several times in the course of explaining this project to journalists and members of Congress, I found that the same question kept coming up: "Instead of spending billions of dollars on this accelerator, why not use a supercomputer to simulate these particle collisions?"

I had to explain that we can use computers to simulate what happens in the explosion of a supernova or a nuclear weapon because we understand the rules that govern matter on all scales from stars to atomic nuclei. Accelerators like the Superconducting Super Collider are built precisely to study the behavior of matter under conditions in which our understanding of the laws of physics is not adequate to calculate what will happen. The collisions in these accelerators probe features of elementary particles a thousand times smaller than an atomic nucleus, and at these scales our present theories become ambiguous. We can no more program a computer to tell us what happens in these collisions than we can program a computer to play chess without telling it how the pieces are allowed to move.

And that is the whole point of these experiments. No one really cares about the collisions or the particles in themselves—the rules of the game are what interest us, and we cannot learn about them without doing experiments that take us beyond the rules as we already know them. The Superconducting Super Collider project was canceled in 1993 by Congress, but a similar accelerator is being built near Geneva by a European consortium. The work of searching for a final theory of physics will continue.

Suppose we reach our goal—what then? It depends on what sort of world we find we are in. If we were to discover that the laws of nature at their deepest level give some special role to life or intelligence, we might derive from this some sense of purpose, some standard of conduct. My own guess is that this will not happen.

Nearly a century and a half ago, Charles Darwin and Alfred Wallace took the crucial step of explaining that the wonderful capabilities of living things could arise by natural selection of inheritable variations, with no advance plan. Since then biologists have made great progress in working out just how this happens in terms of the ordinary processes of physics and chemistry, which are themselves explained within the standard model.

We have not yet understood consciousness or intelligence, but there is no reason to suppose that these are anything but the workings of physics and chemistry within the brain. As far as we can tell, there is nothing in the fundamental laws of nature that will suggest any special role for life or intelligence in the plan of things.

This austere view of nature has horrified many people. In the preface to his play *Heartbreak House,* George Bernard Shaw gave credit to Darwin for starting "a reaction against a barbarous pseudoevangelical teleology intolerably obstructive to all scientific progress," but he went on to conclude that "there was only one result possible in the ethical sphere, and that was the banishment of conscience from human affairs."

Shaw's conclusion seems to make sense only if one supposes that we have to look for something objective, something outside ourselves, to give us a sense of values. But there is no reason not to find our values in our own hearts. If the laws of nature cannot give us a sense of conscience, neither can they take it away. And one of the values that is important to some of us is the search for the laws of nature, a search in which human insight and experimental facilities as well as computers will continue to be needed.

My own feeling is that there will be something healthy in coming to grips with the knowledge that we, like the rest of nature, are the way we are because of impersonal natural laws. Suppose you were the parent of a child who believed in Santa Claus and the Easter Bunny. You might be pleased that your child was made happy by these beliefs, but wouldn't you want them to be put aside as your child grows up? It may be that science can do no greater service to humanity than to help our species grow up and put aside childish beliefs.

WILLIAM F. BUCKLEY, JR.

The Evolution of a True Believer

WILLIAM F. BUCKLEY, JR. *is a nationally syndicated columnist, former host of the PBS show* Firing Line, *and the author of numerous novels and nonfiction books. He founded the* National Review *in 1955 and remains its editor at large.*

I HAVE TROUBLE WITH some of my fellow conservatives who rail against computer technology. There are two categories of these. The first, those who refuse to avail themselves, e.g.—and primarily—of the word processor. The second, those who harbor deep, even apocalyptic misgivings about the loss of privacy. These last deserve consideration, the first, mere pity.

But a word, as a matter of obeisance to the muse, about what word-people lose if they continue in their refusal to buy sliced bread. When I was nineteen, in the army, I wanted to dance with my girl all night, but she stopped me, after a week's gluttony, and said she would have to go home to begin reading for her senior thesis. I grandly told her not to worry her pretty little head, I would write it for her. The next afternoon, in my BOQ (Bachelor Officers' Quarters) I found waiting for me about twenty-seven books about the life and times of Sam Houston: She needed a paper on the subject, between seventy and a hundred single-spaced pages. . . . Five months later I finished typing it out on my Royal portable and presented it to her, so to speak, gift-wrapped. I had made my brownie points, but the next day it was waiting for me in my quarters, a heavy pencil mark circling typographical errors in a dozen pages: Her college would not permit any typos.

Such memories cause me to wonder whether it is possible even to communicate with those lost souls who won't use a word processor. What can you say to them? *Nothing,* actually. It's like undertaking to tell somebody that music is really fun to listen to or that colors please the eyes.

But the philosophical critics must be taken seriously. For a substantial part of my life I acknowledged the philosopher and strategist James Burnham (RIP) as my all-around mentor. On the one hand he was empirically curious, and I don't doubt he'd be using a word processor today. But back then technology was The Enemy. He proposed to his fellow editors that we encourage a total defiance of the creeping digital discipline by engaging—and urging our readers to do as much—in the most rudimentary disruptions, like always putting down the wrong Social Security number or, when speed of delivery didn't matter, the wrong ZIP code. Already there stirred in the libertarian/anarchic community what soon would be fire-breathing at the mere notion of individual identifying numbers. Suppose the Nazis had such facilities! But of course that is a good argument against having Nazis, not against having positive IDs. You can blow willowy air into those steaming furnaces by pointing out that there are empirical inexorabilities on the march that can be halted only if you come up with a contaminant that destroys all paper, everywhere in the world. History's most serious effort to frustrate technological progress was Pol Pot's. Cambodia wasn't teeming with computer IDs during his little reign (1975–79), so all he did was try to kill every Cambodian who could read and write. He managed to do away with one-third of the population.

What one does have to acknowledge, and without equivocation, is that the technological revolution has given us the resources to invade privacy. What does that mean? It means that we should not permit the invasion of privacy. Not that we should jettison technology capable of invading privacy. I am very much in favor of violating the privacy of John Gotti and other part-time killers. I'd like it if we invented a computer virus that, if it came across any combination of letters that authorized a killing or a bombing, would explode in the face of the theretofore sedate executioner. Sure, you would have to make exceptions: John Grisham would need a code that would let him keep on killing people on his word processor. Also the clerks of courts that give the final okay to judicial executions.

And anyway, why is it the doomsayers are so confident that computer and associated technology will remove the keenness of life's experience? Sure, it used to be gratifying when at sea in blue water to figure out just where you were, before there were satellites up there to relieve you of the required fuss. And, yes, celestial navigation should continue to be taught in the naval schools, and, yes, the art will continue to delight inquisitive amateurs.

But what is the shouting all about? No question about it, the Internet culture is going to waste a lot of time and seduce a lot of young people away from the greater nutritional alternative of sustained reading. But far better that Junior should spend three hours a day on the Internet than watching television, and television is much better than the vacuity one associated with old people's homes, back then.

The dispositive point is always the same, whether we're talking about technology or bread or cheese, wine, sex, play, or work: Don't let it take over. It always serves to restore perspective, my formula: If you observe a nerd wasting his life away at the computer terminal, tell him to ease up. If you see Hiroshima disappear, be God-awful careful to avoid doing it again. You don't tell the computer to stop accommodating the fanatic. You don't defame the muse. That would be ingratitude, a terribly sinful offense.

Back when I launched *National Review,* an editorial associate complained about the modern age, but from a perspective entirely different from that of the Luddites. He was an expatriate Viennese intellectual who lived in Vermont and attempted to commute regularly to New York. He swooped into the office one day—he liked noticeable entries—haggard from hours of waiting at various airports. "I dreamed a dream," he told me, dramatically. "Somebody in that dream came up with the idea of: parallel steel rails. You run these rails from town to town and you construct a vehicle that rolls over those rails and takes you from town to town, no traffic problem, no weather, no airport delays! Just smooth travel, from wherever you are, to wherever you're going."

Yes, and don't we all lament the slow death of the railroad. But, once again, you can't blame airplanes for this development. What you blame is people who stop using railroads. What's to be done about that? Nothing, because railroads are *eo ipso* collective enterprises, and one man's decision to patronize them isn't enough to cause them to spring to life. The individual can shut down his computer and go back to a typewriter, or to pen and pencil, but he can't cause others to do it.

That is the marvelous aspect of the computer age. If you insist, you can decline to avail yourself of it, but only when you are directly in charge of the situation. What you can't do is prevent other people from using it, and you can't ward off the derivative advantages of other people's use of technology. When you present your Mars bar to the lady at the counter, she spotlights the bar code and tells you that will be 59 cents, and you're on your way. She might have had to look it up, like in the Yellow Pages. And you would stand there impatiently because, you see, she's not all that good at working the alphabet: So you're silently cursing her miseducation.

But, dear Miniver Cheevy, don't sit there weeping as you assail the seasons. Flick on the Digital Satellite System and help yourself to twenty-five to thirty-five channels of music, just to begin with, and if it makes you feel more useful, concentrate on ways to keep the Nazis sequestered in the fever swamps. And take it easy. They're not likely to get to you just because they know your Social Security number. I personally think it's great, and if ever my faith wavers, all I need to do is read an essay by George Gilder in *Forbes ASAP*.

SIMON SCHAMA

⟹·◦·⟸

Hot-Wired History . . . Unplugged

SIMON SCHAMA *is a history professor at Columbia University and an art critic for the New Yorker. He is the author of* Citizens: A Chronicle of the French Revolution, Dead Certainties (Unwarranted Speculations), *and, more recently,* Rembrandt's Eyes.

NEVER CONFUSE HISTORY with nostalgia. In its Greek origins, *historia* meant inquiry, and from Thucydides onward, the past has been studied to understand its connections with the present. For all the elaborateness of modern scholarship, we still do what the Greeks and Romans did: figure out how we got from there to here. Electronic technology is only the latest (and most potent) tool in that work. With the arrival of the digitized archive, or the historical hypertext, manipulating alternative eventualities, the record of the past faces a brave new future.

Traditionally, historians have come in two basic models: the hang glider and the truffle hunter, and both can be helped out by electronic technology. Truffle hunters are excavators, resolute at extracting some small savory gobbet of truth from an improbably hidden source, but so committed to going from hole to hole that they miss the broad landscape in between. Hang gliders, by contrast, bob about on breezy thermals of generalization, taking in the lay of the land, but never actually descending to inspect its gritty details. But with the computer's help, the truffle hunter's horizons can be broadened and the hang glider's focus sharpened. Digitized archival data—for example, letters, diaries, tax or census statistics, and increasingly, visual evidence from illuminated manuscripts to prints, posters, and photographs—can all be downloaded and scanned for flagged items of special interest. The dedicated historian of the North American widget, for example, could, at a click (or squeak) of a mouse, compare its invention, business history, and cultural significance with its counterpart in, say, Chinese history or its prototype in Moorish Islam.

Other giddy prospects suggest themselves. Who needs scholarly publications in print and paper, when devoted subscribers to the *Journal of Widget History,* as few in number as they are passionate in vocation, can have them made available electronically, thus releasing desperately needed shelf space in crowded libraries? And with the possibility of lectures and seminars being opened electronically to all (who have paid their professional dues), annual conventions of historians can revert to their essential, honest-to-goodness function as guild gatherings, assembled for feasting, gossip, and hiring inspections.

Liberated from these chores, the historian can resume his role as Grand Arbiter between what has been and what is to be. The inexhaustible electronic serf will nail down the database wherever it may be hiding, rummage through its content, flag the significant item, and produce for the analytical scrutiny of his mistress discrete threads of the past, expertly scissored away from the endless ribbon of the time continuum.

So what should we fear? What is there to lose? Nothing but our imagination. The trouble is, though, that history without imagination is just so much data processing of the dead.

For all the things that the computer does brilliantly—the searching, sifting, flagging, storing—constitute the beginning, not the end, of historical wisdom. It gets the historian to the starting line of his real job: the resurrection of a vanished past; its reconstitution into something as real, as vivid, and as important as the fleeting present. And for the tricky, invaluable business, the electronic archive is still a weak collaborator, for it lacks all the properties that trigger the historian's precious intuition of recall: the smell, the feel, the instinct of the past. Bulldozing broad, straight highways through the chaotic tangle of the past carries with it the peril of losing its messy authenticity; of obliterating the accidental nature of so many fateful turns in history. Had

Archduke Francis Ferdinand's chauffeur not gotten lost in the streets of Sarajevo . . . had President Lincoln not been fond of theater . . . without a keen sense of these tragic pratfalls with which the past is littered, the historian threatens to turn into the most overdetermined political scientist, addicted to an unrealistically net relationship between cause and effect.

At its most prosaic, history is supposed to tell us how to avoid the next calamity—recession, revolution, war. It has never done this well, and there is absolutely no reason to suppose that electronically enhanced history will do the job any better. But the true value of history should be seen in a different way: as a meditation in time that better helps us to understand the nature of human behavior. This makes history's true neighbor, not economics or politics, but poetry and philosophy. And it cannot work as it should (and cannot tell the vivid stories it must) unless it truly inhabits an archive where we can touch the ink and the sealing wax; smell the must and the dust; and sense our dim kinship with the long lost. Only this direct, physical exposure to the fragile relics of vanished worlds has the power to summon the ghosts and make them substantial and eloquent. So while you can wire Clio till she's red-hot and cybercool, if you make her virtual, the lady crashes.

BILL McKIBBEN

———≫◆≪———

Out There in the Middle of the Buzz

BILL MCKIBBEN, *a former staff writer for the New Yorker, is the author of* The End of Nature, The Age of Missing Information, *and, more recently,* Long Distance: A Year of Living Strenuously. *He lives with his wife and daughter in the Adirondack Mountains of upstate New York.*

O UT ON A RECENT HIKE, I stopped for lunch at the edge of a high mountain pond. I could see another solitary hiker on the other side of the water, stretched out on a shelving rock about a hundred yards away. And I could hear him talking (sound carries extremely well across water; never negotiate a deal in a canoe). "It's so beautiful up here," he was saying. "It's so peaceful. What's happening with you?"

What I couldn't figure out was who he was talking to. Until I pulled out my binoculars and saw, of course, that he had a cell phone. For a moment I felt vastly superior—and then I reflected a bit. It's true I wouldn't carry a phone with me up a mountain. But I had carried my world with me nonetheless, marched right up there with my eyes fixed on the same vague middle distance that you see when you drive. My mind was abuzz with images, opinions; my mind was its own Bloomberg box, happily chattering away with a thousand dispatches an hour.

We live in the middle of the Buzz. Those billions of microprocessors that have spawned like springtime frogs in the last quarter century are constantly sending us information, data, images. Our minds marinate in it, till we're worried when it shuts off. What do you do first when you walk into an empty hotel room? Savor the silence? Or turn on the TV? And even when we get away from the machines for a while—even when we leave the phone at home—the Buzz comes with us. Quiet, solitude, calm: These are no longer automatic parts of the human experience. You have to fight as hard for them as a farm boy had to fight for novelty and thrill a century ago. How many minutes can you watch a sunset before your mind grows hungry for some faster diversion? How long can you stare up into the night sky?

This constant whispering in our ears, this constant dancing in front of our eyes—that's how technology changes us, weaning us away from ourselves. How can you figure out what you really want when someone's always talking to you, when there's always another home page to click through? When you can't warm yourself by a mountain lake without checking in at home? Electronic communication, for the first time, makes culture ubiquitous. Almost nobody read books five hours a day, or went to the theater every night. We live in the first moment when humans receive more of their information secondhand than first; instead of relying primarily on contact with nature and with each other, we rely primarily on the prechewed, on someone else's experience. Our life is, quite literally, mediated.

Maybe that's a good thing; maybe it's the direction in which we need to evolve on an ever more crowded planet. But I think it may be breeding a kind of desperation in us, too, a frantic, reactive nervousness. That low, rumbling broadcast that comes constantly from ourselves, the broadcast that tells us who we are, what we want from life—that broadcast is jammed by all the other noise around us, the lush static of our electronic age. We look for solitude in our (expensively silent) cars, but first the radio, then the phone, then the computer and the fax intrude. We look for peace in the mountains, but we drag the world along on a tether.

To quote Thoreau is to risk rejection as a romantic. But here goes. "Let us spend one day as deliberately as Nature, and not be thrown off the track by every nutshell and mosquito's wing that falls on the rails," he writes. Now that we've built a technosphere to amplify the sound of every nutshell and to broadcast high-quality pictures of each mosquito's wing, it's even better advice, albeit harder than ever to follow. Solitude, silence, darkness—these are the rarest commodities after a half century of electronics. The incredible economics of the information age mean that almost anyone can afford a large-screen television, a 28.8 modem. But how many can afford peace and quiet?

JEREMY RIFKIN

———◆———

A Radically Different World

JEREMY RIFKIN, *founder and president of the Foundation on Economic Trends, is an outspoken critic of technology. He is the author of the best-selling book* The Biotech Century: Harnessing the Gene and Remaking the World *and, more recently,* The Age of Access: The New Culture of Hypercapitalism Where All of Life is a Paid-For Experience.

THERE EXISTS A long-standing fiction that tools and technologies have no inherent value built into them, but only reflect the values of the people who use them. In fact, that's never been the case. There has never been a neutral technology. All technologies are power. A lance gives us more projectile power than our throwing arm. An automobile gives us more locomotive power than our legs and feet. The Internet provides us with more communication power than is possible through face-to-face interaction.

Every tool we use has power built into it by the very nature of the task for which it was designed. The very exercise of this power secures an advantage over others. This being the case, the introduction of every new technology into society demands a thoughtful discussion of how best to address the inherent inequities created by its use. The new technologies of the information age are a case in point.

The global economy is undergoing a fundamental transformation that will reshape civilization in the twenty-first century. Sophisticated computers, telecommunications, robotics, and other information-age technologies are fast replacing human beings in virtually every sector and industry.

The hard reality that economists and politicians are reluctant to acknowledge is that manufacturing and much of the service sector are undergoing a transformation as profound as the one experienced by the agricultural sector earlier in this century, when machines boosted production and displaced millions of farmers. Many jobs are never coming back. Blue-collar workers, secretaries, receptionists, clerical workers, salesclerks, bank tellers, telephone operators, librarians, wholesalers, and middle managers are just a few of the many occupations destined for near extinction.

Earlier industrial technologies replaced the physical power of human labor, substituting machines for body and brawn. The new computer-based technologies promise to replace the human mind itself, substituting thinking machines for human beings throughout the economy.

Acknowledging this trend, many mainstream economists and politicians have turned to the emerging knowledge sector, pinning their hopes on new job opportunities along the information superhighway and in cyberspace. While the "knowledge sector" will create some new jobs, they will be too few to absorb the millions of workers displaced by the new technologies. That's because the knowledge sector demands an elite workforce and not a mass-labor workforce. Engineers, highly skilled technicians, computer programmers, scientists, and professionals will never be needed in "mass" numbers to produce goods and services in the information age. Indeed, the shift from mass to elite labor forces is what distinguishes work in the information age from that of the Industrial Age.

With near-workerless factories and virtual companies already looming on the horizon, every nation will have to grapple with the question of what to do with the millions of people whose labor is needed less, or not at all, in an ever more automated global economy.

While mainstream Democrats and Republicans have embraced the information age, extolling the virtues of cyberspace and virtual reality, they have, for the most part, steadfastly refused to address the equally important question of how to ensure that the dramatic productivity gains of the new economy will be shared by every segment of the population. Until now, those productivity gains have been used primarily to enhance corporate profit, to the exclusive benefit of stockholders, top corporate managers, and the emerging elite of high tech knowledge workers. If the trend continues, chances are that the widening gap between the haves and have-nots is going to lead to greater social unrest and more crime and violence on the streets of America. Millions of middle- and working-class Americans, caught in between and worried over their own eroding economic fortunes, including loss of job security and falling real wages, are going to become easy prey for extremist political movements at both ends of the political spectrum.

The antidote to politics of paranoia and hate is an open and sober discussion of the underlying technological and economic forces that are leading to increased productivity on one hand, and a diminishing need for mass human labor on the other. That discussion needs to be accompanied by a bold new social vision that can speak directly to the challenges facing us in the new economic era. In short, we need to begin thinking seriously about what a radically different world might look like in an era when less human labor is needed to produce the goods and services of an increasingly automated global economy.

In the past, when new technologies dramatically increased productivity, U.S. workers sought a share of the productivity gains and organized collectively to demand a shorter workweek and better pay and benefits. Today, instead of reducing the workweek, employers are reducing the workforce.

The new labor-saving technologies of the information age should be used to free us for greater leisure, not result in less pay and growing underemployment. Of course, employers argue that shortening the workweek and sharing the productivity gains with workers will be too costly and will threaten their ability to compete both domestically and abroad.

That need not be so. Companies like Hewlett-Packard in France have reduced their workweek from thirty-seven to thirty-five hours while continuing to pay workers at the thirty-seven-hour rate. In return, the workers have agreed to work in shifts. The companies' reason? If they can keep the new high tech plants operating on a twenty-four-hour basis, they can double or triple productivity and thus pay workers more for working less.

In France, government officials are considering rescinding payroll taxes for the employer if management voluntarily reduces the workweek. While the government will lose tax revenue, economists argue that it will make up the difference in other ways. With a reduced workweek more people will be working and fewer will be on welfare. And the new workers will buy goods and pay taxes, all of which will benefit employers, the economy, and the government.

In this country, the federal government ought to consider extending tax credits to any company willing to do two things: voluntarily reduce its workweek and implement a profit-sharing plan so that its employees will benefit directly from the productivity gains. With tax incentives, employers would be more inclined to make the transition, especially if it gave them a marked advantage over their competitors.

The thirty-hour workweek ought to become a rallying cry for millions of U.S. workers. Shorter workweeks and better pay and benefits were the benchmarks for measuring the success of the Industrial Revolution in the past century. We should demand no less of the information age in the century to come.

TOM WOLFE

❧

Sorry, but Your Soul Just Died

TOM WOLFE *has chronicled American popular culture for more than three decades. His best-selling books include* The Electric Kool-Aid Acid Test, The Right Stuff, The Bonfire of the Vanities, *and* A Man in Full. *His next novel is about collegiate life.*

Being a bit behind the curve, I had only just heard of the digital revolution last February when Louis Rossetto, cofounder of *Wired* magazine, wearing a shirt with no collar and his hair as long as Felix Mendelssohn's, looking every inch the young California visionary, gave a speech before the Cato Institute announcing the dawn of the twenty-first century's digital civilization. As his text, he chose the maverick Jesuit scientist and philosopher Pierre Teilhard de Chardin, who fifty years ago prophesied that radio, television, and computers would create a "noösphere," an electronic membrane covering the earth and wiring all humanity together in a single nervous system. Geographic locations, national boundaries, the old notions of markets and political processes—all would become irrelevant. With the Internet spreading over the globe at an astonishing pace, said Rossetto, that marvelous modem-driven moment is almost at hand.

Could be. But something tells me that within ten years, by 2006, the entire digital universe is going to seem like pretty mundane stuff compared to a new technology that right now is but a mere glow radiating from a tiny number of American and Cuban (yes, Cuban) hospitals and laboratories. It is called brain imaging, and anyone who cares to get up early and catch a truly blinding twenty-first-century dawn will want to keep an eye on it.

Brain imaging refers to techniques for watching the human brain as it functions, in real time. The most advanced forms currently are three-dimensional electroencephalography using mathematical models; the more familiar PET scan (positron-emission tomography); the new fMRI (functional magnetic resonance imaging), which shows brain blood-flow patterns, and MRS (magnetic resonance spectroscopy), which measures biochemical changes in the brain; and the even newer PET reporter gene/PET reporter probe, which is, in fact, so new that it still has that length of heavy lumber for a name. Used so far only in animals and a few desperately sick children, the PET reporter gene/PET reporter probe pinpoints and follows the activity of specific genes. On a scanner screen you can actually see the genes light up inside the brain.

By 1996 standards, these are sophisticated devices. Ten years from now, however, they may seem primitive compared to the stunning new windows into the brain that will have been developed.

Brain imaging was invented for medical diagnosis. But its far greater importance is that it may very well confirm, in ways too precise to be disputed, certain theories about "the mind," "the self," "the soul," and "free will" that are already devoutly believed in by scholars in what is now the hottest field in the academic world, neuroscience. Granted, all those skeptical quotation marks are enough to put anybody on the *qui vive* right away, but Ultimate Skepticism is part of the brilliance of the dawn I have promised.

Neuroscience, the science of the brain and the central nervous system, is on the threshold of a unified theory that will have an impact as powerful as that of Darwinism a hundred years ago. Already there is a new Darwin, or perhaps I should say an updated Darwin, since no one ever believed more religiously in Darwin I than he does. His name is Edward O. Wilson. He teaches zoology at Harvard, and he is the author of two books of extraordinary influence, *The Insect Societies* and *Sociobiology: The New Synthesis*. Not *A* new synthesis but *The* new synthesis; in terms of his stature in neuroscience, it is not a mere boast.

Wilson has created and named the new field of sociobiology, and he has compressed its underlying premise into a single sentence.

Every human brain, he says, is born not as a blank tablet (a *tabula rasa*) waiting to be filled in by experience but as "an exposed negative waiting to be slipped into developer fluid." You can develop the negative well or you can develop it poorly, but either way you are going to get precious little that is not already imprinted on the film. The print is the individual's genetic history, over thousands of years of evolution, and there is not much anybody can do about it. Furthermore, says Wilson, genetics determine not only things such as temperament, role preferences, emotional responses, and levels of aggression, but also many of our most revered moral choices, which are not choices at all in any free-will sense but tendencies imprinted in the hypothalamus and limbic regions of the brain, a concept expanded upon in 1993 in a much-talked-about book, *The Moral Sense,* by James Q. Wilson (no kin to Edward O.).

This, the neuroscientific view of life, has become the strategic high ground in the academic world, and the battle for it has already spread well beyond the scientific disciplines and, for that matter, out into the general public. Both liberals and conservatives without a scientific bone in their bodies are busy trying to seize the terrain. The gay rights movement, for example, has fastened onto a study published in July of 1993 by the highly respected Dean Hamer of the National Institutes of Health, announcing the discovery of "the gay gene." Obviously, if homosexuality is a genetically determined trait, like left-handedness or hazel eyes, then laws and sanctions against it are attempts to legislate against Nature. Conservatives, meantime, have fastened upon studies indicating that men's and women's brains are wired so differently, thanks to the long haul of evolution, that feminist attempts to open up traditionally male roles to women are the same thing: a doomed violation of Nature.

Wilson himself has wound up in deep water on this score; or cold water, if one need edit. In his personal life Wilson is a conventional liberal, PC, as the saying goes—he *is*, after all, a member of the Harvard faculty—concerned about environmental issues and all the usual things. But he has said that "forcing similar role identities" on both men and women "flies in the face of thousands of years in which mammals demonstrated a strong tendency for sexual division of labor. Since this division of labor is persistent from hunter-gatherer through agricultural and industrial societies, it suggests a genetic origin. We do not know when this trait evolved in human evolution or how resistant it is to the continuing and justified pressures for human rights."

"Resistant" was Darwin II, the neuroscientist, speaking. "Justified" was the PC Harvard liberal. He was not PC or liberal enough. Feminist protesters invaded a conference where Wilson was appearing, dumped a pitcher of ice water, cubes and all, over his head, and began chanting, "You're all wet! You're all wet!" The most prominent feminist in America, Gloria Steinem, went on television and, in an interview with John Stossel of ABC, insisted that studies of genetic differences between male and female nervous systems should cease forthwith.

But that turned out to be mild stuff in the current political panic over neuroscience. In February of 1992, Frederick K. Goodwin, a renowned psychiatrist, head of the federal Alcohol, Drug Abuse, and Mental Health Administration, and a certified yokel in the field of public relations, made the mistake of describing, at a public meeting in Washington, the National Institute of Mental Health's ten-year-old Violence Initiative. This was an experimental program whose hypothesis was that, as among monkeys in the jungle—Goodwin was noted for his monkey studies—much of the criminal mayhem in the United States was caused by a relatively few young males who were genetically predisposed to it; who were hardwired for violent crime, in short. Out in the jungle, among mankind's closest animal relatives, the chimpanzees, it seemed that a handful of genetically twisted young males were the ones who committed practically *all* of the wanton murders of other males and the physical abuse of females. What if the same were true among human beings? What if, in any given community, it turned out to be a handful of young males with toxic DNA who were pushing statistics for violent crime up to such high levels? The Violence Initiative envisioned identifying these individuals in childhood, somehow, some way, someday, and treating them therapeutically with drugs. The notion that crime-ridden urban America was a "jungle," said Goodwin, was perhaps more than just a tired old metaphor.

That did it. That may have been the stupidest single word uttered by an American public official in the year 1992. The outcry was immediate. Senator Edward Kennedy of Massachusetts and Representative John Dingell of Michigan (who, it became obvious later, suffered from hydrophobia when it came to science projects) not only condemned Goodwin's remarks as racist but also delivered their scientific verdict: Research among primates "is a preposterous basis" for analyzing anything as complex as "the crime and violence that plagues our country today." (This came as surprising news to NASA scientists who had first trained and sent a chimpanzee called Ham up on top of a Redstone rocket into suborbital space flight and then trained and sent another one, called Enos, which is Greek for "man," up on an Atlas rocket and around the earth in orbital space flight and had thereby accurately and completely predicted the physical, psychological, and task-motor responses of the human astronauts, Alan Shepard and John Glenn, who repeated the chimpanzees' flights and tasks months later.) The Violence Initiative was compared to Nazi eugenic proposals for the extermination of undesirables. Dingell's Michigan colleague, Representative John Conyers, then chairman of the Government Operations Committee and senior member of the Congressional Black Caucus, demanded Goodwin's resignation—and got it two days later, whereupon the government, with the Department of Health and Human Services now doing the talking, denied that the Violence Initiative had ever existed. It disappeared down the memory hole, to use Orwell's term.

A conference of criminologists and other academics interested in the neuroscientific studies done so far for the Violence Initiative—a conference underwritten in part by a grant from the National Institutes of Health—had been scheduled for May of 1993 at the University of Maryland. Down went the conference, too; the NIH drowned it like a kitten. Last year, a University of Maryland legal scholar named David Wasserman tried to reassemble the troops on the QT, as it were, in a hall all but hidden from human purview in a hamlet called Queenstown in the foggy, boggy boondocks of Queen Annes County on Maryland's Eastern Shore. The NIH, proving it was a hard learner, quietly provided $133,000 for the event but only after Wasserman promised to fireproof the proceedings by also inviting scholars who rejected the notion of a possible genetic genesis of crime and scheduling a cold-shower session dwelling on the evils of the eugenics movement of the early twentieth century. No use, boys! An army of protesters found the poor cringing devils anyway and stormed into the auditorium chanting, "Maryland conference, you can't hide—we know you're pushing genocide!" It took two hours for them to get bored enough to leave, and the conference ended in a complete muddle with the specially recruited fireproofing PC faction issuing a statement that said: "Scientists as well as historians and sociologists must not allow themselves to provide academic respectability for racist pseudoscience." Today, at the NIH, the term Violence Initiative is a synonym for *taboo*. The present moment resembles that moment in the Middle Ages when the Catholic Church forbade the dissection of human bodies, for fear that what was discovered inside might cast doubt on the Christian doctrine that God created man in his own image.

Even more radioactive is the matter of intelligence, as measured by IQ tests. Privately—not many care to speak out—the vast majority of neuroscientists believe the genetic component of an individual's intelligence is remarkably high. Your intelligence can be improved upon, by skilled and devoted mentors, or it can be held back by a poor upbringing—i.e., the negative can be well developed or poorly developed—but your genes are what really make the difference. The recent ruckus over Charles Murray and Richard Herrnstein's *The Bell Curve* is probably just the beginning of the bitterness the subject is going to create.

Not long ago, according to two neuroscientists I interviewed, a firm called Neurometrics sought out investors and tried to market an amazing but simple invention known as the IQ Cap. The idea was to provide a way of testing intelligence that would be free of "cultural bias," one that would not force anyone to deal with words or concepts that might be familiar to people from one culture but not to people from another. The IQ Cap recorded only brain waves; and a computer, not a potentially biased human test-giver, analyzed the results. It was based on the work of neuroscientists such as E. Roy John,* who is now one of the major pioneers of electroencephalographic brain

---

* The term neurometric is closely identified with John, who has devised both the Neurometric Battery, a comprehensive system for analyzing brain functions, and the Neurometric Analyzer, a patented instrument for making use of the Battery; but John had nothing to do with Neurometrics, Inc. He describes the Battery in *Neurometric Evaluation of Brain Function in Normal and Learning-Disabled Children* (Ann Arbor, University of Michigan Press, 1989).

imaging; Duilio Giannitrapani, author of *The Electrophysiology of Intellectual Functions;* and David Robinson, author of *The Wechsler Adult Intelligence Scale and Personality Assessment: Toward a Biologically Based Theory of Intelligence and Cognition* and many other monographs famous among neuroscientists. I spoke to one researcher who had devised an IQ Cap himself by replicating an experiment described by Giannitrapani in *The Electrophysiology of Intellectual Functions.* It was not a complicated process. You attached sixteen electrodes to the scalp of the person you wanted to test. You had to muss up his hair a little, but you didn't have to cut it, much less shave it. Then you had him stare at a marker on a blank wall. This particular researcher used a raspberry-red thumbtack. Then you pushed a toggle switch. In sixteen seconds the Cap's computer box gave you an accurate prediction (within one-half of a standard deviation) of what the subject would score on all eleven subtests of the Wechsler Adult Intelligence Scale or, in the case of children, the Wechsler Intelligence Scale for Children—all from sixteen seconds' worth of brain waves. There was nothing culturally biased about the test whatsoever. What could be cultural about staring at a thumbtack on a wall? The savings in time and money were breathtaking. The conventional IQ test took two hours to complete; and the overhead, in terms of paying test-givers, test-scorers, test-preparers, and the rent, was $100 an hour at the very least. The IQ Cap required about fifteen minutes and sixteen seconds—it took about fifteen minutes to put the electrodes on the scalp—and about a tenth of a penny's worth of electricity. Neurometrics's investors were rubbing their hands and licking their chops. They were about to make a killing.

In fact—*nobody wanted their damnable IQ Cap!*

It wasn't simply that no one *believed* you could derive IQ scores from brainwaves—it was that nobody *wanted* to believe it could be done. Nobody *wanted* to believe that human brainpower is . . . *that hardwired.* Nobody wanted to learn in a flash that . . . the genetic fix is in. Nobody wanted to learn that he was . . . *a hardwired genetic mediocrity* . . . and that the best he could hope for in this Trough of Mortal Error was to live out his mediocre life as a stress-free dim bulb. Barry Sterman of UCLA, chief scientist for a firm called Cognitive Neurometrics, who has devised his own brain-wave technology for market research and focus groups, regards brain-wave IQ testing as possible—but in the current atmosphere you "wouldn't have a Chinaman's chance of getting a grant" to develop it.

Here we begin to sense the chill that emanates from the hottest field in the academic world. The unspoken and largely unconscious premise of the wrangling over neuroscience's strategic high ground is: We now live in an age in which science is a court from which there is no appeal. And the issue this time around, at the end of the twentieth century, is not the evolution of the species, which can seem a remote business, but the nature of our own precious inner selves.

The elders of the field, such as Wilson, are well aware of all this and are cautious, or cautious compared to the new generation. Wilson still holds out the possibility—I think he doubts it, but he still holds out the possibility—that at some point in evolutionary history, culture began to influence the development of the human brain in ways that cannot be explained by strict Darwinian theory. But the new generation of neuroscientists are not cautious for a second. In private conversations, the bull sessions, as it were, that create the mental atmosphere of any hot new science—and I love talking to these people—they express an uncompromising determinism.

They start with the most famous statement in all of modern philosophy, Descartes's "Cogito ergo sum," "I think, therefore I am," which they regard as the essence of "dualism," the old-fashioned notion that the mind is something distinct from its mechanism, the brain and the body. (I will get to the second most famous statement in a moment.) This is also known as the "ghost in the machine" fallacy, the quaint belief that there is a ghostly "self" somewhere inside the brain that interprets and directs its operations. Neuroscientists involved in three-dimensional electroencephalography will tell you that there is not even any one place in the brain where consciousness or self-consciousness (*Cogito ergo sum*) is located. This is merely an illusion created by a medley of neurological systems acting in concert. The young generation takes this yet one step further. Since consciousness and thought are entirely physical products of your brain and nervous system—and since your brain arrived fully imprinted at birth—what makes you think you have free will? Where is it going to come from? What "ghost," what "mind," what "self," what "soul," what anything that will not be immediately grabbed by those scornful quotation marks, is going to bubble up your brain stem to give it to you? I have heard neuroscientists theorize that, given computers of sufficient power and sophistication, it would be possible to predict the course of any human being's life moment by moment, including the fact that the poor devil was about to shake his head over the very idea. I doubt that any Calvinist of the sixteenth century ever believed so completely in predestination as these, the hottest and most intensely rational young scientists in the United States at the end of the twentieth.

Since the late 1970s, in the Age of Wilson, college students have been heading into neuroscience in job lots. The Society for Neuroscience was founded in 1970 with 1,100 members. Today, one generation later, its membership exceeds 26,000. The Society's latest convention, in San Diego, drew 23,052 souls, making it one of the biggest professional conventions in the country. In the venerable field of academic philosophy, young faculty members are jumping ship in embarrassing numbers and shifting into neuroscience. They are heading for the laboratories. Why wrestle with Kant's God, Freedom, and Immortality when it is only a matter of time before neuroscience, probably through brain imaging, reveals the actual physical mechanism that sends these mental constructs, these illusions, synapsing up into the Broca's and Wernicke's areas of the brain?

Which brings us to the second most famous statement in all of modern philosophy: Nietzsche's "God is dead." The year was 1882. (The book was *Die Fröhliche Wissenschaft* [*The Gay Science*].) Nietzsche said this was not a declaration of atheism, although he was in fact an atheist, but simply the news of an event. He called the death of God a "tremendous event," the greatest event of modern history. The news was that educated people no longer believed in God, as a result of the rise of rationalism and scientific thought, including Darwinism, over the preceding 250 years. But before you atheists run up your flags of triumph, he said, think of the implications. "The story I have to tell," wrote Nietzsche, "is the history of the next two centuries." He predicted (in *Ecce Homo*) that the twentieth century would be a century of "wars such as have never happened on earth," wars catastrophic beyond all imagining. And why? Because human beings would no longer have a god to turn to, to absolve them of their guilt; but they would still be racked by guilt, since guilt is an impulse instilled in children when they are very young, before the age of reason. As a result, people would loathe not only one another but themselves. The blind and reassuring faith they formerly poured into their belief in God, said Nietzsche, they would now pour into a belief in barbaric nationalistic brotherhoods: "If the doctrines . . . of the lack of any cardinal distinction between man and animal, doctrines I consider true but deadly"—he says in an allusion to Darwinism in *Untimely Meditations*—"are hurled into the people for another generation . . . then nobody should be surprised when . . . brotherhoods with the aim of the robbery and exploitation of the non-brothers . . . will appear in the arena of the future."

Nietzsche's view of guilt, incidentally, is also that of neuroscientists a century later. They regard guilt as one of those tendencies imprinted in the brain at birth. In some people the genetic work is not complete, and they engage in criminal behavior without a twinge of remorse— thereby intriguing criminologists, who then want to create Violence Initiatives and hold conferences on the subject.

Nietzsche said that mankind would limp on through the twentieth century "on the mere pittance" of the old decaying God-based moral codes. But then, in the twenty-first, would come a period more dreadful than the great wars, a time of "the total eclipse of all values" (in *The Will to Power*). This would also be a frantic period of "revaluation," in which people would try to find new systems of values to replace the osteoporotic skeletons of the old. But you will fail, he warned, because you cannot believe in moral codes without simultaneously believing in a god who points at you with his fearsome forefinger and says "Thou shalt" or "Thou shalt not."

Why should we bother ourselves with a dire prediction that seems so far-fetched as "the total eclipse of all values"? Because of man's track record, I should think. After all, in Europe, in the peaceful decade of the 1880s, it must have seemed even more far-fetched to predict the world wars of the twentieth century and the barbaric brotherhoods of Nazism and Communism. Ecce vates! *Ecce vates!* Behold the prophet! How much more proof can one demand of a man's powers of prediction?

A hundred years ago those who worried about the death of God could console one another with the fact that they still had their own bright selves and their own inviolable souls for moral ballast and the marvels of modern science to chart the way. But what if, as seems likely, the greatest marvel of modern science turns out to be brain imaging? And what if, ten years from now, brain imaging has proved, beyond any doubt, that not only Edward O. Wilson but also the young generation are, in fact, correct?

The elders, such as Wilson himself and Daniel C. Dennett, the author of *Darwin's Dangerous Idea: Evolution and the Meanings of Life,* and Richard Dawkins, author of *The Selfish Gene* and *The Blind Watchmaker,* insist that there is nothing to fear from the truth, from the ultimate extension of Darwin's dangerous idea. They present elegant arguments as to why neuroscience should in no way diminish the richness of life, the magic of art, or the righteousness of political causes, including, if one need edit, political correctness at Harvard or Tufts, where Dennett is Director of the Center for Cognitive Studies, or Oxford, where Dawkins is something called Professor of Public Understanding of Science. (Dennett and Dawkins, every bit as much as Wilson, are earnestly, feverishly, politically correct.) Despite their best efforts, however, neuroscience is not rippling out into the public on waves of scholarly reassurance. But rippling out it is, rapidly. The conclusion people out beyond the laboratory walls are drawing is: *The fix is in! We're all hardwired!* That, and: *Don't blame me! I'm wired wrong!*

This sudden switch from a belief in Nurture, in the form of social conditioning, to Nature, in the form of genetics and brain physiology, is the great intellectual event, to borrow Nietzsche's term, of the late twentieth century. Up to now the two most influential ideas of the century have been Marxism and Freudianism. Both were founded upon the premise that human beings and their "ideals"—Marx and Freud knew about quotation marks, too—are completely molded by their environment. To Marx, the crucial environment was one's social class; "ideals" and "faiths" were notions foisted by the upper orders upon the lower as instruments of social control. To Freud, the crucial environment was the Oedipal drama, the unconscious sexual plot that was played out in the family early in a child's existence. The "ideals" and "faiths" you prize so much are merely the parlor furniture you feature for receiving your guests, said Freud; I will show you the cellar, the furnace, the pipes, the sexual steam that actually runs the house. By the mid-1950s even anti-Marxists and anti-Freudians had come to assume the centrality of class domination and Oedipally conditioned sexual drives. On top of this came Pavlov, with his "stimulus-response bonds," and B. F. Skinner, with his "operant conditioning," turning the supremacy of conditioning into something approaching a precise form of engineering.

So how did this brilliant intellectual fashion come to so screeching and ignominious an end?

The demise of Freudianism can be summed up in a single word: lithium. In 1949 an Australian psychiatrist, John Cade, gave five days of lithium therapy—for entirely the wrong reasons—to a fifty-one-year-old mental patient who was so manic-depressive, so hyperactive, unintelligible, and uncontrollable, he had been kept locked up in asylums for twenty years. By the sixth day, thanks to the lithium buildup in his blood, he was a normal human being. Three months later he was released and lived happily ever after in his own home. This was a man who had been locked up and subjected to two decades of Freudian logorrhea to no avail whatsoever. Over the next twenty years antidepressant and tranquilizing drugs completely replaced Freudian talk-talk as treatment for serious mental disturbances. By the mid-1980s, neuroscientists looked upon Freudian psychiatry as a quaint relic based largely upon superstition (such as dream analysis—*dream* analysis!), like phrenology or mesmerism. In fact, among neuroscientists, phrenology now has a higher reputation than Freudian psychiatry, since phrenology was in a certain crude way a precursor of electroencephalography. Freudian psychiatrists are now regarded as old crocks with sham medical degrees, as ears with wire hairs sprouting out of them that people with more money than sense can hire to talk into.

Marxism was finished off even more suddenly—in a single year, 1973—with the smuggling out of the Soviet Union and the publication in France of the first of the three volumes of Aleksandr Solzhenitsyn's *The Gulag Archipelago*. Other writers, notably the British historian Robert Conquest, had already exposed the Soviet Union's vast network of concentration camps, but their work was based largely on the testimony of refugees, and refugees were routinely discounted as biased and bitter observers. Solzhenitsyn, on the other hand, was a Soviet citizen, still living on Soviet soil, a *zek* himself for eleven years, *zek* being Russian slang for concentration camp prisoner. His credibility had been vouched for by none other than Nikita Khrushchev, who in 1962 had permitted the publication of Solzhenitsyn's novella of the gulag, *One Day in the Life of Ivan Denisovich,* as a means of cutting down to size the daunting shadow of his predecessor Stalin. "Yes," Khrushchev had said in effect, "what this man Solzhenitsyn has to say is true. Such were Stalin's crimes." Solzhenitsyn's brief fictional description of the Soviet slave labor system was damaging enough. But *The Gulag Archipelago,* a two-thousand-page, densely detailed, nonfiction account of the Soviet Communist Party's systematic extermination of its enemies, real and imagined, of its own countrymen, *by the tens of millions* through an enormous, methodical, bureaucratically controlled "human sewage disposal system," as Solzhenitsyn called it—*The Gulag Archipelago* was devastating. After all, this was a century in which there was no longer any possible ideological detour around the concentration camp. Among European intellectuals, even French intellectuals, Marxism collapsed as a spiritual force immediately. Ironically, it survived longer in the United States before suffering a final, merciful *coup de grâce* on November 9, 1989, with the breaching of the Berlin Wall, which signaled in an unmistakable fashion what a debacle the Soviets' seventy-two-year field experiment in socialism had been. (Marxism still hangs on, barely, acrobatically, in American universities in a Mannerist form known as Deconstruction, a literary doctrine that depicts language itself as an insidious tool used by The Powers That Be to deceive the proles and peasants.)

Freudianism and Marxism—and with them, the entire belief in social conditioning—were demolished so swiftly, so suddenly, that neuroscience has surged in, as if into an intellectual vacuum. Nor do you have to be a scientist to detect the rush.

Anyone with a child in school knows the signs all too well. I have children in school, and I am intrigued by the faith parents now invest—the craze began about 1990—in psychologists who diagnose their children as suffering from a defect known as attention deficit disorder, or ADD. Of course, I have no way of knowing whether this "disorder" is an actual, physical, neurological condition or not, but neither does anybody else in this early stage of neuroscience. The symptoms of this supposed malady are always the same. The child, or, rather, the boy—forty-nine out of fifty cases are boys—fidgets around in school, slides off his chair, doesn't pay attention, distracts his classmates during class, and performs poorly. In an earlier era he would have been pressured to pay attention, work harder, show some self-discipline. To parents caught up in the new intellectual climate of the 1990s, that approach seems cruel, because my little boy's problem is . . . *he's wired wrong!* The poor little tyke—*the fix has been in since birth!* Invariably the parents complain, "All he wants to do is sit in front of the television set and watch cartoons and play Sega Genesis." For how long? "How long? For hours at a time." Hours at a time; as even any young neuroscientist will tell you, that boy may have a problem, but it is not an attention deficit.

Nevertheless, all across America we have the spectacle of an entire generation of little boys, by the tens of thousands, being dosed up on ADD's magic bullet of choice, Ritalin, the CIBA-Geneva Corporation's brand name for the stimulant methylphenidate. I first encountered Ritalin in 1966 when I was in San Francisco doing research for a book on the psychedelic or hippie movement. A certain species of the genus hippie was known as the Speed Freak, and a certain strain of Speed Freak was known as the Ritalin Head. The Ritalin Heads *loved* Ritalin. You'd see them in the throes of absolute Ritalin raptures . . . Not a wiggle, not a peep . . . They would sit engrossed in *anything at all* . . . a manhole cover, their own palm wrinkles . . . indefinitely . . . through shoulda-been mealtime after mealtime . . . through raging insomnias . . . Pure methylphenidate nirvana . . . From 1990 to 1995, CIBA-Geneva's sales of Ritalin rose 600 percent; and not because of the appetites of subsets of the species Speed Freak in San Francisco, either. It was because an entire generation of American boys, from the best private schools of the Northeast to the worst sludge-trap public schools of Los Angeles and San Diego, was now strung out on methylphenidate, diligently doled out to them every day by their connection, the school nurse. America is a wonderful country! I mean it! No honest writer would challenge that statement! The human comedy never runs out of material! It never lets you down!

Meantime, the notion of a self—a self who exercises self-discipline, postpones gratification, curbs the sexual appetite, stops short of aggression and criminal behavior—a self who can become more intelligent and lift itself to the very peaks of life by its own bootstraps through study, practice, perseverance, and refusal to give up in the face of great odds—this old-fashioned notion (what's a *boot*strap, for God's sake?) of success through enterprise and true grit is already slipping away, slipping away . . . slipping away. . . .   The peculiarly American faith in the power of the individual to transform himself from a helpless cypher into a giant among men, a faith that ran from Emerson ("Self-Reliance") to Horatio Alger's *Luck and Pluck* stories to Dale Carnegie's *How to Win Friends and Influence People* to Norman Vincent Peale's *The Power of Positive Thinking* to Og Mandino's *The Greatest Salesman in the World*—that faith is now as moribund as the god for whom Nietzsche wrote an obituary in 1882. It lives on today only in the decrepit form of the "motivational talk," as lecture agents refer to it, given by retired football stars such as Fran Tarkenton to audiences of businessmen, most of them woulda-been athletes (like the author of this article), about how life is like a football game. "It's late in the fourth period and you're down by thirteen points and the Cowboys got you hemmed in on your own one-yard line and it's third and twenty-three. Whaddaya do? . . . "

Sorry, Fran, but it's third and twenty-three and the genetic fix is in, and the new message is now being pumped out into the popular press and onto television at a stupefying rate. Who are the pumps? They are a new breed who call themselves "evolutionary psychologists." You can be sure that twenty years ago the same people would have been calling themselves Freudian; but today they are genetic determinists, and the press has a voracious appetite for whatever they come up with.

The most popular study currently—it is *still* being featured on television news shows, months later—is David Lykken and Auke Tellegen's study at the University of Minnesota of two thousand twins that shows, according to these two evolutionary psychologists, that an individual's happiness is largely genetic. Some people are hardwired to be happy and some are not. Success (or failure) in matters of love, money, reputation, or power is transient stuff; you soon settle back down (or up) to the level of happiness you were born with genetically. Three months ago *Fortune* devoted a long takeout, elaborately illustrated, of a study by evolutionary psychologists at Britain's University of Saint Andrews showing that you judge the facial beauty or handsomeness of people you meet not by any social standards of the age you live in but by criteria hardwired in your brain from the moment you were born. Or, to put it another way, beauty is not in the eye of the beholder but embedded in his genes. In fact, today, in the year 1996, barely three years before the end of the millennium, if your appetite for newspapers, magazines, and television is big enough, you will quickly get the impression that there is nothing in your life, including the fat content of your body, that is not genetically predetermined. If I may mention just a few things the evolutionary psychologists have illuminated for me over the past two months:

The male of the human species is genetically hardwired to be polygamous, i.e., unfaithful to his legal mate. Any magazine-reading male gets the picture soon enough. (Three million years of evolution made me do it!) Women lust after male celebrities, because they are genetically hardwired to sense that alpha males will take better care of their offspring. (I'm just a lifeguard in the gene pool, honey.) Teenage girls are genetically hardwired to be promiscuous and are as helpless to stop themselves as dogs in the park. (The school provides the condoms.) Most murders are the result of genetically hardwired compulsions. (Convicts can read, too, and they report to the prison psychiatrist: "Something came over me . . . and then the knife went in."*)

Where does that leave self-control? Where, indeed, if people believe this ghostly self does not even exist, and brain imaging proves it, once and for all?

So far, neuroscientific theory is based largely on indirect evidence, from studies of animals or of how a normal brain changes when it is invaded (by accidents, disease, radical surgery, or experimental needles). Darwin II himself, Edward O. Wilson, has only limited direct knowledge of the human brain. He is a zoologist, not a neurologist, and his theories are extrapolations from the exhaustive work he has done in his specialty, the study of insects. The French surgeon Paul Broca discovered Broca's area, one of the two speech centers of the left hemisphere of the brain, only after one of his patients suffered a stroke. Even the PET scan and the PET reporter gene/PET reporter probe are technically medical invasions, since they require the injection of chemicals or viruses into the body. But they offer glimpses of what the noninvasive imaging of the future will probably look like. A

* Recounted by the British prison psychiatrist Theodore Dalrymple in the magazine *City Journal*.

neuroradiologist can read a list of topics out loud to a person being given a PET scan, topics pertaining to sports, music, business, history, whatever, and when he finally hits one the person is interested in, a particular area of the cerebral cortex actually lights up on the screen. Eventually, as brain imaging is refined, the picture may become as clear and complete as those see-through exhibitions, at auto shows, of the inner workings of the internal combustion engine. At that point it may become obvious to everyone that all we are looking at is a piece of machinery, an analog chemical computer, that processes information from the environment. "All," since you can look and look and you will not find any ghostly self inside, or any mind, or any soul.

Thereupon, in the year 2006 or 2026, some new Nietzsche will step forward to announce: "The self is dead"—except that being prone to the poetic, like Nietzsche I, he will probably say: "The soul is dead." He will say that he is merely bringing the news, the news of the greatest event of the millennium: "The soul, that last refuge of values, is dead, because educated people no longer believe it exists." Unless the assurances of the Wilsons and the Dennetts and the Dawkinses also start rippling out, the lurid carnival that will ensue may make the phrase "the total eclipse of all values" seem tame.

If I were a college student today, I don't think I could resist going into neuroscience. Here we have the two most fascinating riddles of the twenty-first century: the riddle of the human mind and the riddle of what happens to the human mind when it comes to know itself absolutely. In any case, we live in an age in which it is impossible and pointless to avert your eyes from the truth.

Ironically, said Nietzsche, this unflinching eye for truth, this zest for skepticism, is the legacy of Christianity (for complicated reasons that needn't detain us here). Then he added one final and perhaps ultimate piece of irony in a fragmentary passage in a notebook shortly before he lost his mind (to the late-nineteenth-century's great venereal scourge, syphilis). He predicted that eventually modern science would turn its juggernaut of skepticism upon itself, question the validity of its own foundations, tear them apart, and self-destruct. I thought about that in the summer of 1994 when a group of mathematicians and computer scientists held a conference at the Santa Fe Institute on "Limits to Scientific Knowledge." The consensus was that since the human mind is, after all, an entirely physical apparatus, a form of computer, the product of a particular genetic history, it is finite in its capabilities. Being finite, hardwired, it will probably never have the power to comprehend human existence in any complete way. It would be as if a group of dogs were to call a conference to try to understand The Dog. They could try as hard as they wanted, but they wouldn't get very far. Dogs can communicate only about forty notions, all of them primitive, and they can't record anything. The project would be doomed from the start. The human brain is far superior to the dog's, but it is limited nonetheless. So any hope of human beings arriving at some final, complete, self-enclosed theory of human existence is doomed, too.

This, science's Ultimate Skepticism, has been spreading ever since then. Over the past two years even Darwinism, a sacred tenet among American scientists for the past seventy years, has been beset by . . . doubts. Scientists—not religiosi—notably the mathematician David Berlinski ("The Deniable Darwin," *Commentary,* June 1996) and the biochemist Michael Behe (*Darwin's Black Box,* 1996), have begun attacking Darwinism as a mere theory, not a scientific discovery, a theory woefully unsupported by fossil evidence and featuring, at the core of its logic, sheer mush. (Dennett and Dawkins, for whom Darwin is the Only Begotten, the Messiah, are already screaming. They're beside themselves, utterly apoplectic. Wilson, the giant, keeping his cool, has remained above the battle.) By 1990 the physicist Petr Beckmann of the University of Colorado had already begun going after Einstein. He greatly admired Einstein for his famous equation of matter and energy, $E = mc^2$, but called his theory of relativity mostly absurd and grotesquely untestable. Beckmann died in 1993. His Fool Killer's cudgel has been taken up by Howard Hayden of the University of Connecticut, who has many admirers among the upcoming generation of Ultimately Skeptical young physicists. The scorn the new breed heaps upon quantum mechanics ("has no real-world applications" . . . "depends entirely on fairies sprinkling goofball equations in your eyes"), Unified Field Theory ("Nobel worm bait"), and the Big Bang Theory ("creationism for nerds") has become withering. If only Nietzsche were alive! He would have relished every minute of it!

Recently I happened to be talking to a prominent California geologist, and she told me: "When I first went into geology, we all thought that in science you create a solid layer of findings, through experiment and careful investigation, and then you add a second layer, like a second layer of bricks, all very carefully, and so on. Occasionally some adventurous scientist stacks the bricks up in towers, and these towers turn out to be insubstantial and they get torn down, and you proceed again with the careful layers. But we now realize that the very first layers aren't even resting on solid ground. They are balanced on bubbles, on concepts that are full of air, and those bubbles are being burst today, one after the other."

I suddenly had a picture of the entire astonishing edifice collapsing and modern man plunging headlong back into the primordial ooze. He's floundering, sloshing about, gulping for air, frantically treading ooze, when he feels something huge and smooth swim beneath him and boost him up, like some almighty dolphin. He can't see it, but he's much impressed. He names it God.

Part

II

AT WORK
IN THE DIGITAL AGE

≫━◆━≪

Rodes Fishburne

A

FTER THE TRIUMPH of the first *Big Issue, Forbes ASAP*'s tiny staff breathed a collective sigh of relief and immediately set off to top its success. The idea hatched in the spring of 1997 was to pull together a collection of everyday voices that would capture the digital zeitgeist. It would be modeled on Studs Terkel's legendary 1974 book, *Working.* Terkel, in time-honored journalistic tradition, had walked around Chicago with a notepad and simply asked people to talk, in their own voices and styles, about how they felt about what they did for a living. From stockbrokers to streetwalkers, Terkel gathered insight after insight, building them into a narrative that read like gritty poetry.

Hoping to reproduce Terkel's achievement, *Forbes ASAP*'s staff asked seventy people to talk "in the frankest terms" about their work lives in the era of the networked economy. Even the titles of the jobs—chief information officer, Webmaster, video game champion—revealed just how much work (and play) in the new economy had changed in a quarter century.

A striking difference between *Working* and the second *Big Issue* was that while Terkel found many of his subjects bored with their industrial-age jobs, the new economy workers polled by *Forbes ASAP* reported the opposite problem. They were, in fact, overwhelmed by technology's demands and constant stimulation. Everyone was short of time, of sleep, and of breath—and fearful that things would only get worse. As Michael S. Malone noted in 1998, the most terrifying phrase of modern working life is "24-7."

Big Issue II was a work of art different from its predecessor. It was darker, the voices plainer, the black and white images harsh and unforgiving. It was a magazine that you read with a wince, even as it documented our lives for generations to come.

ANDY GROVE

———◆———

Only the Productive Survive

ANDY GROVE *is chairman and cofounder of Intel Corporation, which is responsible for 85% of the microprocessors used in the world's PCs. Having famously said, "Only the paranoid survive," he exemplifies, perhaps more than anyone else in technology, the driven man.*

IT IS REALLY very simple. Computers sped up the tempo of work. They sped up decision making and information flow. Then the Internet came, and sped things up in the sense that we can now have tomorrow's newspaper today.

I get annoyed when people write articles about how the computer hasn't improved productivity. How do you measure productivity when, with a computer, you can get 200,000 transactions three times as fast? Or you can reach people it otherwise would take you a week to reach? How do you measure the value of that? Another example: I can now do personal research online. Am I more productive than if I had to go to the library? Of course I am.

So the value of the computer is that you can have information at your fingertips at any given time. You never have to send anybody out, to anywhere, to get it. From now on, when you call a government office or you have a question from a company or need support, you will expect that the reply is going to be handled online and handled expeditiously.

Everything is moving in that direction. Society has got to go on a "store-and-forward" paradigm that is completely oblivious to time and place. With 800 numbers, we're already kind of oblivious to place. No one knows where the people you're talking to are. But we are still very aware of the time element of it. We have to fit our interactions into the necessity of two people being on the end of that phone line at the same moment. The next step will mean that time and distance don't matter in our interactions.

If you can telecommute from Boise, somebody else can do it from India. This can cut every which way. Medical advice can go from Memorial Sloan-Kettering back to India. That's a fascinating aspect. A lot of work can be imported and exported. It won't matter where people work. Trade concepts and pricing will apply to nonphysical work.

I held off on cell phones for a long time because I kind of thought it was a stupid yuppie thing. My commute time has gotten longer, and now I rack up the better part of the commute making calls. Some of this is personal, by the way. It's not all work. The cell phone has become part of my life.

It is only this year that I've started to send messages from work to my wife at home. She had email before, but it wasn't part of her daily routine to check it. Usually, I'd get home before she would read the email. But now instead of writing myself a note to talk to her, I send her an email.

It's so much easier to reach people on email. It's so much easier to get through, and there's also no way to get away from it. You can go practically anywhere, and there's no escape. There just aren't any excuses. It's almost an embarrassment to say that I couldn't get online. People want to know, "What's the matter with you? Just because you were in Germany, you couldn't get online?"

Everybody expects you to always be there. I happen to be a fairly busy guy and every once in a while I can't catch up with my day's email before I go home. A lot of the time I do it at home because I don't want to come in the morning and leave yesterday's emails unanswered. I get 50, 60, and 70 emails a day. It's not terribly hard, but I have to deal with them all. I get very few junk emails, very few that I can delete without doing something about. It usually takes a couple of hours to answer my email. But I have to say that email does make things much more productive and much more involving, if not necessarily easier.

I have measured these things every decade. In the '70s I spent exactly the same amount of time on paper mail as I do now on email. Now I spend minutes on paper mail and most of it is junk.

We have a sabbatical program at Intel that is very interesting. Every seven years we get two months off. The first sabbatical I took was in 1983, and I had zero contact with Intel. I didn't call in, and nobody called me. Some of the time I was home and some of the time I was promoting a book. I was around in the U.S. I came back to Intel and spent the first week reading paper stuff and catching up. The second sabbatical was in 1986. I was already on email but not in a mobile sense. We didn't have remote connections. In 1986 I did get a phone call and had to come back a little early. After that I had two half-sabbaticals. It was against the rules, but I wasn't comfortable with taking two months off, and I was on email at that time. I didn't particularly get involved, and I didn't have to be on it. I was off skiing. I was going to get on anyway to get junk news. I couldn't resist. I pulled up my mailbox and got the stuff and answered a few things. It was like I never left.

JERRY YANG

⟾•◆•⟽

Turn On, Type In, and Drop Out

JERRY YANG *is cofounder of Yahoo. In 1994, together with David Filo, he started the company to keep track of his personal interests on the Web. Since then, Yahoo has reached a market cap of more than $18 billion. Yang serves as the company's Chief Yahoo and director.*

IT WAS REALLY, really hard to leave the Ph.D. program at Stanford. I'm not a quitter. We—David Filo and I—could have put Yahoo off for six months, finished our dissertations. But we thought we might miss the time window. It still bothers me. It's a personal goal that I never finished. But on the other hand, had I finished my thesis, what impact would I have had? Maybe 100 people in the world would have read it. And understood it? Maybe 5. And I probably wouldn't use the thesis much because I would go out and work on something completely different. Whereas the attraction to Yahoo was that millions of people were going to read what we produced. And that, to me, is sort of like a drug.

There was a lot of information out there on the Web that nobody could tame, but we were really able to. David was great at it. He was really good at being able to consolidate that information. That was when we realized the power of the Internet. The more information became networked, the more people used the Internet, the more powerful it became.

So we began to index all of the information we were finding on the Web just for fun. You could call it a hobby, you could call it a passion.

Call it instinct. But it wasn't really business. We weren't making money doing it, and we were actually forsaking our schoolwork to do it. In the end it was sort of just the purity of the Internet, and its ability to influence tens of millions of people very rapidly, that got us really, really jazzed about doing what we were doing.

In many ways, we outlasted our earlier competitors. We had so much time to work on it because we were being paid by our grant. We were more rigorous and we had time to waste. If we were writing a newspaper or even writing a magazine—where it took a while for us to see the results—it probably wouldn't have been as interesting to us. The fact was, when we published something, the hits came. When we were tired and didn't want to do it anymore, we'd see the logs going up like crazy. Well, we couldn't stop.

In 1994 we heard about Netscape Communications being funded and how they were releasing Navigator as a commercial product. It was amazing how many Internet startup ideas were being generated within a very close community of friends at school. And for a while, we were sitting there literally writing business plans for Internet-based businesses while on the side working on Yahoo, thinking, That's never going to be a business. So we did shopping malls. We did booksellers. We actually designed a system where you could inventory and order books, similar to Amazon.com today.

But at the time, we didn't realize the thing that we'd been working on for fun was going to be the one that succeeded. But finally we realized that if we stopped, then all those people using Yahoo would go away and they wouldn't have anything. We felt we were offering a service that people really wanted. And that's what got us thinking about it as a business.

Our biggest challenge was the change from grad students to entrepreneurs. We'd never done any of these things before. We didn't know the right protocols. We said things that we weren't supposed to say. And the whole money thing, it's still weird. People don't believe it when I say we didn't do it for the money. But I lived on $19,000 a year as a grad student and I could live on $19,000 today. It's nice to know that your family is provided for, but the money isn't that important.

My family is very close. My brother and I still go home every Sunday to Mom. She cooks dinner. And she packs it up for us to take for the rest of the week. I think that a lot of people who meet me say I'm basically a normal guy. I am. I don't know how else to be other than who I am. Hopefully, no amount of money or fame will change that. It's unfortunate that people do change because of external circumstances. If I want to change, it should be an intrinsic change. Maybe that came out of all the years in the Ph.D. program—just sort of thinking.

DENNIS FONG

———>•<———

Is This Your Life or What?

DENNIS FONG *was the best computer game player in the world when this essay was written. In the summer of 1997 Fong won $5,000, a computer system, and a Ferrari for being the Quake champ at the E3 computer-gaming conference in Atlanta.*

SOMETIMES PEOPLE ASK me for my autograph, and it's just too strange, you know? Like, huh? You want my autograph? And then, when I'm signing it, it's like: Am I supposed to sign it Dennis Fong or *Thresh?*

I was nicknamed Threshold. Like threshold of fear, threshold of pain. But then, when I went to an online game server, it wouldn't let me fit my whole name. So, I shortened it. I mean, people used to call me Thresh anyway because Threshold is kind of a long name to type. But you know, I just shortened it to Thresh, and then like a week later, I looked it up and the definition was "to strike repeatedly." I thought it was pretty cool.

Gaming's a good way to vent your frustrations. If you want to kick someone's ass because they did something to you, you can go online and blow away a whole bunch of people—have fun, start laughing, right? Oh, yeah, that's so fun. You don't shoot someone online and then think you're going to actually go off and kill someone. Then I'd probably be like the most violent person in the world, you know?

The whole point of Quake is to grab a weapon and then hunt down your opponent. I usually warm up by shooting nothing. Then I'll just jump into a game—that's how I practice. I'm currently the best game player in the world because of natural ability. I mean, not to sound cocky or anything, but everyone has a certain plateau they can reach. Someone can play 12 to 15 hours a day, and they don't really get any better. But me, you know, I have an inhuman ability to know my opponents' next move.

I always know where my opponent is. And there's no way to really outsmart that ability. I have really, really quick reflexes. Even if someone is hiding, I can hear where the shot came from and shoot back a split second later. I just pick up on things. I kind of know what the other person's feeling. I'm always one step ahead of them. I'm good on all the levels, whereas some of the people are only good on one level. And I'm good with all the weapons. And I'm good against all styles. You know, some people are really, really aggressive, and some people are really, really defensive. I'm good against either one, and I mix mine up.

Going into E3 in Atlanta, I wasn't really expecting to win. I didn't want to go in expecting to win and then be disappointed, even though I was the favorite. So I said, well, as long as I place in the top four, I'll at least get some cash. I'd still be a little bit upset with myself. But, you know, whatever.

All of the top players were there. But there wasn't quite as much animosity as I expected. Sometimes there are people you don't get along with online. And then you have a rift. But everyone had cleared the slate. We all started new and it was really cool. It was like one of my greatest competitors, whose name is Entropy, was interesting. I had breakfast with him several times.

The final match was pretty intense. You know, I could see the change of styles. In a semifinal match, Entropy was down. With only a few minutes left, I saw him charge recklessly. He was able to kill the guy, and he ended up winning. So when I was playing him, I was up 7 to 0 with about seven minutes left. I knew right away he would be coming after me. So I changed my style and waited for him to come. Like I would trap him in a room, and then he'd be forced—because he was down—to be the one that comes around the corner and starts shooting. But I'd be shooting at the corner, so he had nothing to do but take the first shot in the face. That's how I ended up winning.

A kid winning a Ferrari is a pretty big deal. It doesn't happen every day. It's weird. I'm learning how to drive a stick shift. I'm just kind of driving the car around. I haven't driven very far, just because I'm not totally sure of my stick skills.

JAMES JAMIESON

—=>·◆·<=—

A Rake's Progress

At the time this essay was written, JAMES JAMIESON was a gardener at Microsoft, although he did not work directly for the company.

YEAH, I'VE ACTUALLY seen Bill a couple times. He's really nice. There was one time, about six years ago, he was sitting outside and our crew was coming in to work in that area. Usually, in a situation where we see Microsoft people outside, we go and work in another place. You know, we don't want to disturb them.

Anyway, we came upon Bill, and we were going to go somewhere else. But you know something? He got up and left so we could do our job. Which, you know, was real nice, because he wasn't a prima donna. He respected the fact that, yeah, we had a job to do, too.

TIM BERNERS-LEE

———◆———

The Founder's Message

TIM BERNERS-LEE *is the inventor of the World Wide Web. He is currently director of the World Wide Web Consortium at the Massachusetts Institute of Technology.*

MANY PEOPLE ASK why I didn't commercialize the Web. It's a strange question. By asking the question, people are suggesting that they respect people as a function of their net worth. That's worrying. It's not an assumption I was brought up with, and it is disturbing the extent to which it pervades this country.

I developed the Web with three purposes in mind. The first was to give people up-to-date information at their fingertips by giving them the personal power to hypertext. The second goal was the realization of an information space that everyone could share and contribute their ideas and solutions to. Part three was the creation of agents to integrate the information that is out there with real life. Enormous amounts of information would no longer be lost.

Initially it was very hard trying to persuade people that global hypertext was going to be a good idea and not too complicated. It's very gratifying to see an idea take off like that. Although sometimes I wish I hadn't put the double slash in the URL address because it is a bit unwieldy.

We have to be careful because the sort of Web we end up with and the society we end up building on top of it will be determined by the decisions we make. All the decisions—the protocols we design within the consortium, the ways we implement them within companies, as well as the decisions people make when they browse—will shape the Web. When you browse a site containing a picture of a celebrity, you are affecting the development of the Web. When you set up a Web site in a particular way and make policies about linking only to your own information versus linking to other people's information, you're affecting the way the Web develops. People have to be aware of this. We have the answers in our own hands.

SCOTT ADAMS

——◆——

Funny Business

Cartoonist SCOTT ADAMS *draws the wildly popular* Dilbert *cartoon strip, which appears in 2,000 newspapers in 56 countries, making it one of the most successful syndicated comic strips in history.*

WHEN I MOVED to San Francisco to see an old girlfriend, I knew I wanted to work in a bank. Crocker National Bank had been recommended because of its technology. My economics professor had told me they had this ATM network that was going to really set them apart. I thought, That's cool, they're progressive. I walked into a downtown San Francisco branch, waited in line, and ended up working as a bank teller.

This was 1979. In the next six months I got robbed twice at gunpoint. One robber stuck the gun up to my nose; the other kept it in his pocket. The prospect of death has been a consistent motivator in my life. I decided I really needed to get promoted out of there because I was going to die, and I ended up getting put in a management program.

While all this was happening, I thought I knew how to fix this bank and all of its problems. I wrote up my ideas and sent them off to senior management. It was laughably bad, but it caught the attention of a senior vice president who recognized himself at age 21.

I had actually put jokes in my résumé, and he liked them so much he put me in a branch manager training program. He thought people with a sense of humor have a little extra going for them. A few months later he called me in with another guy and said, "We need a computer system to track performance at all the branches, and we want you guys to do it."

I said, "I really appreciate the opportunity, but I gotta tell ya, I'm not the guy." He said, "All I want to hear from you is whether you think you can do it." My ego was totally bruised, so I said, "Yeah, I can do it."

We didn't have to do any of the technical work. We were just project managers. We put the system together and it kind of worked.

Then they said, "We need somebody to run the system, but it will require some technical skills and it will mean a 35% raise." At that point I'd learned a little, so I said, "Yeah, I can do that." I took the job and I stealthily signed up for a computer programming course. Nobody else in the department knew anything about computers either, so I managed to bluff my way through.

In 1986 I escaped from Crocker Bank. I was looking for big money, and Pacific Bell paid more. I decided computers were just computers, but telecommunications had almost infinite growth potential.

Good analysis. Wrong company.

Pacific Bell always needed more engineers than they had. They would say, "You don't know anything about ISDN, but we need somebody to test ISDN equipment."

I found myself slowly being drawn toward more technical functions because I could bluff my way through and because they were always shorthanded. I quickly discovered I wasn't the only one bluffing.

CAROL BARTZ

⟫⟩◆⟨⟪

No Time to Change Others

As CEO of Autodesk, CAROL BARTZ *is one of high tech's most powerful women. Autodesk is one of the world's leading design software and digital content companies.*

FOR SOMEBODY WHO lives in the middle of technology, I don't use as much as other people. We put in a computerized lighting system at home. Every light is smart. But the truth is it's a little dumb right now because we can't get it programmed right.

I don't sit with my head inside a monitor. I'm a talker. I've got to see people. I'm a person who picks up the subtleties. I think one of my big strengths is I'm a great reader of people. Technology doesn't allow me to do that.

The thing that disappoints me the most about technology is that we've used it in the wrong ways. Technology may give you an extra 45 minutes, but we're not giving that back to our families. Instead we're doing 45 more minutes in meetings. We're way, way, way information overloaded. There's always more information, yet we're already under the gun to look at more information than we can handle. We're being abused by technology rather than using it.

We'll reach a happy medium, I think. When I first got email, way back when I worked at Digital Equipment, each message was like a certified letter coming in. My God, email! Before you knew it, people were abusing it, sending everything to everyone—50-page documents with attachments to the attachments to the attachments. So you stop reading most of it. Now, instead of writing yet another email message, I often think, Wait a minute. I'll use the phone. With the Web or any other technology, you have to have the courage not to use it. Can you just let the phone ring without answering it? I can.

I make time for my family. They would like more. I'm pretty careful, though. People talk about balance, but I don't believe in it. The concept means perfection. Every day I cannot be the perfect CEO, the perfect mom, the perfect wife, the perfect friend, and do a little volunteering. That's not the way it works. If I have a lot going on at work, I've got to be there. When I am home, I spend a lot of time with my family and forget about work for a while.

But when I'm at work, I work hard. Everybody does. We have incredibly short product cycles, which means incredibly intense development cycles. It's the term-paper phenomenon from college. For marketing, the term paper is the product launch. For finance, it's the end of the quarter. We pull all-nighters. We do whatever is required. And then the semester starts again—a new product cycle starts—and you rejuvenate.

We're helping people do their work better, and we're helping to make it more fun. The first love of architects, one segment of our market, is the design of a building. The building also has to be functional—it needs heating ducts, a sound structure. Our programs help architects spend much less time doing the boring part of their job. It allows them to be creative. Certainly people designed and built things before, but technology enables you to try before you buy. You can model almost anything. You can run stress tests and thermal tests and wind tests. You can actually walk into a building before one pier is drilled. We've changed the "what if?" process. Once you build something, the "what if?" process is difficult. You probably won't rip the top off and start over. But you can do that when you're working with a virtual model. You can change it again and again until it is exactly how you want it.

Technology changes the nature of collaboration. You can't make a building without collaboration. Everyone—the architect, the structural engineer, the heating engineer, the electrical engineer—comes together to build a building. In the old days, they had to communicate using FedEx and faxes, and it was very inefficient. "Is this the last thing this guy sent me? Hmmm. I don't know." "By the way, has everybody else been alerted?" Now let's say you're building an office building. You put up a project Web site on the Internet. Everyone involved can go there to find whatever they need—the status of every aspect of the building, the most current revision of the plans.

I'm from Wisconsin, and I got a computer science degree from the University of Wisconsin. I was a real nerd. I love, love, love, love math. Back in the late '60s, math meant being a teacher if you were a woman. I wasn't interested in teaching. Then I took my first computer course. It was crazy. It was like math, only more fun. I switched to computer science. My roommates thought I was nuts. There were only two women in the department.

I went to First Bank System in Saint Paul, where I sold computerized banking services to small banks when computers were just starting to be used in that business. Then I went to 3M as a systems analyst. I went to Digital Equipment and then to Sun Microsystems. There were 100 people at Sun. We had $9 million in revenue. When I left, we had about $3.5 billion. But after 10 years I got a little burned out on the hardware world's mine's-bigger-than-yours race. I thought software was the place to be. I loved Autodesk because it was a company that provided software to solve very interesting problems.

I don't have the male-dominant gene that says you have to run something someday, but I did like the concept of putting an imprint on a company. When this job was offered to me, I thought I should try it. Autodesk had a fabulous franchise. It created a market. The country's infrastructure has to be maintained, and whether that's making sure all of our bridges are working, earthquake-proofing a structure, or remodeling a kitchen, design is central. We're right in the middle of the action.

In the country's biggest companies, there aren't many women CEOs. But more are coming up. Some are starting their own companies. It's better to be a woman in technology than in other industries, but there definitely still is a gap or a glass ceiling. It's there in a lot of subtle and some not-so-subtle ways. It starts with venture funding. It's present in the fact that there are not that many women technologists. It goes back to the fact that young girls still aren't encouraged in the math and science arena. It goes to the fact that white males are still more comfortable with white males.

When I'm with a group of high tech execs, I don't feel anything strange. But when I'm in a group of executives from other industries, they assume I must be somebody's wife. I will go to a meeting of 100 executives from throughout the country, and though there are only 100 people in the room, it is still assumed that I am there for some other reason. They assume that there must be 99 executives and that person in a skirt. I was in Washington, D.C., with Bill Gates and Andy Grove and some other executives last June for a meeting with some senators. It was high-tech-CEOs-come-to-town, and a senator turned to me and asked, "So how are we going to start the meeting?" He thought I must be the moderator.

It's annoying. I don't have time to change these guys, but when it's ridiculous I call them on it. What I do have time to do is try to change the environment so that my daughter has a place.

JOHN PERRY BARLOW

———◈———

Surfing the Fence Line

JOHN PERRY BARLOW *is a retired Wyoming cattle rancher, a former lyricist for the Grateful Dead, a corporate consultant, and cofounder of the Electronic Frontier Foundation. His manifesto,* A Declaration of the Independence of Cyberspace, *can be found on more than 20,000 Web sites.*

CORPORATIONS ARE ENCHANTED by the devil they know. They *are* the devil they know. The information age was supposed to free up our time; we were supposed to work less. But the information age is rich in irony. There are many people who are caught in a transitional phase. They may have the illusion that they are working in the center of the information age—they could even be working for information companies. But they are being treated in the most beastly fashion—right here in Silicon Valley, companies treat their employees as disposable. They take in 22-year-olds and use them like toilet paper. My introduction into this whole world was in 1988. Apple wanted me to write a book about the company. I was excited about Apple, at least the myth of Apple, because I thought it provided a new form of community-cum-business that could have been the way to go in a culture that was losing community.

Apple, as I learned when I arrived, was in fact worse than more traditional industrial organizations. It thought that it was so enlightened that it could treat people really badly and still feel a sense of smugness and superiority. It was just like a dysfunctional family. Nobody dared say they were being treated like dirt because everybody knew that

Apple was enlightened. But the people there had absolutely no job security, and they were worked to the bone. They were not trusted. I don't think I've ever run across security guards that fierce except when I was entering East Germany. And it hasn't changed much, either.

Another great irony of the information age is that people are traveling more than ever to get together and meet. I think that the Internet is going to do for jet fuel what the personal computer did for paper. I originally was under the impression that I was going to get out of agriculture and use all this digital technology to be able to leave my body in Pinedale, Wyoming, and let my mind roam the planet and make a living. But what has happened is that I leave my mind at Barlow@eff.org while my body roams the planet. What I wasn't counting on was the incomplete quality of digital information—its incredible capacity to make connections but its inadequacy when it comes to completing them.

I was at Xerox PARC a while ago and a fellow named Ranjit Makkuni showed me his virtual conferencing room. It had everything: all the bandwidth in the world, high resolution, four-wall screens, and three-dimensional sound. If you were in that room and somebody was in a similar room in Portland, you could see where they were spatially in relation to you; you could hear them as clearly as you'd hear them if they were there. I asked him, "Is it just like actually being in the room together?" and he said, "No, the prana is missing." *Prana* is the Sanskrit word for breath or life force.

Yet for all that, I can recall my first time in cyberspace. I was on The Well, which I thought of as being a self-contained world unto itself. Then somebody told me that I could telnet into this other system and get something. And I didn't quite understand what they meant, but they had given me the line, the telnet, the host name, and a password. I said, telnet so-and-so dot com. And suddenly there's this new log-in prompt and I realized I was making a hard disk spin 3,000 miles away. And I could have the same effect on literally millions of hard disks at any moment. Everything was equally close to me. I have a difficult time describing how it actually felt. But it was just, suddenly, I got it. My God, this whole thing is absolutely of a piece. It is instantaneous, simultaneous, ubiquitous, and growing like crazy. This is the nervous system of the planet. What hath God wrought? I still feel that way. I think something truly profound is taking place here.

LUCY LIPPS

≫◆≪

Ms. Loose Lips

*By her own account, LUCY LIPPS, née Kristi Hoss, Web host-
ess, is "the leading authority on romance and the art of being
a contemporary sex goddess." She lives in Houston but works
in Los Angeles, New York, Aspen, and London.*

YOU THINK YOU'RE worldly, you've got the world by the balls, but
you never do. When that happens, something will blindside you.
I mean, I thought I was big stuff there in New York. I grew up in a port
town in South Texas on the gulf where there are oyster shells in most
people's driveways. The highlight of my adolescent career was being
nominated for "Ms. Quito"—there are so many mosquitoes around
that we actually have a Ms. Quito.

South Texas is where I got the name Lucy Lipps. I'm not sure if it
was my dad or my brother who started calling me that. I was always
tattling on my brother when I was little. It comes from the Walter
Winchell quote, "Loose lips sink ships." My brother is 10 years older.
Every time I was following him, crying, "He won't take me with
him,"—he'd say, "Oh, God, here comes Lucy Lipps." It sounds like a
porn star, which is okay: It makes people check in. The name stuck all
through school, me being the biggest, loudest, most opinionated person in school, even college.

I started out majoring in premed. I wanted to be a plastic surgeon.
I had this thought in my mind: Never trust an ugly plastic surgeon.
These people need me. But I decided I just couldn't shut up long
enough to pay attention for 15 years of school to become a plastic sur-

geon. The next best thing for me was obviously broadcasting. Radio, TV. It was just my temperament.

At home, I'd have to scream really loud to get over everybody else's screaming to get them to pay attention to me. With this one device, a microphone, I could talk and everybody could hear me. I just thought that was the greatest thing in the world. My father describes me with a live mike like a crack addict with a platinum card.

I went to work for a station. It was a Howard Stern-type show. I was talking about the computer on the air one day. People called in about it and I was persuaded to try the computer. I broke it out and got onto America Online. I gave out my email address on the air. That evening I came home and had a thousand emails. I was, "Wow!"

Then somebody at the station took my picture and scanned it in, and you could get it in the AOL gallery and I heard even more. These people were sending me pictures of what they had done with my picture. They had taken it off and made wallpaper. It's weird. I started to realize what a powerful forum it is.

Then I made a Web page. The next month I got 700,000 hits. It was growing at a rate of like 250% a month. Sex is the only thing that really sells on the Internet. It's the only thing that's really making money.

I've picked up and absorbed along the way the ability to read other people. It's probably why I am good at giving advice. I'd say 25% of the questions I get are about sex, 25% are about me, and 50% are just about relationships.

I spend about every waking hour and then three times in the middle of the night on my site, keeping up. I love it. I love it.

The most-asked question about sex is from men who want to know how to get girls to notice them. That and how to make a girl happy. There are so many people out there looking for love.

For some people I'm like having a best friend who says, "Hey, man, you screwed up. It's okay. We all do it. It will be okay." A lot of times people won't go to their friends, especially boys, adolescent boys, because they don't want to be embarrassed. I'm kind of like the father confessor, but just a little saucier version in drag.

BILL GATES

Watching His Windows

BILL GATES *is Microsoft's chairman and chief software architect. He has become an icon for, depending on your point of
view, the best or the worst that technology has to offer. At the
time this essay was written, he was the richest man in the
world, a position that he has since moved in and out of.*

MICROSOFT IS DESIGNED to write great software. We are not designed to be good at other things. We only know how to hire,
how to manage, and how to globalize software products. The key was
to never view ourselves as a service company. We had to be a product
company. But it was an approach that would probably not apply to any
other business. This is a business where you can find people who have
enthusiasm for doing things well. You can create incredible feedback
loops that guide what you do. We have many users who love to tell us
how they do things.

I used to have this memo that I updated every year called The Ten
Great Mistakes of Microsoft, and I would try to make them very stim-
ulating so people would talk about lessons for the company's future.

Many of our mistakes related to markets we didn't get into as early
as we should have. The constraint was always the number of people
we could hire, while still managing everything, and ensuring that we
could meet all of our delivery commitments. We were always on the
edge. We really pushed the limits of how fast we hired people.

The only real disagreement Steve Ballmer [vice president of sales
and marketing] and I ever had was when he joined the company. We

had 25 people. He said, "We have to hire about 50 more people to deal with all this opportunity." I said, "No way, we can't afford it." I thought about it for a day and said, "Okay, you just hire as fast as you can, and only good people, and I'll tell you when you get ahead of the sanity picture." Here we are at 24,000 people now and still the key constraint is bringing in great people.

All successful companies are run by a team of people, and I've been very lucky with the other people who have come in and helped out.

How do you manage the sales force and make sure that those measurement systems are really tracked down to the individual level to encourage the right behavior? I'll sit in meetings where Steve Ballmer talks about how he wants to do it, but that's not my expertise. How do we advertise to get these messages across? I sort of know where we are going long-term. I've got to make sure people are coming up with messages consistent with that future. But I'm not expert in those things.

Even in technology areas it's fun to learn new things: When I'm trying to find out where we are going with asynchronous transfer mode, for example, we have experts who come in and talk to me about those things. I spend two weeks here just doing "think weeks," where I read all the stuff smart people have sent me. I get up-to-date to see how those pieces fit together.

In terms of hiring great people, how do we hire all these people? It's by word of mouth. People say it's great to work here. The stock value has a huge impact on employees, customers, stockholders, everybody, and it reflects the long-term approach and strength of the company.

We've always said that, given our long-term approach, this business will definitely go through cycles. There will be ups and downs. There haven't been any downs yet, but we are still sincere about saying that. We say our profitability, percentage-wise, has grown at an unsustainable rate. We are always telling analysts, "Don't recommend our stock. We sell software, not stock. Lower your earnings estimate, be more conservative." It's not a long-term approach to promote the stock in any way. We are one of the most valuable companies in America, and I think it reflects people's optimism about the people here and what software can be.

I personally work long hours, but not as long as I used to. I certainly haven't expected other people to work as hard as I did. Most days I don't work more than 12 hours. On weekends I rarely work more than 8 hours. There are weekends I take off and I take vacations. My job is the best job there is and I get a lot of variety. I travel around and see customers.

If I left Microsoft today, they'd have to pick somebody else to run the company. Who knows? The guy could do a better job. But a CEO transition is probably very risky for a company. I'm a younger CEO than you'll find in most companies and more committed to my job than most. Nobody is going to get me interested in some other job or activity, so it's very unlikely that we'd face that challenge.

Who knows how the new CEO would do? There are an immense number of good people here. The whole notion in the press of personifying a company through one person or a few people is a gross simplification, and it totally misstates the picture.

RAY OZZIE

———◆———

Breakfast Revolution

Bill Gates has called RAY OZZIE *"one of the top five program-mers in the universe." Ozzie is the creator of Lotus Notes and founder of Groove Networks.*

I N 1993 I DECIDED to do an experiment using myself and my family as guinea pigs. I put a T1 line in my house and put computers every-where. I just wanted to see how it would affect our lives. The biggest thing I discovered is that I was the worst problem. I am a compulsive email checker. When I walked by a computer, I just had to see if there was something new waiting for me. I was afraid I'd fall behind. So I was checking in all the time while my family watched me, shaking their heads, giving me a lot of grief. They, meanwhile, were mostly un-affected.

I talk to my wife in the morning over coffee. Until recently, out of the corner of my eye, I would also sort of watch morning TV and scan my email and drink coffee. Then I stopped sitting at the kitchen table with her. I just went to the corner where the PC was set up, and worked on email and caught up on news on the Web. I was isolating myself further into the technology, away from my home.

Of course, I could have stopped myself, but then technology came along and helped. About a year and a half ago, IBM came out with the ThinkPad 560. It is a small, thin thing. I outfitted my house with a wireless LAN, and now I have the ThinkPad sitting on the table in the kitchen. It sits there unobtrusively, has a great battery life and oper-ates wirelessly. Now I can sit at the table with my wife and sort of browse via the computer, as if I were sitting with her reading the morning paper. It's not as obnoxious. I think she likes it better, too. The ThinkPad absolutely sold me on the notion that information appliances will arrive and make things better, even for compulsive users of technology like me. No, it's not perfect yet. Small is good, but it should be made of rubber. When it falls off the table because one of my kids knocks it off, I should be able to pick it up, as opposed to picking up the pieces. There should be, instead of wires and ugly battery chargers, recharger bowls—something that is more natural to home settings. We always hear about how these things will become an appliance operating in our lives as easily as telephones; that's easier for me to see now.

We're more intolerant of inefficiency. For one example, I needed a certified check the other day. I rarely have to go to the bank anymore, but it took 40 minutes from the time I parked my car to when I drove off, just to get this stupid certified check. In the old days—and this isn't too long ago—it would have been fine, expected. Now, it seemed to take forever; I became so frustrated. We have total control over our ability to get frustrated, but the frustration is self-propagating. The speed that we operate at now is making us more and more impatient.

We will cope with it, eventually, but it may take another generation. Generation Y will cope better than we do. It will probably be second nature for my kids. They are growing into this environment as opposed to having to deal with a transition from a very different world. It will exist and we will take it for granted.

I have a couple of really big concerns. I am really, really concerned that we are not preparing ourselves as a society for the fact that all of this communication is going to create political and social issues that have not been addressed. We talk but don't do anything about the fact that there will be more and more commercial and governmental exploitation of surveillance technologies and digital artifacts.

I don't think we know the questions to ask. I think technologists tend to do things because they can be done. We build little devices without regard to how they will be used. I've built a lot of these devices and I can't stop thinking about the implications. It worries me.

WALTER WRISTON

———◆◆◆———

The Defeat of the Elite

Banker WALTER WRISTON, *retired CEO of Citicorp and Citibank, served as chairman of former President Ronald Reagan's Economic Policy Advisory Board. His books include* Risk and Other Four-Letter Words *and* The Twilight of Sovereignty: How the Information Revolution Is Transforming Our World.

ANYTHING THAT GETS information to people is threatening to existing power structures. I was talking to Peter Drucker about the fact that no one has figured out a way to categorize things on the Internet. He told me about a Czech monk in the 15th century who invented alphabetization. Before that, books were arranged wherever the monks wanted to put them, so nobody else could find them. Then this guy had a brilliant idea to go a-b-c. It revolutionized the organization of information. He broke the monopoly of the monks. And you know what happened to him? He got excommunicated for his trouble.

Whenever there is a shift in how wealth is created, the old elites give up their position and a new group of people arise and control society. We're in the middle of that right now.

Years ago, at the bank, we had a company in Boston working on voice-answerback. You'd call and say your account number, and the voice would say you're overdrawn by $300 or whatever. We bought this busted company, called Scantlin Electronics, from Jack Scantlin, and he said, "You're doing it all wrong."

I asked why, and he said analog technology was yesterday's news;

tomorrow's was going to be digital. Then he asked me what people want to know from their bank, and I told him they want to know how much money they have in their account. And he said, "I'll be back in 90 days with a device that will tell them that." I said, "Sure, right, bye-bye."

But he came back with a terminal and a card, and you could put in the card and get your balance on a screen. That was the basis for ATMs and all the rest of it. It moved us out of analog and into the digital world. Jack repackaged and sold himself to the bank two or three times, and now he's living on his own island in the South Pacific with a big yacht, and I say bless him. He changed the way we looked at things.

HARRY WU

Life in the Labor Camps

Chinese dissident HARRY WU, *a human rights activist, was a political prisoner for 19 years. He is executive director of Laogai Research Foundation, which uses the Internet to provide regular updates on conditions in Chinese labor camps.*

I N THE PAST eight months, I've been home only about three days. The rest of my days I get up and somebody delivers me to the airport where I fly to a speaking engagement. Since August 1995, when I got my release [from Chinese jail], I believe I've made about 250 speeches in Europe and in every American state except, I think, Alabama, Mississippi, and Louisiana. I've talked to everybody from grammar school students to Vietnamese human rights groups to researchers at Yale and Columbia universities.

I can sleep anytime I want. I learned that in prison, because we sometimes had no food. We used to say to ourselves, If you don't have money, don't spend money. That means if you don't have energy, turn down your brain, save your energy. We had to show our performance, otherwise we got in trouble; we got the torture.

My organization is the Laogai Research Foundation. *Laogai* means "labor and reform," which is what the camps in China are called. People ask me, "Why are you so busy? Why do you travel around the world? For what?" I tell them I want to see the word *Laogai* someday appear in the dictionary in every language and in every country, like *Gulag*. Under the name Laogai, 50 million people have been put away. And it still exists today.

The foundation has its own Web site and several offices, in Paris, Washington, and Australia. When I travel I have a lot of people supporting me. I'm not James Bond. But we have a very organized communication system. Every day, wherever I am, I make a phone call and leave a message in code. I also get a lot of protection. Two months ago, when I was in Japan, the government gave me a policeman for protection 24 hours a day. Same in South Korea.

I was arrested the last time I tried to get into China because of a computer. I chose a remote border entry because I thought they wouldn't have the technology. But they had a computer, put my name on it, and identified me and arrested me. Next time I go, I'll take a laptop computer with fax. The Chinese control their communication system, and they watch the Internet, but so far they can't interpret our faxes if we send messages in code.

I have to be careful using Chinese telephones now. I'll tell you a story. One of my guys is Tibetan, and in 1993 he went into China and was betrayed by another Tibetan. So Chinese security followed him. He gave me a call: "I bought a pair of shoes for you." I said, "What kind?" He said, "Sport shoes." "Size?" "Number 7." Perfect. Number 7 was our code. It means everything's perfect. But he was arrested after that call. The Chinese asked about me, and he said, "I don't know anything about Harry Wu." And they played him a tape of the phone call. And they asked him, "What is the meaning of the sport shoes number 7?" They control the communication system. And all the secret police carry cellular phones.

I told Motorola that. Motorola was in the Cold War. They have principles; they didn't do business with the Soviet Union because they said, "We don't want to share our advanced technology with this evil empire." Now they say about China, "But we are just working on the communication system. And if the communication system is going well, it means the people will be more free." And I say, "That's right, but in another part of the Chinese government, they're using that same technology to control people, to monitor them and arrest them." That's why the government is buying all kinds of equipment right now from HP, Bell, and others, so they can get even better at monitoring.

But we will win because technology is also helping us advance our struggle. The world is open now. The door is open, and nobody can close it. Technology is opening people's consciousness.

TODD PRIDY

——⟨⬥⟩——

Playing Jacks

TODD PRIDY, *former first baseman for the Sonoma County Crushers, was a six-year veteran of minor league baseball at the time this essay was written. Upon obtaining a teaching degree in history, he retired from baseball after the 1999 season.*

L AST YEAR I was the hitting instructor at Napa Valley Junior College, and we were playing a fall game against, I don't know, somebody. It was real close to the time my wife was going to have a baby. When I left her that morning, she was fine. But I took my pager with me as well as the cell phone and told her to call me if anything happened. So we're playing. I was coaching first base and it was probably like the third inning when the pager goes off. The phone number was mine and it had the old "911" after it—which meant I better hurry up and call.

So I went over to the dugout and called her on the cell phone. It was showtime. Man, I don't think the wheels touched the ground on my way home. I raced her to the hospital and just like that we had a baby boy. We named him after the slang term players use for a home run—Jack.

I have a cell phone in my truck now. And on nights when my wife and kid don't come to the game, you know, I just pull out of the parking lot and give her a quick call and let her know I'm coming home. It's nice, especially now with the little one, to know that I can always be contacted somehow.

There are times when I come home after a game and jump on the

Internet and look up my buddy in triple A back in North Carolina. You know, to see how he is doing. I check to see how other guys that I've played with are doing, too.

During the '95 off-season, I signed a minor league contract with the Texas Rangers. Well, just before spring training, I'm reading the newspaper and I see: "Texas Rangers sign first baseman Bubba Smith to a minor league contract."

So the wheels start turning, and I jumped on the Internet and looked up Bubba Smith. I checked out his records and his stats and stuff. My first reaction was kind of like, Okay, I have every confidence in my abilities, but damn, look at this guy's numbers. What are they going to do with two first basemen? And then I thought, They're going to need a DH [designated hitter] and . . . well, they'll figure out who can play the sack and who can't, and the other one will DH.

You start playing mental games with yourself and trying to figure out why they signed him when they've already got me . . . eventually I think I just said, Screw it, just go out there and get it on.

TOI

———◆———

One-Trick Engineers

At the time this essay was written, TOI was a prostitute at Cherry Patch Ranch brothel near Las Vegas. She had worked there for four years and claimed to make about $10,000 to $15,000 for three weeks' work.

WE GET MEN from all over the world here, but during Comdex it's just crazy! The girls were just talking about it: When's Comdex? WHEN'S COMDEX? That's our busiest week by far. We get, on average, 70 men a night in here during that show, and Joe [the owner] has to bring in more girls.

We're the closest brothel to Vegas, so they come here in droves—rental cars and limos.

Many of them save up all year to come here. But they're different, yeah, they are cheap! But the money all evens out because there are so many of them.

Comdex guys? I've noticed a lot of lonely guys, yes, that are stressed out. They come here and relax. This is a place where they can get away from it all, kick back, and forget their worries.

GORE VIDAL

———✦———

The View from the Amalfi Coast

Novelist GORE VIDAL *is the author of more than 35 books (from* Myra Breckinridge *to* Lincoln*), in addition to numerous film scripts, articles, and essays. A former candidate for senator of California, Vidal lives in Ravello, Italy, for part of each year.*

I GAVE A COMMENCEMENT address at the University of South Dakota, a state my father fled to go to West Point but which I have seldom visited. Now it is a place to flee to. Sioux Falls is an attractive city, green and lush nowadays. More important, thanks to technology, this faraway Midwestern state once suitable only for cattle and missile sites is becoming a bedroom for Chicago office workers who can work at home and use interactive TV for meetings. Technology has changed my life even here on a cliff overlooking the Tyrrhenian Sea, a view unchanged since Ulysses, as usual off course, came floating by millennia ago.

I write longhand or on a portable manual typewriter and have no intention of going electric, much less to a computer. But even so, everything has changed for me. I fax my longhand or typed pages to a lady in London. She transcribes whatever I'm doing onto a floppy disk. Then she prints it out, faxes it back, and I rewrite until we're ready to send it off to the publisher. In the case of journalism, I can watch a news story on CNN, then send off a story even as it is breaking, in time to make the next issue of the *Nation*. In the old days—as there is no particular postal system in Italy—it would be at least a month before it could be typed up and then sent by pony express across the Atlantic. In 1992 I'd send presidential candidate Jerry Brown in New England lines and thoughts for his speeches and hear him, that night, using them on CNN. This is, simply, a speeded-up process, which means that when I write on politics I am up-to-date instead of, at best, a week or more behind events. The once absolute tyranny of geography has vanished.

So, work for some of us has gotten better. On the other hand, the nature of most work is now make-work, and that may be clearer in the wide-open spaces than it is in the traffic's roar of a great city. Robotizing, digitizing, instant communicating, et al., will eliminate millions of jobs, leaving multitudes to the hell of frying in fast-food restaurants. Work must be rethought in our brave new world. Or even eliminated for some.

In spite of all the talk that this will free us, democratize us, give the poor man the same access to information as the rich man, I doubt much will change. Since the rich are ill-educated at best and the poor kept in perfect ignorance, I don't see what good all this knowledge will do either group.

And writing? As it is, everyone thinks he's a writer, particularly those whose reading skills are minimal. I don't think a hundred million novels in English a year would be in any danger of being downloaded or sent away for.

Novel writing is a slow process in which hands and brain coordinate on a page. I've worked in the same fashion for half a century. Deep, complex ideas are just that: deep and complex, and they work best when you don't try to force them from the deep until they are ready to surface.

I can't imagine the impact on my books if I'd had a computer and access to the Internet all these years. I'd probably store historical data on a computer, as my biographer Fred Kaplan does. The results would be no different, though. In general, people who write on computers don't write nearly as well as those who type or write longhand. They become "easy settlers," as we used to call movie writers who settled for their first notion of a scene. The computer page looks too perfect to alter the first time around. Hence, lousy, repetitive prose.

Theoretically, the Internet might be a forum for good critics, but Grisham's Law will prevail and the critics will be paid to push the same old brand names. The United States is culture-resistant as opposed to gadget-friendly.

Over on the other side of the world, the Russian system collapsed for reasons that had nothing to do with us but indirectly because of technology. The indirection was that no society can shut itself off from satellite TV, bootleg tapes, and word of elsewhere. In the jungles of militarized Burma, rebels, as I write, are watching *Gidget Goes to Waikiki* and are, consequently, revolting.

Part III

TIME IN THE
DIGITAL AGE

❦

Rodes Fishburne

BIG ISSUE III, "Time," was conceived at the birth of the dot-com boom, a year before the phrase "Internet time" entered the vernacular. Yet even then, to those living and working in places such as Silicon Valley, it was apparent that life was accelerating at a dizzying pace.

The modern idea of time and of what we will do to save it, expand it, hoard it, and spend it, has always been fascinating. But now it began to seem threatening as well. The "time-saving" inventions of the past half-century had somehow turned on us. We now held cell phone meetings in traffic jams, checked voicemail during Christmas dinner, and used our technology constantly, perverting its original selling point.

As our authors showed, any attempt to grapple with time inevitably leads to an examination of mortality. So it's not surprising that this series of essays represents the *Big Issue* at its most meditative. Former speechwriter Peggy Noonan deftly demonstrated her gift for examining life with an honesty that is both disarming and bracing, while *Forbes ASAP* consulting editor Owen Edwards wrote eloquently of man's arrogance toward time, even as it slips past. Edwards' piece is a lasting example of the distance a superb writer can travel in just two pages. Shortly after publication it was read one evening by Peter Jennings on the nightly news.

When the Greek mathematician Pythagoras was asked about time 2,500 years ago, he responded that it was "the soul of this world." The essays that follow attempt to trace this idea, like an outline on onionskin paper, capturing the image for a brief, timeless moment.

MICHAEL S. MALONE

⫸◆⫷

The Mission Bell's Toll

MICHAEL S. MALONE, *editor of* Forbes ASAP, *is a business and technology writer who has covered Silicon Valley for more than 20 years. His books include* Infinite Loop, The Big Score, *and* Going Public.

I N THE FRENETIC world of Silicon Valley, where the daily obsession is to shave a microsecond from every transmission, revision, and decision, a vital lesson about time lies unnoticed. As we spend billions struggling to glimpse just one product generation ahead, a prophecy about our future lies with two Ohlone Indian skulls buried to the eyeballs, cranium down, in a box of rice.

At the very heart of Silicon Valley sits Santa Clara University, an oasis of adobe buildings and gardens surrounded by a sea of industrial parks and suburban housing developments. And at the university's heart, literally and emotionally, is Mission Santa Clara, founded by the Franciscan order in 1777.

Around the mission lie rose gardens, wisteria walks, and one old adobe wall. Each tells a story. But the story told by the rose garden is the most terrible. There, beneath the thorns, and yellow and salmon and red petals, trapped within the deep and gnarled roots, are the skeletons of an untold number of Ohlone Indians, young and old, victims of smallpox and chicken pox, mumps and measles . . . but most of all, victims of the passage from one era to the next. They are the first valleyites to be sacrificed to the unforgiving passage of time.

The Ohlones ruled the valley for several thousand years. Yet now all that remains of them is a few dusty fragments tucked away in Tupperware bins in the abandoned football team locker room. There, in the remotest building on campus, archaeologist Russell Skowronek manages a staff of two assistants and five student volunteers as they race to save the artifacts from the oblivion of asphalt parking lots and poured concrete foundations. What they have found and cataloged is the detritus of America's manufacturing history, a rag-and-bone shop of early California culture: a poker chip, slate pencil, crockery toy marble, shriveled peach pits, the lower half of a glass mustard container, and other shattered and yellowed objects pulled from university grounds and the remains of a privy from a forgotten Santa Clara tannery. And, shockingly, the pair of Ohlone skulls in the desiccant.

Sitting in the university's faculty club, Skowronek anxiously stirs his coffee. An energetic man with a long mustache, he speaks quickly, like a man used to not being heard.

"We're sitting right now on ground zero of the modern computer age," he says. "You already knew that. But what you didn't know is that it started 220 years ago."

Skowronek smiles. "Let me explain. Before 1777 the Ohlone Indians lived in a cyclical world. It hadn't changed in 10,000 years, not since the last Ice Age. There was really no sense of time being linear, only circular. The seasons came and went. You hunted or you planted. It was not a time-based world. In fact, despite our arrogance about how much better our lives are today, we estimate that it took only one adult Ohlone just 20 hours per week to feed and shelter his or her family."

It was not a long life, Skowronek continues, nor an especially complex one. The Ohlone lived in clans that rarely interacted—except for the occasional fight or marriage—with neighboring clans just a half mile away. With little east-west trade, clans that lived just a mile from San Francisco Bay might never eat a fish or a clam but instead subsisted largely on deer and on acorns pounded into meal. The early European explorers of the region were frustrated when the guide from one clan would lead them only as far as the next stream and then refuse to go on in fear of losing his life.

"It all ended in January 1777, with the founding of the mission," says Skowronek. "Suddenly, the Ohlone found themselves in time.

Western European time. Life at the mission was run by the bell. You got up, ate, prayed, worked, and signed off the day at midnight with the bell. And from the moment the mission bell rang for the first time, the clocks of Santa Clara Valley began—and they kept going faster every year."

It wasn't just the priests who were trapped in this time but the Ohlone as well. Having lived millennia without time, they had no resistance to the temporal march ringing each day from the mission tower.

Mission Santa Clara soon became the locus for all activity in the valley. Suddenly, clans that hadn't moved more than five miles in 500 years were crossing ancient boundaries and making regular visits to the mission to trade. Many chose to stay and live near the mission grounds. Stunted for generations, trade soon flourished, as did communications between clans. For the first time the Ohlone became a distinct tribe but in the process gave up the 50 subdialects and unique styles of family artisanship that had long distinguished them. Their arts and languages hybridized into single, common forms. In listening to the time bell, the Ohlone had embarked on a path from which there was no going back.

The Ohlone's vulnerability to the bell was emblematic of a lack of resistance to many things Western, most horribly contagion. In the first three decades of the mission's existence, hundreds of Ohlone died from epidemics of childhood diseases to which they had no immunity. Those baptized were buried in what is now the rose garden. But many others died from less obvious causes that nevertheless were tied to the Western European pattern of time: diet, overwork, industrial accidents, medicine, and the stress of living in a timed world.

"This new world not only changed the pace of the valley but even its look," says Skowronek. "The daily demands of commerce, faith, and schooling meant you had to build more and more buildings and homes. That meant roof tiles and adobe bricks, and that in turn meant kilns. And kilns meant charcoal, and that meant oak trees. And that deforested the valley floor, which meant no more acorns for the Ohlone. From now on they had no choice but to eat a Western diet and live a Western life."

By 1827 and the end of the valley's first modern era, Santa Clara Mission was home to 1,462 people. Spanish was now the lingua franca. Tens of thousands of cattle roamed the valley floor, and the first vineyards were planted near the mission. Alta California, because of its unique location on the Pacific Rim, also rapidly became a center for trade in a global economy: The priests wore silk vestments from China, and mission residents regularly bought items imported from Acapulco and Mexico City, the Philippines, Spain, and even England.

The second revolution in valley life, which occurred in the decade after 1845, was as profound as the first, and it teaches the same lessons. One is that technological change not only produces wholly new types of products but it also forces the reorganization of the society around it. Furthermore, this reorganization is not just structural but temporal. Its participants physically and culturally restructure the world and society, and inhabit an irrevocably new timescape with its own unique rhythms and cycles.

The third lesson is the most disturbing: When a society encounters such a point of inflection, it divides into two groups. One group, usually the majority, which cannot or will not cross over to the new world, is lost. The other, the minority that does cross over, to be joined by the next generation and new arrivals, establishes a new identity so complete as to erase all traces of the people they were before.

"You see it at the mission during the first half of the 19th century," says Skowronek. "You start out with 50 clans, and almost overnight they become Ohlone Indians. Then come the Catalonian Spanish priests and the mestizo soldiers. Before long, they are Californians. Then, in the 1840s, the Anglos arrive. They are squatters—at least until the Bear Flag Revolt and the gold rush. Then they become 'pioneers.'

"It would be easy to say these are merely changes in nomenclature, mixed with some public relations. But in fact, these name changes represent a fundamental transformation. These before-and-after groups, even when they include the same people, inhabit very different worlds."

No group felt this change more than the Ohlone. The few who had survived the first revolution in time had, within a few years, stopped being Indians and became, in an odd metamorphosis, Mexicans. "Then," says Skowronek, "after U.S. statehood, they became, basically, nothing. They were disenfranchised, dehumanized. And in response they simply disappeared. They hid as best they could in the ethnic population, losing their Ohlone identity. Their descendants wouldn't emerge again until it was safe, in our time."

Meanwhile, the Spanish/Californians, too, became Mexicans and were largely marginalized as the valley filled with new immigrants— Irish, Italian, Yugoslavian (Americans)—who easily adapted to the new pace of life.

One of these was a German, Jacob Eberhard, who bought a tannery, itself the descendant of a tanning works that was as old as the mission, from his father-in-law. Lasting nearly 170 years until finally closing its doors after the Second World War, the tannery was the most enduring business in valley history. Eberhard brought the latest inventions and consumer products to the factory and his own home. By 1880 his home featured a privy and new Edison lights, and the tannery had become a giant complex of a dozen buildings beneath a towering, belching smokestack. The tannery was a foul-smelling, unpleasant place to work—and wasn't very popular at the new college campus across the street when the wind shifted. Nevertheless, it was on the cutting edge of American technology in the years after the Civil War. Leather was the plastic, the silicon, of the 19th century, and nobody made it better than Eberhard. At its peak, the factory shipped 900,000 pounds of cow, calf, and sheep hides throughout the world, most notably to the shoe factories of Lowell, Massachusetts. But Eberhard wasn't just a mass producer of rendered flesh; he produced some of the best saddle leather on the planet, the finest of which became part of a bejeweled, silvered, and gilded $10,000 saddle ordered by the 101 Wild West Show. It was, according to contemporary accounts, "the most beautiful and high-priced saddle in the United States."

The world of the Eberhard Tannery in the 1880s was one of alarm clocks and pocket watches, factory whistles and train schedules. This was the new timescape, and those who could adapt to its regime survived. Those with a gift for it thrived. Once again, the new time transformed the landscape. An added level of complexity had been bolted to the manufacturing process. Now there was a hierarchy of order processing, from customer to retailer to distributor to manufacturer to supplier (like Eberhard) and back again. This system demanded the rapid transfer of information and material, and soon the valley was crisscrossed with telegraph wires and railroad tracks. And where they and the cattle ranches met, towns appeared. The mission faded in importance to the commercial centers of the valley. Increasingly, the mission became an object of nostalgia for the past, not a part of the active present.

The valley floor itself was now one vast cattle ranch, with the last of the great oak trees felled or killed by grazing. Living in hovels, the surviving ancient Ohlones died out. Meanwhile, in 1881 Martin Murphy Jr., founder of what is now Sunnyvale and owner of most of the ranch land in the valley—indeed, the largest private landowner in the world—celebrated his golden wedding anniversary by inviting the entire state to a party. An arrogant man celebrated not just his own wealth and power but also the victory of the industrial world. Trains were chartered from around the state; hundreds of cattle were slaughtered. Eberhard was there, as were all of the successful businessmen of Santa Clara Valley. This was their moment, the high-water mark of their era.

Yet even as they were celebrating, that era was coming to an end. Within a decade the cattle ranches would almost be gone, replaced by miles of fruit trees. Technology had once again sped up the clock. Thanks to artesian wells and water pumps, mass production, marketing, and reliable railroads and highways, Santa Clara Valley was now the Valley of Heart's Delight, with the most prosperous orchards in the nation. The valley moved on corporate time, the punch clock, and the Taylor Method: In the vast new Del Monte and Libby canneries, workers were shown time-motion films on how to cut apricots and boil cherries and pit prunes. The flats of goods were wrapped in colorful promotional labels, sold according to Chicago Board of Options Exchange prices, and shipped by rail to markets in Minneapolis and Manhattan.

The children of the deceased Martin Murphy and Jacob Eberhard now lived in turreted gingerbread homes in downtown San Jose and sent their well-dressed sons to Santa Clara University and their daughters to the College of Notre Dame. The local towns swelled with the new cannery workers from Portugal and Eastern Europe, who deposited their wages at the new Bank of Italy (soon to be Bank of America). Mansions now lined the Alameda from the old mission to San Jose, the very path once taken by the Franciscans. And in the spring, the streets would whiteout from a blizzard of blowing fruit blossoms. Busy drivers, rushing to work in the new corporate time, complained about the nuisance to city magistrates.

Once again, as time accelerated and the valley floor was transformed, and as the production process grew more subtle and complex, the people again changed. The aging pioneers, now distinguished but anachronistic, were trotted out at museum openings and interviewed by the local paper about how it was in the old days. And thanks to a new generation of writers like Jack London and local publications like *Sunset* magazine, a cult of nostalgia sprang up, creating an enduring myth of graciousness out of the hard life of the mission era. By the 1920s, houses in a growing number of new valley developments featured walls painted in adobe hue, tile roofs, and even little ersatz bell towers—along with a garage to house that most representative object of the new timescape. Yet even as the Valley of Heart's Delight was celebrating its newfound luxury, two young men, Bill Hewlett and David Packard, were turning on the switch of their new audio oscillator, in whose high-frequency waves could be heard the squeal of the valley's next era. Then, in 1955, two years after a feeble Eberhard Tannery finally shut its doors, William Shockley, armed with a team of brilliant young men and a Nobel Prize for creating the transistor, returned to his old hometown to reset the clock and, in doing so, annihilate the valley of his childhood.

It is a curious fact, long known to biologists, that every animal—from the torpid giant tortoise to the frantic housefly—is given as its birthright about 1 billion heartbeats. Even that cynosure of the ephemeral, the mayfly, gets its 10^9 as a larva before its brief fling at flight.

Why a billion—2 at most—and not more? The answer seems to lie in some kind of clock within the cells. It is as if the Almighty, with uncharacteristic democracy, ordained that every species would have its same threescore and ten, the same span of experiences, no matter how quickly or slowly it was forced to live them. Clotho may change the content of each life's thread, but Lachesis always draws out the same length for Atropos to cut. And all of our vast and costly struggles—medicine, nutrition, safety, genetic engineering—to extend this deadly timer will, it seems, at most improve our fateful number of heartbeats by a factor of two.

But in the digital, solid-state world that is the new metronome of valley life, it is a different story. The modern integrated circuit chip will soon be able to perform approximately 1 billion operations per second. One gigahertz. A billion electronic heartbeats: the equivalent of a lifetime in a single second. And, of course, at the end of those billion beats, there won't be a tiny electronic death but another billion-beat second, and another. And, since silicon is incredibly stable and invulnerable to almost everything but cosmic rays, there will be a billion more of these digital lifetimes for each chip—more than all the generations of life on earth—before it goes dark.

This is the new clock, our clock, the timepiece of the valley's digital era. This is the mission bell that tolls quicker than the synapses can arc across our brains, that counts out an eternity of silicon days in the time it takes to blink your eye. And thanks to Moore's Law—that defining rule of our lives and augury of our future superfluity—this new silicon clock will grow faster and faster, doubling in speed every few years, until it too produces whole cosmologies of change that are beyond human comprehension. And what then? What happens when the next clock resets the time once again? Who gets through the next time, and what do they become?

Look at any newspaper, magazine, or television show; surf the Net; shop at the local department store; listen to the words you use in daily speech: Silicon Valley is now the center of the world, the greatest creator of new wealth and employment in human history, the dynamo of innovation transforming the modern world, the creator of a new paradigm that is redefining the way we speak, live our daily lives, even how we see the world. And in this digital universe, Silicon Valley is the new Greenwich: We build the clocks and set the pace; the world revolves around our time. We are sui generis, we are unique in all the world and all of history, we are without precedent, and without end. The '90s have been our golden age—this has been our great party, and we have invited the whole world to attend. We speak knowingly of long booms and perpetual prosperity as if God himself has blessed our good works with immortality.

Yet the lesson of the past is that none of this is new, only the magnitude. In fact, in the 220 years of modern Santa Clara Valley history, there have been three other such eras. Each of them was kicked off by a technological revolution, each of them operated to a different and faster clock, each of them was global in scope, each of them transformed the nature of the valley itself and the self-image of its residents, and each effectively erased all real memory of what came before. And at the moment of each era's greatest arrogance and self-assurance, each was within a decade or two of coming to an end. The clock shifted again and they were as effectively erased as Minos or Carthage. Their children lived in a different world, spoke different words, and bore different names. If the cycles of the past hold, the end of Silicon Valley and of the digital revolution as we know it lies sometime in the years just beyond 2010. And then? The clocks reset themselves once more, this time perhaps to the speed of nucleotides forming and re-forming a trillion times each second in biological computers, or quantum dots, or perhaps one vast global computer, humming away in 100 billion interconnected computers and chips, bearing all the world's knowledge in a new kind of silicon consciousness.

But whatever the clock, the pace will be unimaginably fast. And under such a blazing discipline, who among us will be able to cross over to the other side? A few will, perhaps our children and our children's children who have spent their entire lives as navigators of cyberspace. But it is also not hard to imagine that no one, at least no one human, will enter this new world, or the next one that arrives in the final decades of the 21st century.

Who, or more accurately what, will this new era, this new timescape, belong to? Intuitively, we already know: the machines themselves. Chips can live a lifetime in a second, then live a billion lifetimes more. For them the pace of this new clock is almost pastoral. Eventually, anthropomorphic software agents will be our surrogates into this world . . . until they need us no more. They will in time take over cyberspace as their own universe—real ghosts in the machine. Unlike us, they will be able to change their identities and their roles in microseconds and, thanks to Moore's Law, will grow ever smarter and faster and more capable of dealing with this hyperaccelerated timescape. Then the tool will become the toolmaker, and perhaps the toolmaker the tool. And the numerous objects of our lives will become the broken relics in some future cyberarchive.

We have entered into a kind of Faustian bargain with time: Just join the world of the clock, and we'll give you progress, we'll give you hope.

And medicine. A longer life span. Libraries of knowledge. The ability to reach around the world. And fly to the moon. Just listen for the bell and attend to its call. . . .

We have listened, and we have been rewarded in extraordinary ways. But it has come at an enormous cost—perhaps none greater than the one that lies ahead. Time is about to speed up again. Soon the pace will leave us behind.

And then, as for the Ohlone, the mission bell may signal the end of our day.

PEGGY NOONAN

———◆———

There Is No Time, There Will Be Time

PEGGY NOONAN *was a special assistant to President Reagan and chief speechwriter for George Bush in 1988. She is the author of* Simply Speaking *and, more recently,* The Case Against Hillary Clinton.

I SUPPOSE IT IS commonplace to say it, but it's true: There is no such thing as time. The past is gone and no longer exists, the future is an assumption that has not yet come, all you have is the moment—this one—but it too has passed . . . just now.

The moment we are having is an awfully good one, though. History has handed us one of the easiest rides in all the story of man. It has handed us a wave of wealth so broad and deep that it would be almost disorienting if we thought about it a lot, which we don't. But: We know such comfort! We sleep on beds that are soft and supporting, eat food that is both good and plentiful. We touch small levers and heat our homes to exactly the degree we desire; the pores of our bare arms are open and relaxed as we read the *Times* in our T-shirts, while two feet away, on the other side of the plate glass window, a blizzard rages. We turn levers and get clean water, push a button for hot coffee, open doors and get ice cream, take short car trips to places where planes wait before whisking us across continents as we nap. It is all so fantastically fine.

Lately this leaves me uneasy. Does it you? Do you wonder how and why exactly we have it so different, so nice compared to thousands of years of peasants eating rocks? Is it possible that we, the people of the world, are being given a last great gift before everything changes? To me it feels like a gift. Only three generations ago, my family had to sweat in the sun to pull food from the ground.

Another thing. The marvels that are part of our everyday lives—computers, machines that can look into your body and see everything but your soul—are so astounding that most of us who use them don't really understand exactly what they're doing or how they do it. This too is strange. The day the wheel was invented, the crowd watching understood immediately what it was and how it worked. But I cannot explain with any true command how the MRI that finds a tumor works. Or how, for that matter, the fax works. We would feel amazement, or even, again, a mild disorientation, if we were busy feeling and thinking long thoughts instead of doing—planning the next meeting, appointment, consultation, presentation, vacation. We are too busy doing these things to take time to see, feel, parse, and explain amazement.

Which gets me to time.

We have no time! Is it that way for you? Everyone seems so busy. Once, a few years ago, I sat on the Spanish Steps in Rome. Suddenly I realized that everyone, all the people going up and down the steps, was hurrying along on his or her way somewhere. I thought, Everyone is doing something. On the streets of Manhattan, they hurry along and I think, Everyone is busy. I don't think I've seen anyone amble, except at a summer place, in a long time. I am thinking here of a man I saw four years ago at a little pier in Martha's Vineyard. He had plaid shorts and white legs, and he was walking sort of stiffly, jerkily. Maybe he had mild Parkinson's, but I think: Maybe he's just arrived and trying to get out of his sprint and into a stroll.

All our splendor, our comfort, takes time to pay for. And affluence wants to increase; it carries within it an unspoken command: More! Affluence is like nature, which always moves toward new life. Nature does its job; affluence enlists us to do it. We hear the command for "More!" with immigrant ears that also hear "Do better!" or old American ears that hear, "Sutter is rich, there's gold in them hills, onward to California!" We carry California within us; that is what it is to be human, and American.

So we work. The more you have, the more you need, the more you work and plan. This is odd in part because of all the spare time we should have. We don't, after all, have to haul water from the crick. We don't have to kill an antelope for dinner. I can microwave a Lean Cuisine in four minutes and eat in five. I should have a lot of extra time—more, say, than a cavewoman. And yet I feel I do not. And I think: That cavewoman watching the antelope turn on the spit, she was probably happily daydreaming about how shadows played on the walls of her cave. She had time.

It's not just work. We all know the applications of Parkinson's Law, that work expands to fill the time allotted to complete it. This isn't new. But this is: So many of us feel we have no time to cook and serve a lovely three-course dinner, to write the long, thoughtful letter, to ever so patiently tutor the child. But other generations, not so long ago, did. And we have more timesaving devices than they did.

We invented new technologies so that work could be done more efficiently, more quickly. We wished it done more quickly so we could have more leisure time. (Wasn't that the plan? Or was it to increase our productivity?)

But we have less leisure time, it seems, because these technologies encroach on our leisure time.

You can be beeped on safari! Be faxed while riding an elephant and receive email while menaced by a tiger. And if you *can* be beeped on safari, you *will* be beeped on safari. This gives you less time to enjoy being away from the demands of time.

Twenty years ago when I was starting out at CBS on the radio desk, we would try each day to track down our roving foreign correspondents and get them to file on the phone for our morning news broadcasts. I would go to the daily log to see who was where. And not infrequently it would say that Smith, in Beirut, is "out of pocket," i.e., unreachable, unfindable for a few days. The official implication was that Smith was out in the field traveling with the guerrillas. But I thought it was code for Smith is drunk, or Smith is on deep background with a really cute source. I'd think, Oh, to be an out-of-pocket correspondent on the loose in Cairo, Jerusalem, Paris—what a thing.

But now there is no out of pocket. Now everyone can be reached and found, anywhere, anytime. Now there is no hiding place.

We are "in the pocket." What are we in the pocket of? An illusion, perhaps, or rather many illusions: that we must know the latest, that we must have a say, that we are players, are needed, that the next score will change things, that through work we can quench our thirst, that, as they said in the sign over the entrance of Auschwitz, "Work Brings Freedom." That we must bow to "More!" and pay homage to California.

I live a life of only average intensity, and yet by 9 P.M. I am quite stupid, struck dumb with stimuli fatigue. I am tired from 10 hours of the unconscious strain of planning, meeting, talking, thinking. If you clench your fist for 10 hours and then let go, your hand will jerk and tremble. My brain trembles. I sit on the couch at night with my son. He watches TV as I read the *National Enquirer* and the *Star*. This is wicked of me, I know, but the *Enquirer* and the *Star* have almost more pictures than words; there are bright pictures of movie stars, of television anchors, of the woman who almost choked to death when, in a state of morning confusion, she accidentally put spermicidal jelly on her toast. These stories are just right for the mind that wants to be diverted by something that makes no demands.

I have time at 9. But I am so flat-lined that I find it very hard to make the heartening phone call to the nephew, to write the long letter. Often I don't. I feel guilty and treat myself with Häagen-Dazs therapy. I will join a gym if I get time.

When a man can work while at home, he will work while at home. When a man works at home, the wall between workplace and living place, between colleague and family, is lowered or removed. Does family life spill over into work life? No. Work life spills over into family life. You do not wind up taking your son for a walk at work, you wind up teleconferencing during softball practice. This is not progress. It is not more time but less. Maybe our kids will remember us as there but not there, physically present but carrying the faces of men and women who are strategizing the sale.

I often think how much I'd like to have a horse. Not that I ride, but often think I'd like to learn. But if I had a horse, I wouldn't be making room for the one hour a day in which I would ride. I would be losing hours, seeing to Flicka's feeding and housing and cleaning and loving and overall well-being. This would cost money. I would have to work hard to get it. I would have less time.

Who could do this? The rich. The rich have time because they buy it. They buy the grooms and stable keepers and accountants and bill payers and negotiators for the price of oats. Do they enjoy it? Do they think, It's great to be rich, I get to ride a horse? Oh, I hope so. If you can buy time, you should buy it. This year I am going to work very hard to get some.

During the summer, when you were a kid, your dad worked a few towns away and left at 8:30; Mom stayed home smoking and talking and ironing. You biked to the local school yard for summer activities—twirling, lanyard making, dodgeball—until afternoon. Then you'd go home and play in the street. At 5:30 Dad was home and at 6 there was dinner, meat loaf, mashed potatoes, and canned corn. Then TV and lights out.

Now it's more like this: Dad goes to work at 6:15, to the city, where he is an executive; Mom goes to work at the bank where she's a vice president, but not before giving the sitter the keys and bundling the kids into the car to go to, respectively, soccer camp, arts camp, Chinese lessons, therapy, the swim meet, computer camp, a birthday party, a play date. Then home for an impromptu barbecue of turkey burgers and a salad with fresh Parmesan cheese followed by summer homework, Nintendo, and TV—the kids lying splayed on the couch, dead-eyed, like denizens of a Chinese opium den—followed by "Hi, Mom," "Hi, Dad," and bed.

Life is so much more interesting now! It's not boring, like 1957. There are things to do: The culture is broader, more sophisticated; there's more wit and creativity to be witnessed and enjoyed. Moms, kids, and dads have more options, more possibilities. This is good. The bad news is that our options leave us exhausted when we pursue them and embarrassed when we don't.

Good news: Mothers do not become secret Valium addicts out of boredom and loneliness, as they did 30 and 40 years ago. And Dad's conversation is more interesting than his father's. He knows how Michael Jordan acted on the Nike shoot, and tells us. The other night Dad worked late and then they all went to a celebratory dinner at Rao's where they sat in a booth next to Warren Beatty, who was discussing with his publicist the media campaign for *Bulworth*. Beatty looked great, had a certain watchful dignity, had the vodka penne.

Bad news: Mom hasn't noticed but she's half mad from stress. Her face is older than her mother's, less innocent, because she has burned through her facial subcutaneous fat and because she unconsciously holds her jaw muscles in a tense way. But it's okay because the collagen, the Botox, the Retin-A and alpha hydroxy, and a better diet than her mother's (Mom lived on starch, it was the all-carbo diet) leave her looking more . . . fit. She does not have her mother's soft, maternal weight. The kids do not feel a pillowy yielding when they hug her; they feel muscles and smell Chanel body moisturizer.

When Mother makes fund-raising calls for the school, she does not know it but she barks: "Yeah, this is Claire Marietta on the cookie drive we need your cookies tomorrow at 3 in the gym if you're late the office is open 'til 4 or you can write a check for $12 any questions call me." Click.

Mom never wanted to be Barbara Billingsley. Mom got her wish.

What will happen? How will the future play out? Well, we're going to get more time. But it's not pretty how it will happen, so if you're in a good mood, stop reading here and go hug the kids and relax and have a drink and a nice pointless conversation with your spouse.

Here goes: It has been said that when an idea's time has come a lot of people are likely to get it at the same time. In the same way, when something begins to flicker out there in the cosmos, a number of people, a small group at first, begin to pick up the signals. They start to see what's coming.

Our entertainment industry, interestingly enough, has plucked something from the unconscious of a small collective. For about 30 years now, but accelerating quickly this decade, the industry has been telling us about The Big Terrible Thing. Space aliens come and scare us, nuts with nukes try to blow us up.

This is not new: In the '50s Michael Rennie came from space to tell us in *The Day the Earth Stood Still* that if we don't become more peaceful our planet will be obliterated. But now in movies the monsters aren't coming close, they're hitting us directly. Meteors the size of Texas come down and take out the eastern seaboard, volcanoes swallow Los Angeles, Martians blow up the White House. The biggest-grosser of all time was about the end of a world, the catastrophic sinking of an unsinkable entity.

Something's up. And deep down, where the body meets the soul, we are fearful. We fear, down so deep it hasn't even risen to the point of articulation, that with all our comforts and amusements, with all our toys and bells and whistles . . . we wonder if what we really have is . . . a first-class stateroom on the *Titanic*. Everything's wonderful, but a world is ending and we sense it.

I don't mean: "Uh-oh, there's a depression coming." I mean: We live in a world of 3 billion men and hundreds of thousands of nuclear bombs, missiles, warheads. It's a world of extraordinary germs that can be harnessed and used to kill whole populations, a world of extraordinary chemicals that can be harnessed and used to do the same.

Three billion men, and it takes only half a dozen bright and evil ones to harness and deploy.

What are the odds it will happen? Put it another way: What are the odds it will not? Low. Nonexistent, I think.

When you consider who is gifted and crazed with rage . . . when you think of the terrorist places and the terrorist countries . . . who do they hate most? The Great Satan, the United States. What is its most important place? Some would say Washington. I would say the great city of the United States is the great city of the world, the dense 10-mile-long island called Manhattan, where the economic and media power of the nation resides, the city that is the psychological center of our modernity, our hedonism, our creativity, our hard-shouldered hipness, our unthinking arrogance.

If someone does the big, terrible thing to New York or Washington, there will be a lot of chaos and a lot of lines going down, a lot of damage, and a lot of things won't be working so well anymore. And thus a lot more . . . time. Something tells me we won't be teleconferencing and faxing about the Ford account for a while! The psychic blow—and that is what it will be as people absorb it, a blow, an insult that reorders and changes—will shift our perspective and priorities, dramatically, and for longer than a while. Something tells me more of us will be praying, and hard (one side benefit of which is: There is sometimes a quality of stopped time when you pray. You get outside time).

Maybe, of course, I'm wrong. But I think of the friend who lives on Park Avenue who turned to me once and said, out of nowhere, "If ever something bad is going to happen to the city, I pray each day that God will give me a sign. That He will let me see a rat stand up on the sidewalk. So I'll know to gather the kids and go."

I absorbed this and, two years later, just a month ago, poured out my fears to a former high official of the United States government. His face turned grim. I apologized for being morbid. He said no, he thinks the same thing. He thinks it will happen in the next year and a half. I was surprised, and more surprised when he said that an acquaintance, a former arms expert for another country, thinks it will happen in a matter of months.

So now I have frightened you. But we must not sit around and be depressed. "Don't cry," Jimmy Cagney once said. "There's enough water in the goulash already."

We must take the time to do some things. We must press government officials to face the big, terrible thing. They know it could happen tomorrow; they just haven't focused on it because there's no Armageddon constituency. We should press for more from our foreign intelligence and our defense systems, and press local, state, and federal leaders to become more serious about civil defense and emergency management.

The other thing we must do is the most important. I once talked to a man who had a friend who'd done something that took his breath away. She was single, middle-aged and middle class, and wanted to find a child to love. She searched the orphanages of South America and took the child who was in the most trouble, sick and emotionally unwell. She took the little girl home and loved her hard, and in time the little girl grew and became strong, became in fact the kind of person who could and did help others. Twelve years later, at the girl's high school graduation, she won the award for best all-around student. She played the piano for the recessional. Now she's at college.

The man's eyes grew moist. He'd just been to the graduation. "These are the things that stay God's hand," he told me. I didn't know what that meant. He explained: These are the things that keep God from letting us kill us all.

So be good. Do good. Stay his hand. And pray. When the Virgin Mary makes her visitations—she's never made so many in all of recorded history as she has in this century—she says: Pray! Pray unceasingly!

I myself don't, but I think about it a lot and sometimes pray when I think. But you don't have to be Catholic to take this advice.

Pray. Unceasingly. Take the time.

PETER ROBINSON

Sincerely, Mom

PETER ROBINSON *is a research fellow at the Hoover Institution. He is the author of the best-selling* Snapshots from Hell: The Making of an MBA *and hosts the PBS television program* Uncommon Knowledge.

Notice how we are perpetually surprised at Time. ("How time flies! Fancy John being grown-up and married! I can hardly believe it!") In heaven's name, why? Unless, indeed, there is something in us which is not temporal.

—C.S. Lewis

MY 5-YEAR-OLD, Pedro, has reached the stage at which children repeat phrases they only imperfectly understand. The other day I found him intently studying an insect. "Look, Daddy, a dumb beetle!"

It turned out he had been watching a program on African animals. "Dumb beetle" was the way he had heard "dung beetle."

Most of Pedro's mistakes are funny—he calls his potatoes "smashed," and he's convinced his favorite *Star Wars* character is named "Dark Raider." But a couple of weeks ago, he used a phrase that hurt. Showing me how quickly he could dash across the living room, he sang out, "Look, Daddy! Faster than the speed of life!"

Faster than the speed of life.

Although the passage of time certainly has its benefits—I wouldn't want to change diapers forever—it has begun doing things to me that are distinctly unpleasant. I'm alarmed to discover how gray I've become. At a restaurant the other day, the kid at the cash register asked in all innocence whether I'd like the 55-and-over discount.

Wasn't technology supposed to help with this? Now that I'm middle-aged (41, not 55, thank you), I don't want any more cell phones, beepers, palm-held personal assistants, or other "timesaving" high tech devices. They only make time move *faster*. I want technology that makes time stand still.

Oddly, just such a technology exists. It was my mother, until recently one of the most untechnological people I know, who brought it to my attention.

Last year Mom announced that she wanted to buy herself a computer. I tried to talk her out of it. She was 80, and during her Christmas visit, I sat next to her as she attempted to use my computer. The icons confused her. She typed slowly (her brief career as a secretary ended almost five decades ago). She found even the most basic terminology difficult.

"A floppy disk? Why is it called 'floppy'? It looks rigid to me," she asked.

"Because the first disks, in use a dozen years ago, really were floppy," I replied.

"Oh," she answered. She smiled sweetly, as if indulging me.

She bought a computer anyway. A member of her church gave her lessons. (The high tech age has produced a new work of corporal mercy—teaching computers to the elderly—to go along with feeding the hungry and clothing the naked.) It took less than a month for Mom to master email so completely that she turned into a spammer; one morning she sent me five emails before I told her to knock it off.

For years my mother had been planning to write her memoirs. She had put together a fat file of notes and newspaper clippings, but she had never started. Now I suggested that instead of writing a book, she might tell her story by email. I advised her to keep it simple, sending two or three emails a week to my 7-year-old daughter, Edita.

Would you like to hear about when I was born? October 27, 1916, I came into the world. The doctor drove his horse and buggy the 10 miles from the little town of Montrose, Pennsylvania, where he lived, to the hamlet of Forest Lake, where our farm was. (When my sister, Ethel, was born, it was January and there was so much snow the doctor couldn't get there. My father had to ask a neighbor how to cut the cord that connects the baby to her mother.)

Soon Edita and I were reading about the one-room schoolhouse, about the woodstove on which her mother cooked, about the icebox that her father kept stocked with blocks of ice from the pond near his water-powered sawmill, and about the plumbing—water was piped from a spring downhill to the farmhouse where it ran into the kitchen sink 24 hours a day, and the outhouse ("It was mighty snowy and cold to get there in the winter!!").

For my daughter, the fascination lies in reading about the animals—the collie, Drummie, who rounded up the cows every evening and brought them back to the barn, and the horses, Roxy, Major, and Jewel.

Roxy and Major were huge workhorses. Roxy, a female, was quite cross and I didn't dare go near her. She was likely to bite or kick. Major was a male, a handsome horse, deep black with white around the feet and down the middle of his face. He was happy-natured and never would bite or kick. They did look beautiful when hitched up together.

Jewel was a pony. She was black and white, much the same coloring as Major. My sister and I would put a saddle on her. I loved riding off into the country on Jewel. In the summer she also pulled a wagon for us.

For me the fascination lies elsewhere. My mother's emails present an America that no longer exists. The hardness of life comes through. Mom was the only member of her school to go on to high school. ("I had to leave home to room in Montrose, where the high school was located, because Montrose was 10 miles away and too far to drive every day.") Although her father owned six farms, none of his tenants could pay their rent.

One farmer gave us a turkey every year for Thanksgiving, and that was his rent. There was another who had a BIG family but wasn't a very successful farmer. I don't think he ever paid us any rent, and sometimes in the middle of the night my mother would go to his farm to help his wife, who was having another baby.

The sense of faith is palpable. School days began with a Bible verse and the Lord's Prayer. In high school, students wrote religious inscriptions in each other's "autograph books."

One inscription read:

A place for me in your album,
A place for me in your heart,
A place for us in Heaven,
Where true friends never part.

Each story my mother tells represents a victory over time, a fragment of the old world she has snatched from oblivion to give to her grandchildren. Yet her emails convey a still more decisive victory. It lies not in what she writes but in her voice.

Mom is now 82. She uses a cane indoors and a walker outdoors. On good days, she paints—she's working on portraits of my children—but she has to tuck her walker under her easel for support. On bad days, she sits in her easy chair. Her age presents itself in the quavery handwriting in her letters, the phrases she misses when we speak over the telephone. The exception is her emails. The voice they convey is the voice that I knew as a child. Her sense of humor, her pleasure in telling a story, her eye for detail and color—all are present, unmediated by old age. When I read my mother's emails, time stands still.

Or rather, my mother stands outside time. It is Aristotle's distinction between "accidents" and "substance." Accidents are the inessential aspects of an entity, substance is its essence. In humans, accidents include eye color, hair color, height, weight, and age. Substance is the voice in Mom's emails. Email—prosaic email—has permitted me to glimpse that which, in C.S. Lewis's words, is "not temporal."

For now my mother's emails continue to arrive, faster, so to speak, than the speed of life. Even when they cease, I will know that despite the accidents of old age—despite the accident of death itself—time never touched her.

OWEN EDWARDS

Running Out

OWEN EDWARDS *is a consulting editor for* Forbes ASAP, *a contributing writer for* GQ, *and the founding editor of* Parenting *magazine. He is currently working on his next book, a memoir of life in the Greek Isles.*

THE FIRST MECHANICAL CLOCKS, appearing in the 13th century, signaled a subtle shift in the way we comprehend the nature of time. This paradigm shift, while giving the world a remarkable concept we now call "exact time," usurped one of the great temporal metaphors: the hourglass.

Sand flows through the neck of an hourglass at a constant rate, but creates the opposite illusion. When the top is full, it is as if nothing is changing. Then as the sand passes the halfway point, the rate of change appears to accelerate, until, at the point when the top chamber empties, the pace seems frantically fast. This, of course, is exactly how time passes in life.

When we're young, years unfold at such a leisurely pace that we constantly hurry them along, unable to wait until we're seventh graders, or 16, or finally in college, or at the legal drinking age. At some point, perhaps when we're 30 or 40 (or even 50 for the reality challenged), we realize the top glass is half empty, and the falling sand is picking up speed. From this point on, acceleration rules. By the time we're old, the grains are so few we feel we can count them—if only they'd hold still. The last pinch of sand races down so fast that no one could have warned us how precious those few grains would become. For monks, princes, poets, and anyone else who could watch an hourglass, a fundamental irony of time stood revealed: It is a constant that always varies.

Conversely, the round face of a mechanical clock seduces us with different and false impressions of time. The first of these is that time is circular, not linear, and that it endlessly repeats itself. This may be true in a cosmic sense, but in the intimate span of a single human life, not one minute will be repeated at the same time tomorrow. In fact, even in an age that has invented "exact time," the reassuring term "same time" is a hoax, elevating routine to the level of holy meditation. Because of modern clocks, we are suckered into believing that the double orbit of hands during the passage of 24 hours brings us back to where we were yesterday.

I remember an old woman saying to me with real surprise, as if she'd just come out of a long sleep, "How did I get here?" What she meant by "here" was old age—the final destination we somehow imagine we'll travel toward forever but, with time circling around and around, somehow never reach. Fooled by the slow passage of minute and hour hands, we are able to deny all the things—the graying hair, aching knees, sagging chins—that try to remind us that the sand is running out.

A clock's second false impression is that its smooth regularity describes a continuum that we assume will move at a dependable rate whether we're young or old, feeling joy or pain, anticipating the future or clinging desperately to the present, facing a firing squad or taking a spring walk in the woods. Capable as we are of chalking off seconds, minutes, hours, days, and months, we imagine we can also measure life. And so we become the victims of a joke as old as . . . well, as old as time.

Think of how arrogantly we deal with time, as we infer that the ability to track its increments gives us the power to manipulate its unimaginable totality. Such hubris is famously punished by the gods, and so we are sentenced to endless confusion in time's mind-boggling taffy pull. We constantly look forward to things, taking our minds off the present to obsess about the future. Then, like the broken lines in the middle of a highway devoured by a speeding car, moment after moment slips by unnoticed. We push time along, and when we finally reach our goal—the big birthday, the month's vacation in "timeless"

Venice, the cool autumn after a suffocating summer ("If only October would come!")—we then try to bring time to a halt. "I hope this day never ends." Which, of course, it does, all the faster because we're so determined to hold it in place.

Then comes the punch line of this crushing chronological joke: nostalgia. The awaited day, or week, goes by at an unvarying pace, and we begin to think that our backward longing, with its entourage of snapshots, postcards, and videotapes, can slow time's inevitable disappearance. And, again, as we crane around to see behind us, the present rushes past unobserved. The next thing we know, it is we who are asking, "How did I get here?"

As if the classic clock weren't misleading enough, we now have digital time, with its idiot savant accuracy and total lack of context. Looking at the disembodied numbers in the margins of our computer screens or on the control panels in our coffeemakers, we see a kind of icy, soulless time, with no "then" and no "later," but only a relentless, meaningless *now, now, now.* Plucked out of the continuum, seen naked, the pointless present is time at its most monstrous. There was a time, only a few centuries ago (the blink of a fruit fly's eye in the stately march of epochs), when few humans knew the hour or even the year. Now we can never avoid it, with cheap digital clocks winking off the minutes and seconds in every "timesaving" device known to man.

Which brings us to the well-known but always vexing modern conspiracy to take away what little time we have while proffering the illusion that we'll have more. Just as the clock defines our civilization, the dream of beating the clock defines the latter half of the 20th century. Everything from the automobile to the vacuum cleaner has been sold with the promise of shimmering green fields of leisure. Yet today many of us spend hours in our cars, trapped on sludge-filled moving rivers of traffic, as time passes with its usual remorseless momentum. And, since more and more people work, and the workweek takes up more and more of our lives, most of us do our housekeeping chores during the hours once devoted to relaxation. Wasting time, a once honorable anti-endeavor, is now a source of shame.

With the rapid approach of the millennium, the longest measurement of human time, the computer has raised the stakes. In the irresistible guise of the ultimate productivity machine, this technology may have the power to steal time in a way not even automobiles and television managed to do. Given the pervasiveness of wired and wireless connection, some of us—the slavishly computer savvy—can now work almost every waking hour. And, since time is money, many of us do. I remember the days when my father would come home from his office at 6 in the evening, mix a couple of vespers martinis for himself and my mother, and embark on evenings that belonged to him (and his family), not his business. Thirty years later, I rarely turn off my computer until 10 P.M. And, in order to deal with that new time-saver, email, I turn on the machine half an hour earlier each morning. Weekends? They are becoming weekdays in disguise. The Web, perhaps the most appropriately named medium of our age, has already caught millions in its sticky strands of vanished time. Because of this pernicious pleasure drain, some of us—a recent study suggests—are slightly depressed when we use the Internet. So we go off to the old cities of Europe, where the sight of ruins and peeling frescoes reminds us not that time is of the essence but that time *has* an essence.

Recently the GartnerGroup, eminent computer consultants, created a peculiar device, as unnatural as the centaur, mermaid, or griffin: a large hourglass that incorporates a digital clock counting down to January 1, 2000—Y2K. Presumably, the irony of this mixed metaphor will not be missed. That most of the world's computers can't tell the difference between one century and another seems an important message. To be able to do things faster, to accomplish feats of calculation in nanoseconds, to compress what once took months into a few minutes, is not to understand time. To understand time, even to experience what we now knowingly refer to as "real time," *takes* time. Even to get a hint of what it does and what it means may take all the years of a long life.

No doubt we know we should step back, take a while, and think about why a minute can last forever or why a month can pass in an instant. But we won't. Our eyes will be on that digital countdown to 2000 A.D., a date we anticipate variously with dread or delight. It will be here before we know it. *Where did the time go?*

MICHAEL LEWIS

━━━◦◦◦◦━━━

25-7?

MICHAEL LEWIS *is author of the best-selling books* Liar's Poker, The Money Culture, *and* The New New Thing. *His most recent book,* Next: The Invisible Revolution, *is about the Internet boom.*

I CAN STILL REMEMBER when time was too abundant to seem valuable. As a boy in New Orleans, I could flush whole months down the drain without concern that I was depleting a scarce resource, that I was somehow *spending* time. Of course, to a child, time is the gray brick wall that stands between you and Christmas morning.

But it wasn't just childhood. Old Southern attitudes, especially when united, as they were in New Orleans, with economic impotence, encourage the opposite of urgency. In New Orleans even the grown-ups seemed to have all the time in the world. When two New Orleaneans bumped into each other on the street, they didn't exchange pleasantries, they exchanged genealogies. Old New Orleaneans could be almost ironic in their timelessness. A simple telephone call, the ostensible purpose of which was to find a time to visit, could last an hour, at the end of which both parties would apologize for not having more time to talk.

The first inkling I had that time could be something other than infinite was when I saw my college roommate, a Korean immigrant, plan his day. His life was as synchronized as the Normandy invasion. Every night before he went to bed, he laid a single sheet of white typing paper out on his immaculate desk. Using a ruler and a No. 2 pencil, he divided the paper into perfect little rectangles. Each rectangle represented 15 minutes of the following day. Into these blocks went everything he would do, including three visits to the men's room. To a Korean immigrant, time was so precious it could not be left to chance.

In their attitudes toward time, the new Korean immigrant and the old New Orleanean probably describe the two ends of the American spectrum. The behavior at each end makes sense, in its way. On one end is the quintessential climber, spurred on by his fear that he will somehow fail to gain a grip on his society. On the other end is the quintessential faller, unaware of the erosion of the toehold his forebears have taken for granted for a hundred years.

Less comprehensible is the behavior across the rest of this American spectrum, especially where fortunes are essentially secure. In the great arenas of American ambition—Wall Street, Capitol Hill, Hollywood, Silicon Valley—you can see the richest and most powerful Americans treating time with something akin to the grim fanaticism of the Korean immigrant. Consider the following examples (which I have numbered to save time):

1. A dozen engineers join a new Silicon Valley startup company. These young men are not quite millionaires, but they are about as permanently employable as people can be. When hired, they agree to the most onerous terms: For the first nine months of the startup, they must forsake their private lives. Sunday is officially a workday; there is no such thing as quitting time, and so on. All quite happily agree. And for the next nine months, the young engineers spend 100 hours a week in their cubicles. They tell friends and family they have no time for anything else. But later, when they share war stories, they will recall the countless hours in the office they spent shooting the shit and playing field hockey with each other in the hallways.

2. A New York financier who has made hundreds of millions of dollars buying companies and carving them up, leaving ordinary workers with a great deal of time on their hands, does not have time to fit everyone he must see into normal working hours. Many mornings he schedules not one but two breakfast meetings. He does not eat breakfast. He hasn't time. Indeed, he does not remain at either breakfast long enough for the people to eat. He lets all who have arisen at 5:30 in the morning to meet with him know how sorry he is that he must hurry off.

3. A freshman congressman from Arizona sleeps on the floor of his Capitol Hill office. He could easily afford to rent an apartment and sleep in a bed, but he claims he doesn't want to waste time by going home. Oddly, he is a libertarian Republican. That is, the government of his dreams is a government in which congressmen do nothing but drive back and forth from home to office.

4. A leading Silicon Valley venture capitalist finds he has no time for his family. Specifically, he is unable to do both his job and his life. To avoid becoming a stranger in his own household, he announces that he will take a six-month leave of absence from work. At a time when the average German worker finds it unthinkable to be granted fewer than five weeks of vacation a year, an American male with a quarter of a billion dollars to his name cannot afford to take a week off without guilt.

5. A famous American magazine editor telephones writers to commission articles. He does not place these calls himself. His secretary does it for him. When she reaches the writers, she says, "Mr. K—— is calling for you. Please hold." The editor keeps the writers waiting on the line for three minutes before he picks up.

These five examples may be extreme, but they are not atypical of the treatment of time at the top of the American pyramid. They illustrate several unspoken truths. The first is that even the most successful Americans—perhaps especially the most successful Americans—have no free time. Or perhaps they consider that free time indicates second-rate behavior.

On the face of it, this comes as a shock: You would think that rich and powerful people would have much more free time than lesser mortals. And once upon a time they did. But in what once was called the leisure class there is now no leisure.

The second related point is that time is not merely a matter of minutes and hours and days. It is, in and of itself, a status good. And a strange status good it is, because it is a negative status good. The more one appears to have of it, the worse off one appears to be. Only through a conspicuous absence of free time can one signal the value of one's time, and thus of oneself. No self-respecting billionaire would be caught dead with holes in his schedule.

Of course, once it is firmly established as a status symbol, time can be manipulated in all sorts of interesting ways. Consider examples 2 and 5. These illustrate a common technique for signaling one's place in the world: wasting other people's time without spending a moment of one's own. Another technique of manipulating time to boost one's stature is to band together with a group to deceive others about your time (example 1). Actually to work all the time is unpleasant; people rarely do it. Instead, they fake it. Silicon Valley startup companies and Hollywood movies are especially useful for this purpose. As long as everyone involved agrees to make a secret of his leisure, the world will believe all to be perfectly free of time.

This tacit agreement among the rich and the powerful to transform time into a negative status good has all sorts of interesting little social effects. It boosts the credibility of things that happen quickly, for instance. After all, no truly inspired decision or event could take . . . time. It also infuses with wonderful new prestige any new timesaving device. After all, who most needs such a device? People who have no time! And who has the least time? The best people! One of the young geniuses at Xerox PARC—the research facility where most of what we now know as the personal computer was dreamed up—has created an interesting timesaving device. His name is Ramana Rao, and he is the founder of a Xerox startup company called Inxight Software, which shows how the contents of the World Wide Web are arranged in ways that enable the user to get at them more quickly. When Rao gets up in front of attentive crowds, as he often does, to explain the amount of time his invention saves, he opens with a self-deprecating comment. "I would trade everything we have done at PARC for one simple invention," he says. "The 25th hour of the day."

You can almost hear the shrieks. Yet another hour that must be jammed to the hilt with pointless meetings! Another hour in which one must scheme to waste lesser people's time! Another hour to hide from the wife and kids! Another empty hour in the diary! An hour! Please, God. . . . Nooooooo!

JAMES J. CRAMER

≫•≪

Early

JAMES J. CRAMER *is a hedge-fund manager and cofounder of* TheStreet.com *and* SmartMoney *magazine. He writes a column called "The Bottom Line" for* New York *magazine.*

TIME STARTS FOR me earlier than for most people. Maybe earlier than everybody. For much of my life I could not sleep past 3:15 A.M. I would wake up, startled by some bizarre inner alarm clock that would go off in a most unpleasant and untimely fashion. For years I lay awake at night, alternately trying to read or attempting to go back to sleep. Sometimes I would drip with sweat, worrying about what would happen in the stock market that day. Was I prepared? Was I ready? Sometimes I would simply try to block everything from my brain in a desperate attempt to go back to sleep.

The futility of it all only increased as I reached my 40s. (I am now 43.) The 3:15 hurdle simply couldn't be passed. But what was I supposed to do? The paper didn't hit the driveway for another 90 minutes. You can't call anybody in this hemisphere without chaos and fury erupting on the other end of the line. I already had done all my homework the evening before, or I wouldn't have been able to fall asleep.

Then I discovered the Internet and now I cannot live without it. I am one of those people whose life will never be the same, postmodem. Like clockwork I still get up at 3:15. But now I go to work.

So let me give you a diary of my life from 3:15 A.M. to 4:15 A.M. because that's when I get everything done. After taking almost exactly 10 minutes to shower, shave, and get dressed, I saunter down to the kitchen and flip on the PC. It opens immediately to www.thestreet.com, where I scan the story I wrote the previous day that got posted when I was asleep. I check other late stories and then it's off to the email box.

In the five hours I sleep, I usually get about 50 emails. None of them is junk. All deserve to be answered. I tell everyone to email me because I have no time for calls once the market opens at 9:30 A.M. in New York.

I type like racer Jeff Gordon drives, so I have banged out all the email answers by 3:40 A.M., pausing only to make a pot of coffee for my wife (its timer set for a lazy 6:15 A.M.) and take out the trash. At 3:40 A.M. I go to www.wsj.com and read the *Wall Street Journal.* To save time, I read only what I want to know, rather than reading every page. That lets me get to www.nytimes.com by 4 A.M. Business, sports, and the front page, and then it's off to quote.yahoo.com for Reuters headlines and world markets. I am out the door by 4:15 A.M. and on my way to work.

In one bizarre, lonely, distraction-free hour, I now accomplish everything that used to take me until 8:30 A.M. For that one hour I have conquered time, vanquished and beaten it beyond recognition. And what was once the darkest, most depressing time of night is now the most productive time I possess.

EDWARD O. WILSON

E.T. Stayed Home

EDWARD O. WILSON *is a two-time Pulitzer Prize winner and Pellegrino University Professor Emeritus in entomology at Harvard University's Museum of Comparative Zoology. He is the author of* Consilience: The Unity of Knowledge.

YES, THE CYBERWORLD is truly wonderful, and within it humanity has seized an infinite new possibility for imagination and simulacrum. But that is all the more reason to stay intellectually sober. Let us remember the fundamental constraint of our species: We are organisms. We evolved biologically, like other organisms, and as a consequence are closely adapted in body and mind to the earth. No matter how far afield in space and time imagination may now lead, our genetic origin will always pull us home to this cradling planet.

A feeble sense of time is part of this constraint. Every person's direct experience of reality is squeezed down to a span reaching from a few thousandths of a second, the minimum interval required for an electrical and chemical transmission among cells of the brain, to about a century, the maximum life span of a brain. From our mortal perspective the span seems immense. After all, a full lifetime is equal to a sequence of about a trillion brain events. But its reach shrinks to the infinitesimal when placed within the whole spectrum of conceivable time—that is, from quantum events among subatomic particles to the potentially infinite duration of the universe. Some of the trip from one end of this spectrum to the other can be simulated with the aid of computers, by altering the parameters of equations and then

143

the velocity of changing images. What our brains see, however, is no more than a highly distorted glimpse. Like starlight collected in the mirror of a reflecting telescope, the data represents the real world, but it must be bent and focused, then filtered and coded by our cellular systems.

Our perception of time is trapped this way because the human body is essentially an aqueous suspension of giant organic molecules. The human engine is prescribed by nucleic acid polymers (DNA) and then driven by enzymes, the proteins that catalyze its chemical reactions. To function at a sustainable rate, vast numbers of these molecules and other vital substances must be packaged precisely into cells. The cells in turn are bounded by active membranes that draw in nutrients while passing out wastes and other substances. Simple physics dictates that to reach a life-sustaining rate, the cell must be small enough for substances to diffuse across it in short periods of time. All larger organisms like us are built from masses of such cells, which are aggregated into specialized tissues and organs that exchange materials by membrane pumps and fluid circulation. The most advanced of these specializations is the act of thinking. To create a thinking person requires tens of billions of nerve cells, intricately connected to one another by networks of cables (axons) and terminal branches (dendrites). All this mass together forms the quart-sized brain.

The demanding architectural requirements of thought in particular explain why human beings are among the largest animals on earth. And why insects cannot think. You have to be big to be smart. Our six-legged companions have had more than 350 million years to try it, ever since their origin in the late Paleozoic era. But their lack of an internal skeleton that would grow steadily while still permitting uninterrupted support and movement has kept insects small. And even though they have miniaturized their nerve cells drastically and packed as many as possible into their tiny crania, they still come up short. The relative geniuses among insects, the ants and honeybees, appear able to learn little more than the distinctive smell of their nestmates ("Me and you sisters, she enemy") and the way home after foraging trips. The rest of their repertory consists of hardwired instinct.

The human brain, more than a million times larger than that of an ant, performs prodigiously better. Yet, like that of all animals, it is trapped in a small box of time. To trigger the encrypted message of one cell requires thousandths of a second, and to summon complex conscious thought by the action of multitudes of such cells consumes at least tenths of a second. Consequently, the brain works far too slowly to monitor the quantum-level events of physics and chemistry, and far too swiftly to sense the geological history transforming the planet.

Could evolution have done better? Somewhere in the universe there may be microscopic organisms whose brains, made not from giant molecules but from nanoelectronic atomic arrays, can think in millionths of a second. Elsewhere there may be planet-sized living clouds that take years to compose equally sophisticated thoughts. But I doubt it. More likely, extraterrestrials (E.T.'s) everywhere are carbon based, cellular, and moderately big in comparison with other motile organisms around them. In other words, they are similar to us in the fundamentals.

I suspect their scientists also would say something like the following: Modern biology teaches that all intelligent life must ground knowledge of its own existence on four levels of time. The first is molecular time, the passage of atomic and molecular events that compose the foundation of life but are too small and swift to be perceived by the unaided senses. The second is organismic time, which is operational from seconds to years and where we truly live in conscious experience. Ecological time, the next level, passes too slowly to be comprehended by direct observation. In an evolving ecosystem, most organisms come and go across flurries of generations. To visualize a vegetation-choked pond metamorphosing into a bog, for example, or a forest emerging from an abandoned field requires a succession of photographs or maps made over a period of years.

Finally, in evolutionary time, embracing centuries to millennia, even the rotation of local ecosystems is an indecipherable blur. Only the genes of entire populations (such as red maples, house finches, and human beings) persist as an unbroken continuum. Yet if, godlike, we could watch them for long enough periods of time, we would see them changing, because heredity itself is modified in response to challenges from the inconstant ecosystems.

These divisions in space-time require that the science of biology be sliced into corresponding specialties. That is the reason molecular, cell, organismic, and evolutionary biology are treated academically as disciplines unto themselves. Scientists simultaneously dice the same biological knowledge at right angles to distinguish the kind of plant, animal, or microorganism under scrutiny. It is quite common, indeed it is the rule, for researchers to spend their entire careers inside such specialties as the molecular genetics of colon bacteria or the evolution of birds.

To think about the multiple levels of space-time, and ourselves as organisms, is to align our self-perception truthfully and fundamentally. It also suggests, incidentally, that we are unlikely ever to travel physically to the stars or to sustain indefinitely much interest in life beyond the solar system. The argument for this conservative (and admittedly fallible) view is the following: In a century or two, biology will be a mature science, able not just to take the full measure of life on earth but also to imagine in detail the possible range of life-forms that have evolved elsewhere. As biology matures we will ask ourselves, "Why wait thousands of years, longer than the average life span of civilizations, for a round trip expected to add relatively little to knowledge?" The window is opening now for venturing into deep space. I predict that within a generation or two it will close, and by intellectual choice.

The same reasoning, if correct, may explain why earth has evidently never been visited by extraterrestrials. Chance alone dictates that we are not the first in our part of the galaxy to have achieved space travel. Other civilizations could have reached the same competence as humankind and taken the leap anytime during the past billion years. But they have not, dreams of alien abductees notwithstanding. There has been, moreover, no sign yet that any are trying to make contact through interstellar broadcasts.

Why not? Pessimists might conclude that all technoscientific cultures quickly self-destruct, and ours will be no exception. In opposition, I like to think that the E.T.'s have found wisdom and fulfillment in their own solar systems, and so will we.

LOUIS AUCHINCLOSS

The Persistence of the WASP

LOUIS AUCHINCLOSS *is famous for exploring the world of America's moneyed class. His best-selling novels include* The House of Five Talents *and* Portrait in Brownstone.

THE TERM *WASP* has often been used to describe the managerial class in America as it existed from the 1880s to the 1929 market crash. The term is inaccurate, for this class included large enclaves of Roman Catholics and Jews, but it is safe to say that it was made up of whites, mostly rich, whose earned or inherited money was usually derived from business or finance, and who protected their world and their descendants from intruders by the use of clubs, private schools, restricted summer resorts, and a code of manners.

How has this class survived in a world of rapid change, where astronomical fortunes in electronics are made overnight, where the sexual revolution has smashed every old rule of chastity or even restraint, where discrimination in matters of sex, creed, or color has become a moral crime, and where people have actually begun to take seriously the old democratic dogma that one man is the equal of another?

The answer is: not badly.

Of course, there always will be the small, unconvertible minority that sits back, with shaking heads, and finds that the world has gone to the dogs and there is no bringing it back. But on the whole, the old managerial elect have shrewdly adapted themselves to the new ways. What they have given up is not so much their power as their monopoly. They have had, so to speak, to share the wealth. Or rather they have had to move over to make room for those who have amassed new and greater fortunes.

New markets provided what the new tycoons needed. They did not, as in most revolutions, have to plunder the property of their predecessors. The old managers saw that they could stay rich even if they had lost their rank. It was all they really wanted, and they set about to keep what they had and even to amplify it. A booming stock market had room for all. Most of the privileged children with whom I was reared are richer now than they were then, a fact only obscured by the presence around them of new arrivals far wealthier than they.

The clubs, tottering on the verge of extinction in the 1930s and 1940s, have been saved; many now have long waiting lists of applicants. This was accomplished by a judicious compromise: Old barriers to admission were lifted. Discrimination against women, religious minorities, and, in some cases, blacks, was barred or at least modified. In similar fashion the private schools, even the Protestant church academies of New England, have been expanded to include all sects and races, and millions of dollars have been raised for scholarships for the financially disadvantaged.

In so-called high society, the value of genealogy has been completely wiped out. No new millionaire would feel his position improved by marriage to a Boston Lowell or a New York Livingston. But in giving this up, the old world gave up nothing that hurt it. Indeed, the whole transformation has been accomplished in such a way that the new rich can boast with a smug satisfaction that the old WASP world is dead and gone. Yet the corpse breathes merrily on. If the *ancien régime* in France had shown anything like the adaptability of the American old guard, the Reign of Terror never would have occurred.

Of course, one can say that the old guard had no choice. Laws had to be obeyed. And, after all, there was no unbridgeable distance between the old and the new. But even so, I think people should get some credit for resilience. And the children of the old guard, particularly the daughters, have shown a distinct taste for new ways and new freedoms and even new excesses.

There is, however, another aspect to our swiftly changing society that has presented some difficulty to the old managerial guard: the loss of any clear division of time into separate compartments. A generation ago there was still an obvious distinction between the workweek and the weekend, between the downtown office and the vacation getaway, between shoptalk in the locker room and dinner party conversation. But now our days and nights are fused into a kind of industrial timelessness; electronic gadgets have extended the office to the home, and indeed, we can no longer tell whether our telephone interlocutor is at his desk or in his swimming pool. Similarly, his wife may be his brilliant hostess or his brilliant law partner—or both. If we work around the clock, we also play around it: As much can be accomplished on a golf course or on a yacht as in the glass cube of an office building. We can chase the dollar even in our dreams.

This is, however, essentially a generational problem. And, after all, there is nothing radically novel about it. It boils down to the persistence of work, and that has always been a part of the American ethic.

DOUGLAS COUPLAND

─═──◆──═─

Lost in Solitaire

DOUGLAS COUPLAND *is the author of* Generation X. *His fourth book,* Microserfs, *explores the lives of computer geeks. His more recent novel is* Miss Wyoming.

I'M IN A 737 right now headed south from Vancouver, my home-town, to Los Angeles, a three-hour flight. Out the window to my right the sun is shining. A meal has just been served—beef with vermicelli—"beef south, chicken north," as the old saying goes. My laptop PC tells me I've just finished my 1,523rd game of Eric's Ultimate Solitaire. My total playing time has been 61 hours, or roughly 2 minutes, 24 seconds per game. I've won 10% of my games, and my average score is 11 out of a possible 52. But to my credit, I've been having much higher scores lately. Somewhere around game 800 or 900 my brain kicked into total game fluency.

But yes, 61 hours of solitaire—the game that ate my brain.

That's two full days of my life spent piling phantom electronic cards atop one another. I'm unsure if this is pathetic or cool. Maybe it's both. But life is short; time is precious—why did I do this? And why will I, in all likelihood, continue to cheerfully waste thousands of more hours playing solitaire?

I fly more than most people. This is partly because of my work, and partly because my father was a Canadian Armed Forces jet pilot who still spends his weekends flying up and down the British Columbia coast in a seaplane. I have no memories of ever *not* flying. Taking a taxi is weirder to me than flying from Vancouver to Frankfurt over Greenland and seeing the aurora borealis dance. A quick and very conservative tabulation tells me that I've spent well over a solid *year* of my life either in the air or in airports—several hundred times more hours than I've spent playing Eric's Ultimate Solitaire.

A decade ago, flying was *fun*. Destinations were still glamorous, and no seat uncomfortable. And the meals! Well, the meals honestly haven't changed much. Ten years ago the in-flight meal would have been beef and "noodles." Over the years, however, my zest for air travel has eroded. Anybody who's flown much knows the progression: You stop speaking to the person next to you; you get addicted to business class and first class; you perfect your carry-on luggage strategy. And so on. Flying becomes a deglamorized chore. The final step is the prayer that, as a species, we invent the *Star Trek* teleportation device: "Beam me into O'Hare, Scotty!"

Like some people, I'm unable to either read or sleep on planes, and until recently I was at my wit's end as to how to make my hours in the air more tolerable. Flying, at a certain point, had become hours spent staring at the seat-back in front of me. A big change came when I got my first laptop PC—*whee!* I thought my in-flight time problems were over, and they were, until the battery died after 37 minutes of use. So I got another laptop, and the salesman lied to me, and *it* died after 38 minutes. So finally I bought the laptop I now use, not because it has any glitzy features but merely because (are you listening, manufacturers?) it provides two hours of flat-out usability. And with this new PC came my big discovery this year: Time spent playing computer solitaire is time that *vanishes*. Completely. I get on a plane, I turn it on, I play, I blink, and two hours are gone. Wow. Finally, a way to genuinely erase time.

To judge from my internal excitement, one would think I'd discovered uranium or invented the wheel. But then my father quickly brought me down to earth. "Solitaire?" he said. "We used to kill whole days at a time playing solitaire when I was stationed in Thule up in Greenland in 1958. I would have gone crazy without it."

A genetic link!

Last Christmas, at about the same time I got my new laptop, my brother got my dad a small PC loaded with, yes, solitaire. My father now plays it almost daily in his den. I asked him last week why he keeps on playing even though he's a busy guy. He said, "That's easy.

Every time I push the key and it deals me a new round, I get this immense burst of satisfaction knowing that I didn't have to shuffle the cards and deal them myself. It's payback time for all the hours I've ever wasted in my life shuffling and dealing cards."

Some West Coast Indians in British Columbia believe that when you travel, whether on a canoe or in the Concorde, your soul can follow you only as fast as you're able to walk. I think of the times I've flown to Australia or Chile or Italy and there's my plucky little soul chugging along, only miles away from the Vancouver airport where the trip began. I think about this, and about the need to kill time in the air, and I wonder if there's a connection—if there's a need to kill time in the absence of a guiding internal spirit. We're all so willing to accept the strange reality of geographical displacement when we travel—waking up in Vancouver and going to bed in Oslo—yet we're unwilling to believe in time sickness. Not just jet lag but genuine damage done to the sense of time and the spirit as we hop between continents. We look for salves. We look for the aurora borealis. We look for a red eight to slap onto a black nine. I look for the 61 hours I lost in computerized solitaire, but I know I'll never find it. And I know I'll lose far more time in the future.

The captain just announced we'll be landing at LAX in 20 minutes. This flight has been "fast" because I was writing this, and it involved emotion and reflection. Maybe I should start talking to the people sitting beside me more. Maybe I should start believing that instead of just shuffling these glowing kings and queens and jacks and aces every time I push the Return key, I'm building a beautiful house of cards instead. It'd be a beautiful place, and my soul could go there instead of forever traipsing its way out of the city and back. I'm 37. I've flown a whack of miles and I'm going to fly a whole whack more. My soul must have awfully sore feet by now.

DANNY HILLIS

⤜⬥⬥⤛

Impatient Pendulum

DANNY HILLIS *is credited with having pioneered the concept of massively parallel computing. He cofounded Thinking Machines and is now chairman and chief technology officer of Applied Minds.*

HANGING IN THE atrium of the Smithsonian Museum of American History, in front of the Star-Spangled Banner, is a great pendulum stretching 52 feet from its suspension point in the domed roof to the bottom of the second floor. The 240-pound brass bob makes an unhurried swing every two and a half seconds, its path slowly rotating as the earth turns underneath during the course of a day.

This Foucault pendulum is a great crowd pleaser, although I am convinced it is for reasons having nothing much to do with Monsieur Foucault, nor with the principles of physics demonstrated by his pendulum. A patient observer, watching the spectators gather around the pendulum, will occasionally hear parents discuss those topics with their children, but the explanations are always short and usually false.

What is striking is not so much the conversations but the lack of them. The pendulum inspires silence. The same family of rambunctious children and bedraggled parents that races through the Ceremonial Court as if it were an obstacle course will stand in awe at this swinging bob of brass for minutes at a time. I suspect that the real reason that the pendulum is so well loved is because it is slow. Its leisurely swing, just slower than the human breath, calms audiences and entrances them with a slower beat.

When I was a child, the pendulum swung even slower. It was longer then, too. It was shortened (and therefore quickened) in one of those paradoxical compromises of museum management: People stood mesmerized for so long that they blocked the flow of traffic. To me, this speedup of an icon of slowness is symbolically fitting. The tempo of life has quickened.

But it is not just the slowness that attracts the crowd, it is the promise of order. Temporal disorientation is an unwanted side effect of modern life. We are dazzled by progress, rushed by events, and disconnected from the stable rhythms of time. Our technology has isolated us from the natural cycles (day, month, year) that once governed the pace of life.

Anyone who has survived a long power blackout or a camping trip knows that the proverbial difference between night and day is much more dramatic without electric lights. In true darkness, the stars become important. In a world without flashlights, the lunar month governs what can be seen and hidden. A full moon allowed our ancestors to work all night to bring in the harvest. A new moon kept them from travel. Not so long ago life was ruled by the moon's phases, yet today we are hardly aware of them.

The year, too, means less than it once did. In a world with artificial climate, even the seasons lose their power to regulate. We go about our business much the same in every season. The shortening of winter days is a curiosity, not a serious constraint. The patterns of rain and temperature, once issues of life and death, are now reduced to topics of idle social banter. In the dead of winter, we play tennis and eat strawberries shipped from the other hemisphere, where it is still summer.

One might suppose that weakening our ties to the natural cycles of time would cause our artificial substitutes to gain importance, but as nearly as I can tell, these too have lost authority. Our annual cycle of holidays now serves more to stimulate commerce than to regulate lives. Feasts and days of fast mean little in times of plenty. Rituals, once our most powerful device for restraining the passage of time, seem to have lost their potency.

In the time of my childhood, Monday was wash day, Tuesday was market day, and Sunday was worship and a day for rest. In this age of 24-hour-a-day, seven-day-a-week convenience, I have begun to lose my bearings. I fly from time zone to time zone, living in CNN time, out of touch even with the rhythms of my own flesh.

I have a recurring dream of a big, slow clock in a faraway place—somewhere empty and difficult to reach, perhaps in the middle of a desert, or on a mountaintop, or in a deep, cool cave. This is the clock that connects the motions of the sun and the moon and the stars to the mundane calendars of humankind. Wound by human caretakers in quiet ceremony, it patiently counts the millennia.

This is the clock that provides what the pendulum only promises: the calibration of the rhythm of life, the definition of Now. I am certain that if I could only visit it . . . I would regain my sense of time.

CHUCK YEAGER

———◆———

Ripping the Envelope

CHUCK YEAGER *became the world's first supersonic pilot by breaking the sound barrier in 1947. He is the author of* Yeager: An Autobiography *and* Press On: Further Adventures in the Good Life.

———

M Y LIFE HAS been spent converting speed into time. When I first entered the army air corps in September 1941, I was an 18-year-old kid, and speed was just the thrill of driving a pickup truck at 50 miles per hour. But when I became a fighter pilot, speed became time, and time was an advantage over the enemy. In World War II our P-51 Mustangs not only had tremendous range but, just as important, were a little faster than the German Me 109s and Fw 190s that we were fighting. Speed meant that you could catch the enemy and destroy him. Since our job was to escort B-17s, which were not very fast in relation to the fighters, we would take bomber groups all the way to the target and back, protecting them from the Germans.

When jet aviation arrived at the end of the war, many people asked why pilots wanted to go faster and faster. Once again the answer was *time*. Our objective was to either catch the enemy or outrun him—to close or extend the distance in time. But we ran into a problem. Approaching the speed of sound, airplanes suffered a tremendous amount of buffeting and shaking. In our P-51s this wasn't a hazard, merely a nuisance as we tried to track some guy at high speed. But jets were a different story. In 1944 the army air corps, realizing that the problem had to be solved, awarded a contract to Bell Aircraft in New

York to build a little rocket airplane called the Bell X-1. The airplane's single mission was to somehow fly faster than sound.

When I returned from the war in the spring of 1945, I was assigned to Wright Field as a maintenance officer, then was sent to test-pilot school. When the air force took over the X-1 program from Bell Aircraft and the National Advisory Committee for Aeronautics (NACA), I was selected as primary pilot because I understood systems, and the X-1 was a very complex airplane. My backup was a first lieutenant named Bob Hoover, who was one of the better pilots in the Flight Test Division.

It took nine flights in the X-1 over a period of 69 days before we had accomplished our mission and flew the airplane faster than the speed of sound. That was October 14, 1947. Once again, we were in control of time.

Breaking the sound barrier meant that we could develop fighters that had greater speed capability and could either escape from or catch the enemy. But my thoughts and feelings at that time went beyond combat. Controlling time also meant we had finally opened up the whole universe to travel.

After getting the X-1 above the speed of sound, we developed swept wings, delta wings, thin wings, and jet engines with afterburners. We were able to smoke right on out to twice the speed of sound. As time went on, we were even able to cruise at speeds three times the speed of sound and fly across the United States in an hour's time. This was a great advantage for the military because it meant that we could fly reconnaissance planes at various altitudes and at very high speeds and get data on the military readiness of different countries—and do it so quickly the enemy had no time to respond.

Today we have the capability to develop aircraft that can not only fly easily at four or five times the speed of sound but also carry passengers. Now the control of time is not just in the hands of fighter pilots.

People talk about going into space, traveling to the moon in two or three days, or to Mars in a few weeks. I suppose that is controlling time, too. But in my opinion, there is no reason to travel to Mars, especially when we pretty much know what's there.

Time remains for me a very difficult concept. Time is a period that elapses between your birth and your death. What you accomplish during this time is your legacy. My legacy, I suppose, is speed. But look-ing back, I don't think many people really save a lot of time by moving faster from one point to the next, because from the time you're born until the time you die, it's pretty cut-and-dried. When that time comes, that's it. You have to take advantage of time, not speed. That's the way I look at it.

CHARLES VAN DOREN

If We Loved Time . . .

CHARLES VAN DOREN *is a former Columbia University English professor and editor for* Encyclopaedia Britannica. *He is the author of* A History of Knowledge: Past, Present, and Future.

TIME IS MANKIND'S oldest invention. Even before our ancestors tamed fire, they must have recognized the periodicities in human life. The sun rises, sets, rises again; seasons return; children grow to adulthood; death overtakes all.

Awareness of time was what first distinguished us from the animals with whom, until very recently, we shared the world. We knew time; they did not. We could foresee the future and they could not. Time was what made us human.

To be human was both a sorrow and a glory. We envied the animals their ignorance; the invention of time created the expectation of death, an idea no animal had to share. Awareness of time opened to us the idea of eternity, where there is no change. Animals existed in an unchanging now, whereas we did not and had to regain it. Yet the invention of time also opened the way to hope—the last and best gift in Pandora's box—hope for an eternal future no animal could ever conceive.

For aeons, time was not the measure but rather the form of human days, years, and lives. Each was an arc having beautiful words that named its parts: morning, noon, and night; spring, summer, fall, and winter; childhood, maturity, and old age. Time's arc left the earth, reached toward the stars, and returned to earth again. Birth and death were life's limits. All humans everywhere are aware of the arc of time; only recently, in the long history of humankind, have some of us begun to measure time itself. For us, measuring has become an obsession, even a madness. We divide the arc of time into hours, minutes, seconds, even the tiniest parts of seconds. Division without end allows us to schedule, forecast, and predict moments of time and time's events with a precision unimaginable to our ancestors.

Perhaps, if they knew, they would not envy us. For when we measure time, when we divide our days and years into the smallest conceivable units, when we number them with a multitude of zeros and ones, we cease to be aware of the time of our lives.

The parts of a human life are not temporal; they cannot be measured with clocks and watches. They are activities and powers, different kinds of things to do and be. Love is a part of life and so is work; sleep is a part of life and so is learning; thought is a part of life and so is singing. The time for any of these parts cannot be legislated or scientifically determined. These and other parts, like eating and praying, playing and sitting still, make up a good life. Mixed together, they make a life lovely; regimented or required, time itself becomes a prison.

We invented time to be free from the ignorance of the animals, who had no past and no future, but we who measure time are in danger of turning our freedom into slavery.

If we loved time instead of fearing it, we would always have time to do whatever we desired to do. The fear of time—of time lost, of time wasted—is a mortal disease. It shortens a life to an instant—this instant—which will be followed by other instants that are equally fleeting. There can be no joy in moments that are carefully measured and doled out.

It is said that there is not enough time to do everything that has to be done. But what has to be done? There is only one thing; that is to live. There is all the time in the world for that. In fact, there is no time, real time, for anything else.

Part IV

CONVERGENCE
IN THE DIGITAL AGE

Rodes Fishburne

THE GENESIS FOR *Big Issue IV* was a Little League game. There, new ASAP editor in chief Michael Malone watched a fellow father as he consulted a client on a cell phone while simultaneously cheering his son at bat. What disheartened Malone even more was the fact that he'd recently done the same thing.

Everywhere we looked in the winter of 1999, things were flowing together, creating new connections, new ways of seeing the world. Thanks to the Internet, email had fused work and play into one indistinguishable blur, and our private lives were available to any interested hacker with an open phone line. We switched gender for after-dinner conversation in digital chat rooms and connected with people on the other side of the world while never learning our neighbor's last name.

In the last year of the 20th century it seemed as if technology was not only America's story, but the world's story as well. On the lips of visionaries, from Bill Gates to George Gilder, was the prediction that soon we would all be connected in one shimmering electronic net. Everyone and everything was coming together, pulled by the magnetic force of the microprocessor—a chaotic convergence announced by the beeps and squeaks of modems and cell phones. It was a dream that managed to be both thrilling and chilling.

Our essays on convergence ranged from Muhammad Ali's homage to athletic excellence to Jan Morris' very personal tale of switching genders. Tom Wolfe returned to the *Big Issue* to deliver another masterstroke. This time he told the tale of convergence through the life and work of three remarkable men—Pierre Teilhard de Chardin, Marshall McLuhan, and Edward O. Wilson. Wolfe uncovered the roots of convergence in the work of a Jesuit priest, traced its development to the man who coined the term "global village," and completed the triumvirate with Wilson's idea of consilience: "All knowledge of living things will converge . . . under the umbrella of biology. All mental activity, from using allometry to enjoying music, will be understood in biological terms."

But any student of history knows that today's convergence is tomorrow's violent schism. For all our hope that faith and reason will find common ground, our dreams of merging the human with the digital, there is also the tragic understanding that just before things fly apart they come together.

GEORGE GILDER

The Brightest Star

From space, the Web appears as a swirling sphere of light

GEORGE GILDER *is a contributing editor for* Forbes ASAP. *This is an excerpt from a chapter in his recent book* Telecosm. *His other books include* Wealth and Poverty, Life after Television, *and* Microcosm.

IMAGINE GAZING AT THE WEB from far in space. To you, peering through your spectroscope, mapping the mazes of electromagnetism in its path, the Web appears as a global efflorescence, a resonant sphere of light. It is the physical phase space of the telecosm, the radiant chrysalis from which will spring a new global economy.

The luminous ball reflects Maxwell's rainbow, with each arc of light bearing a signatory wavelength. As the mass of the traffic flows through fiber-optic trunks, it glows infrared, with the network backbones looming as focused beams of 1550-nanometer radiance running across continents and under the seas. As more and more people use wireless means to access the Net, this infrared ball grows a penumbra of microwaves, suffused with billions of moving sparks from multimegahertz teleputers or digital cellular phones. Piercing through the penumbra are rich spikes of radio frequencies confined in the coaxial cables circling through neighborhoods and hooking to each household. Spangling the Net are more than 100 million nodes of concentrated standing waves, each an Internet host, a computer with a microprocessor running at a microwave frequency from the hundreds of megahertz to the gigahertz. The radiance reaches upward between 400 and 800 miles to thousands of low-orbit satellites, each sending forth cords of "light" between Earth and sky in the Ku band between 12 and 18 gigahertz.

Now imagine that every 100 days the total brightness doubles. Not only does the total number of screens rise by more than one-third but also the traffic on each of the links rises by 50%. Federal Express ignites a flare in Memphis, and its glow swells into the millennium. AOL customers leave behind their 28-kilobit links and move to 56-kilobit and Ethernet modems: A larger surge ripples across the ball of light. Corporate Ethernets leap up from 10 megabits a second to 100 megabits and then to a gigabit. All pump up the lumens of the encircling radiance.

As the intensity of the light rises—as more and more photons of traffic flash through the webs of glass and air—the change pushes up the overall frequency or average color of the light. So, as the brightness increases, its average color also inches up the spectrum. The global iridescence changes its dominant hues. If it were a rainbow, the center of intensity would move from red through green toward violet. If it were a meteor, the Doppler blueshift of the Internet would suggest it is approaching you.

Ultimately, through this radiant light will run most of the commerce of the world. In fact, more value will move by resonant light than by all the world's supertankers, pipelines, 18-wheeler trucks, and C5A airships put together. Yet all these frequencies, visible on the spectroscope in space, are invisible to you. The Internet is a cloak of many colors for the communications of the world, but human senses can grasp none of its tints and spangles. The 400 terahertz of visible light are absent in the links. On the ball of light of Internet frequencies, visible light sparkles only in the billion phosphorescent spots where there is a screen.

Seeking clues to the meaning of this radiant transformation, I began by thrashing through haystacks of economic literature. I was looking for a needle of insight through which to march all the gaudy caravans of undulating camels, laden with Internet glow. In the end, I found a pin instead.

The pin was a unit of factory output in Adam Smith's *The Wealth of Nations*, exemplifying the power of mass production and the division of labor. Smith showed that a worker specializing in one part of the process of manufacturing pins could be hugely more productive than a worker attempting to produce pins entirely by himself.

Living in a time of transition resembling today's, Smith was boldly explaining the passage from the age of guilds and crafts to the age of mass manufacturing. He showed that the factory workers of the industrial age were not 2 times or 10 times more productive than craftsmen were, but 5,000 times more productive. A key reason that specialized workers can produce so much more is their faster process of learning. Each worker has to master only one part of the process. Because he gets to apply his intelligence to that one component more frequently, he accelerates his learning.

In the time of Adam Smith, the workers could not gain the five thousandfold edge without coming together in a single factory at a single time. Capital and equipment were scarce and costly. Imagine, though, a global cornucopia of capital flowing readily across borders and through the ball of radiance. Imagine the cost of equipment, based on microchips and fiber threads, plummeting to less than a dollar for a million instructions per second or $19.95 for 30 days of access to Internet exabytes. Imagine that any worker could collaborate with any other worker at any time—that the factor of 10^4 could be harvested by any collation of workers in a virtual web anywhere on earth. That is one measure of the meaning of the light. The nodes of creative effort could summon their five thousandfold magic of learning at will in minutes rather than in years.

The Riddler

As an incandescent ball rising up with little overall planning or guidance, the Internet raises again the riddle faced by every sophomore physics student: the rise of civilization in the face of the law of rising entropy. (The second law of thermodynamics, the entropy law defines the tendency of all order and energy to deteriorate into disorder and waste.) Claude Shannon used the same word to designate information content in a communications channel. More entropy in Shannon's code signifies more information. In Shannon's terms, entropy is a measure of unexpected bits, the only part of a message that actually bears information. Otherwise, the signal is only telling you what you already know.

For the message to be high entropy (full of information), the carrier must be low entropy (empty of information). In the ideal system, the complexity is in the message rather than in the medium. By eliminating the entropy from networks, you can increase their ability to bear information. Another word for a low-entropy carrier is a dumb network. The dumber the network, the more intelligence it can carry.

Applying Shannon's theory to an industrial process, an unexpected set of bits usually means something is going wrong. You set it right and you reduce the entropy. You change a series of unexpected bits (information about a breakdown or defect) into a set of predicted bits signifying a smoothly flowing process with no entropy content (no surprises). The process that removes the entropy from the communication is learning or experience.

These gains of learning were conceptualized about 35 years ago by Bruce Henderson in his concept of the learning curve: the approximately 20% increase of efficiency accruing to every doubling of the accumulated unit volume of a product. Henderson's Boston Consulting Group demonstrated this learning effect for thousands of different items, from chicken eggs and tires to insurance policies and telephone calls; Bain & Company refined and extended it as the experience curve; Moore's Law captures its effects in the production of microchips; Michael Rothschild presented evidence that it is a biological truth, applicable to everything from ants and bees to Amazonian slime molds; and Raymond Kurzweil deems it a law of time and chaos by which time—measured by the incidence of salient events—accelerates in every evolutionary process. Now time seems to be racing through the global radiance.

Imagine the mesh of lights as an efflorescence of learning curves as people around the world launch projects and experiments without requiring the physical plant and equipment and the regimented workers in Adam Smith's factory. Without the overhead and geographical friction, entrepreneurial creativity takes off. As network guru David Isenberg puts it, "The Internet offers a near-zero impedance environment for innovation." Imagine the 100-day doubling of the intensity of the light as the spectroscopic effect of the approximately 20% leap in efficiency achieved with every doubling of the accumulated volume of new products.

On the Net, the doubling of new products is manifested by the increase of traffic. On our spectroscope in space, rising traffic is signaled by a rise in the intensity and in the frequency of the light. On Earth, the network becomes dumber and more photonic. All the proliferating protocols and intricacies of electronic networks diminish to one, the Internet Protocol. Increasingly, IP packets run directly on the low-entropy light running down the dumb glass.

With one simple protocol, the network becomes increasingly predictable. It is a low-entropy carrier of ever more voluminous and high-entropy traffic. Swept up into an ever more photonic radiance, the traffic can soar a thousandfold every three to five years, more than a millionfold in a decade—a miracle for our time, dwarfing Adam Smith's pins. As the traffic overflows the smart silicon passages of conventional networks—where it is compressed and coded and celled and queued and framed and corrected electronically—it soars up the spectrum. On the wideband boulevards of photonic glass, everything travels in IP on lambdas.

Answering the sophomore's riddle, Henderson's link of learning and cost is a curve of declining entropy. In yielding about 20% efficiency gains with every doubling of accumulated units produced, the curve affects both forms of entropy: energy entropy and information entropy. At the beginning of any manufacturing process, energy is wasted, materials are squandered, tolerances are large, physical entropy is high. Similarly high is information entropy in the form of unexpected outcomes, surprising effects, bugs, glitches, noise.

The move from Adam Smith's pin factory and its like to the global radiance of the Net is a move from the physical entropy of heavy manufacturing to the nearly costless shuffle of photons. This move, too, effects a dramatic change in the industrial spectrogram. As more and more of the world's commerce climbs ever higher in the spectrum, it leaves behind the huge power lines shaking with the weight of 60-hertz pulses of megawatts and climbs into worldwide Webs of 60-terahertz infrared. The power lines remain indispensable as low-entropy carriers of power, but their contribution to total value shrinks. In the process, the economy becomes physically more efficient and informationally more complex. The central engines of new value are the high-entropy information industries on the fringes of the Net.

As the economy moves from its basis in heavy lifting to its bonanza of learning, its physical entropy tends to disappear into the ball of radiance. The physical costs of new knowledge drop to nearly nothing. The processes of economic growth begin to revolve around the paradox of information entropy. Learning occurs only when information entropy is high—when the surprises multiply. Yet the purpose of the process is to eliminate the entropy, end the learning, in the familiar hum of the perfect machine.

The spectrograms in space thus bear a further lesson of economics. They tell the story of the rise and fall of market power, the oscillating cycles of monopoly and oligopoly. Once a product rises to its point of perfect resonance, it can no longer improve. Once it has found and exhausted its market, it reaches a learning impasse.

Every new product begins as a monopoly. But when products achieve a large global market, they can no longer rapidly double their unit sales and slalom down these steep slopes of learning. They are nearing the bottom of the entropy curve. They mature and no longer contribute substantially to new economic growth and edification. Even when they are heroically advancing their technology, like Intel and Microsoft today, they normally follow a predictable path. Rather than launching new items—new surprises—they are wringing out the last gouts of entropy in their existing products. They are sustainers. Their rate of learning has declined to the reassuring burble of predictable bits, nearly all entropy gone. These companies are then vulnerable to entropic disruption from fast learners below.

This is the tragic rhythm of capitalism, the fatal triumph of enterprise, the vicious circle of learning. But it is also the guarantor of freedom. The radiance does not migrate to one place and stay there, whether Redmond, Washington, or Santa Clara, California. It reaches its point of resonance and then gives way to new flares of learning and creativity.

At the bottom of the entropy curve is the hum of resonance. The goal of every enterprise is the resonant point that defines the end of learning—the sweet spot when the natural frequency, color, or spectrum of a product is in perfect interplay with its customers. The technology, the market, the system of distribution, the feedback loops, are all in sync and in phase. There are no surprises. Most improvements at this point represent overshoot.

A Stupid Network

As the Net moves up the spectrum and becomes dumber and wider, imagine now that the learning accelerates on both ends of the arcs of radiance. Without a high-entropy medium of noise-forming barriers in the middle, the distinctions and categories of conventional commerce break down. Buyers, sellers, producers, consumers, financiers, insurers, and savers merge across the radiant ball, and both the words and the roles lose their edges.

I log on to Amazon.com and a "cookie" on my computer informs the system of my presence. I play a game of literary preferences. It is a service of Amazon. But it allows the company to alert me to new products that I might like. If they are not just right, I correct them. From my purchases and preferences, Amazon learns how to serve other similar customers. I review a book that I have read. Amazon prints the review. From my purchases and the purchases of others, it contrives a best-seller list that is updated every hour. It informs me of the exact performance of all my books. I sell my books from my own Web page, collecting a profit, and Amazon fulfills the orders. I am an Amazon customer, supplier, investor, client, author, audience.

The buyers of Web services supply their own capital in the form of their linked computers. They provide infinite shelf space on their disks. They give or sell their names, their time, their knowledge. They learn how to improve the product. The sellers of Web services use the equipment of their customers and gain knowledge and time from the buyers. Each population learns from the other—is the other. The customers are the product and the product is the customer and both serve each other, in a rhythm of creativity between producers and users, a resonance of buyers and sellers in which the buyers also sell and the sellers also buy in widening webs of commerce. The resonance is the wealth and the light, and there is no impedance in the middle.

Markets grow from the outside in or from the bottom up. One man may contrive an attractive item, such as a wheel or a hammer, an anticancer diet or an interactive Web page format, a butterfly museum or a virtual auction block. Many may go to work to provide an item to trade for it or improve upon it. Many others may use it. A single attractive invention that resonates with the needs of others can unleash a cascade of creativity.

Governing the light is this law of resonance. Supply creates its own demand, and the supplies and demands in themselves create a market. That is the source of Metcalfe's Law. The exponential value of networks is not in the links; it is in the light at the end of the links, suffusing the edges of the Web. The Internet is not merely a radiance of connections; it is a mesh of constant invention. It is not a Web of ever proliferating desires or demands; desires can well proliferate without it. The Net is a seine of collaborative production. It is the capitalist means of production, and it has fallen into the hands of a billion learners and value creators.

Through an endless *tâtonnement* of trial and error, capitalism teaches every venturer the rules of resonance, the laws of right and light. It reveals what efforts reverberate in the minds and hearts and hands of other producers—what ventures enlighten and enrich them. It ruthlessly filters out the ego trips and feckless tries and self-indulgences and investments of disguised consumption, and products that exploit and diminish their customers. They may burn ardently like a short circuit, but they don't resonate. The radiance of the Net rides on trust: predictable waves of unsurprise that can carry the entropic ideas of enterprise. The Net promotes the ideas that yield more than they cost—the ones that are worth more to others than to the producer, the ones that teach more than they lose. Only products that enrich their customers ultimately create the kind of market that compounds its gains.

(People who focus on porn as the propeller of the Net miss its meaning. Porn does not enrich and edify its users; it distracts and impoverishes them and ultimately reduces their buying power. It sucks and sours the saps of love, the source of creativity and new life. Within the glowing radiance, it represents the shadow, not the glow.)

All economic growth depends upon the expansion of learning and information. This economy is uniquely fertile because the products that are plunging most rapidly down the curves of learning are themselves learning machines, information processors in all their forms. The Internet is a network of networks of learning curves and melodies seeking their points of harmonic resonance. It triumphs by proliferating the slopes of learning, the songs of searching, the quests of curiosity that are at the heart of wealth creation.

On the map of incandescence, the light is not evenly distributed. One looks in vain for a "level playing field." The glow radiates most ardently and at highest frequencies in domains of freedom and technological creativity. In countries that have climbed highest on the spectronic ladders toward visible light, the warps and woofs of incandescence can almost be seen. Through most of the 1990s, the center of the radiance was overwhelmingly in the United States. The United States commanded four times as much computer power per capita as the rest of the industrial world, 75% of the computer networks, and 80% of Internet hosts. The radiance is a reflection of political and economic freedom, immigration, and the spirit of enterprise. Nearly half the luminosity remains in the United States, and within the United States, perhaps half is in California, and in California half is in the region of Silicon Valley. But the radiance is now on the move.

At the millennium, the incandescence is diffusing around the world, offering a promise of new freedom and prosperity from Santiago, Chile, to Shanghai, China. Encircling the globe under oceans and beaming from satellites, the radiance is increasingly eroding the powers of despots and bureaucracies, powers and principalities. The crystal cathedrals of light and air are increasingly reachable anywhere on the face of the earth. To stifle links to the global communities of mind and liberty entails increasingly brutal and obvious repression and incurs rising costs of economic stagnation and retardation. Within the market space of the Net, anyone anywhere can issue a petition or publication, utter a cry for help, broadcast a work of art. Anyone can create a product, launch a company, finance its growth, and spin it off into the Web of trust.

Turn off your spectroscope, though, and the Web disappears. It is as invisible as the life of the mind and the laws of liberty that sustain it and that it sustains. Although the sphere of light spans the globe and reaches up as far as 23,000 miles, it appears to humans at their screens as a single point of concentrated light. At any instant, that is all that is present on a cathode-ray tube: a single spot rastering back and forth 60 times a second. It tricks your eye into seeing a full image.

Turn off your spectroscope and if you are in the wrong markets, the Web may seem inconsequential. You decry "the myth of Internet traffic," as did a January 1999 issue of the estimable *Business Communications Journal*. You may call it an "American fad," as have several French executives in my presence. You may compare it to tulipmania. For the colors of visible light are absent. Without your Maxwellian prism, all the frequencies dissolve and, except for an infinitesimal spot of phosphorescence on your screen, disappear from sight.

This trompe l'oeil point of light both symbolizes and embodies the global efflorescence: a light of infinite dimensions concentrated into a single point racing across the screen. Moving up the spectrum toward the visible domain, becoming ever dumber and more capacious, the Internet transcends geography and reduces to a single spot in time and space. As the commerce of the world flows into this global radiance and is distilled into this single point, it resonates with the creative work of the world. Accommodating real-time transactions, it is a market space that can absorb all the business of the new global economy. The smaller the point, the more the room.

As activities move from the surface of the world into this virtual pinpoint of radiance, they accelerate toward a universal resonance— the velocity of light—and converge to a universal medium. The light is both the abundance and the scarcity of the new world economy, the creative interplay of limit and infinite, the flesh and the divine.

MUHAMMAD ALI

⇒»◦«⇐

Me . . . We

The most recognizable man in the global village proves,
once again, that he is the greatest.

MUHAMMAD ALI *has captured the world's attention in many
forms: as a three-time world heavyweight boxing champion, a
civil rights proponent, a draft resister, an Olympic gold medal
winner, and the torchbearer at the 1996 Summer Olympics in
Atlanta.*

WHEN YOU GET to be 57, and you've been world famous and
been called the greatest, met presidents and kings, and had
books written about you, they ask you to write articles on subjects like
convergence. Now, as I understand it, convergence means that society today is no longer pretending that there is any real difference between things like art and nature, science and religion, between the
poetry a man makes out of words and the poetry God makes out of
time and space, between the fight one man may fight for dignity in a
ring and the fight a whole race of people may fight for dignity on the
earth.

Athletes have always known this, from the first Greek Olympics to
today's Special Olympics. Sports has to be the most convergent of all
human activities because athletes know that there is no fundamental
difference between body, mind, and spirit. To be truly great, an ath-
lete must develop all three together, exercise them all together, and
bring the strength of all of them to bear on the contest. Only then is
greatness possible, and only then does victory have universal meaning
because it reflects the fullness and richness of the human heart.

I wanted to be heavyweight champion of the world from an early age. I wanted it not only because it is the greatest title in sports but because the champion is a symbol of greatness itself—of what an individual can achieve through sacrifice and work and faith.

But the title brings heavy responsibility: People all over the world look up to the champ, and whether he wants to or not, he becomes an example to them. Winning the heavyweight championship of the world is not just a great victory, it is a great duty. A man who seeks such greatness for money or other selfish reasons will never be able to inspire others. And a man who achieves such greatness and then is false to his own principles will have turned his victory into a lie.

I won the heavyweight championship for the first time in 1964, when I was 22 years old. I savored the overnight celebrity and basked in the media spotlight. Then almost at once I began to be challenged on my religion and then on my opposition to war. Those media spotlights quickly became interrogation lights, and the people who had celebrated me began ripping at me this way and that, demanding I support their stand. I very quickly found I had to decide what it really meant for me to be world champion.

It's hard to define yourself when you're young and at the summit of a vast and searching world. I had to look deep into myself for the answer. Despite being champ, it was a lonely process, and before it was over, the title itself had been stripped from me, then won back, lost, and won back again. But what I gained was of much greater value.

As I look back on it today, I would say that what I gained was the ability to see the world in something like the way God must see it. To understand that there are no distinctions of any real importance in the affairs of men, that there is only one time and one place and one person and one truth. And that we are all contained in that time and place and person, and that the truth contains us all.

In our daily lives, we may find it convenient to make distinctions, to give numbers and names to things in the world, but that is like counting the drops in the ocean or classifying the leaves on a tree. The beauty of the ocean and the tree remains wondrous nonetheless, and filled with God's glory for the spirit and the mind and the fingers, young and old, that can reach out and discover it anew each day.

JAN MORRIS

──➤◆◄──

Herstory

A famous travel writer explains her journey across gender

JAN MORRIS *has written books on many places around the world, plus works of history, biography, memoir, and fiction. Her recent book is* Lincoln: A Foreigner's Quest.

TWENTY-SEVEN YEARS AGO, almost on the cusp between the third and fourth quarters of the 20th century, I completed what was then simplistically called a change of sex. Nowadays it is more often euphemized as gender reassignment, and this shift of words is not simply semantic. It recognizes that across the civilized world, sex is no longer being seen as something absolute, and that the old immovable opposites of Male and Female may be converging after all.

When this happened to me—for I certainly did not ask for it, only obeyed an irresistible organic urge—it seemed to many people utterly astonishing, if not actually incredible. I was not the first person to undergo such a metamorphosis, but I suppose I seemed an unlikely candidate for it. I was a foreign correspondent and an established author, I had been a soldier, I was happily married with children, I was a staunch advocate of the stiff upper lip, grinning and bearing it, pulling myself together, and many another attitude popularly supposed to be particularly masculine. When it emerged that I had abandoned maleness and would, in the future, be known not as James but as Jan, some of my male acquaintances thought I must have gone off my head. Otherwise, why on earth would anybody rather be a woman than a man?

Gradually, though, it turned out that I was not crazy. I did not run away with a property tycoon or appear topless in nightclubs. My family life remained happy as ever, and I continued to write books. Now the quandary facing people was no longer how best to humor me but how to deal with me as a woman rather than as a man. And that is how it was that I first experienced for myself, in the world of the 1970s, the great gulf that then still lay between the two halves of mankind. The women's movement had long been stirring, but the great mass of people still thought of male and female almost as separate species and treated them as differently as they would a dog and a cat.

Men, in those days, seem to me to have been much more courteous to women (opening doors, taking hats off in elevators), but the dullards among them were also much more condescending. They really did not take women very seriously. I happened at that time to know rather a lot about oil politics in the Arab world (I had been the Middle East correspondent for the *Times* of London), but I remember all too clearly with what patronizing contempt my opinions were dismissed by men I met on airplanes. It just did not seem possible to them that a woman could even be interested in, let alone conversant with, such grown-up, undomestic matters, and the extraordinary thing was that men I had known for years now instantly changed their personalities in my presence.

Women by and large were far less fazed. My change of life did not seem to them so astonishing. They welcomed me as a recruit to the oppressed classes, and they kindly helped me with the transition. Besides, I think some were attracted by the very idea of a conjunction between male and female—for I did not try to disguise the traits of temperament and intellect that remained with me from my previous existence.

And in this they were, I think, far more responsive to the changing times than most men were. For as the last decades of the century passed, that gap between the sexes narrowed, and I began to be seen—to feel myself, too—not just as symbiotic but as symbolic, too. What was so unutterably bizarre, after all, in a sex change? Which is the profounder entity: sex, which is a matter of hormones and ovaries, or gender, which is spirit and taste, the form of talent, and the nature of love? And anyway, are we not all an amalgam of male and female, in one degree or another?

Of course, by then the historic rise of feminism was changing all

the world's attitudes. I could measure in male responses the tremendous shift of balance between the sexes that was happening all around
us—a redistribution of power far greater and more fateful than any
political revolution. No longer would male mediocrities sweetly
change the course of a conversation, if I ventured to insert a thought
about the possibilities of glasnost in the Soviet Union, or the historical origins of Serbian intransigence. (And alas, perhaps only gentle-
men of very uncertain age would remove their bowler hats when one
entered the elevator.)

Slowly, tentatively, often reluctantly, the world was recognizing as
nonsense the antique inequality between the sexes, and the relationship between men and women was achieving a new rationality. All
revolutions are violent, and there was certainly an element of brutal
intolerance to this one. Often enough, standing in the middle as I did,
I felt myself sympathizing first with one party, then with another, as
women rebelling against centuries of unfairness conflicted with men
dazed by the collapse of so many inherited convictions. I could sym-
pathize with women still scorned by damn fool bureaucrats and dis-
gracefully underpaid; I felt sorry for men obliged to admit women
into their cherished clubs, and willy-nilly to adapt their age-old con-
ceptions. But I knew that such discomforts were only incidental to a
vast beneficial rearrangement of humanity, not to be completed for
another generation at least, and I felt a sort of undeserved pride to be
standing as a living symbol of a great reconciliation.

For convergence, of course, is generally reconciliation. When you
come up close, most things are not as bad as they looked from a distance, and men and women turn out to be not so different after all.
Even physically, at the end of the 20th century, they are growing more
alike: the women taller and stronger as they lead newer, freer lives; the
men less macho as the organic need for brute force subsides.

Who would have thought, 50 years ago, that women would be playing soccer, let alone boxing? Or that men would habitually be sharing
the housework—or for that matter, if we are to believe the hi-sci pun-
dits (who are generally right), that they might one day be bearing babies? Who could have foreseen that the toughest politician in 1980s
Europe would be female (Thatcher), and the most conciliatory in
1990s Africa, male (Mandela)?

Divinities of older times were sternly sexist, creating one sex first, elevating one above the other, obliging them to sit in separate parts of the temple. The deities of technology don't give a damn, and today's men and women bow down in perfect equality before the cybergods.

In the age of sperm banks and genetic engineering, nobody is much surprised by my life story. It is no big deal anyway: simply a matter, so the scientists say, of some birth anomaly of the brain. In another half century, I do not doubt, the convergence of the genders will have gone much further, and a good thing, too. By then I shall no longer be able to claim, even to myself, the status of a symbol. For one thing, switching between the sexes will be commonplace. For another, I shall be dead.

STANLEY CROUCH

━━━▷◆◁━━━

Whose Pluribus Equals Whose Unum?

Despite all of our differences, we are Americans still

STANLEY CROUCH *is an award-winning essayist whose books include* Notes of a Hanging Judge, The All-American Skin Game, *and* Don't the Moon Look Lonesome.

THE QUESTION OF RACE is something that, almost always, means less than what is made of it. Sure, we know that Negroes arrived here as African slaves captured by other Africans and sold to Europeans who brought them to the Western Hemisphere, where they endured slavery for almost 400 years—and 90 years of Southern segregation after that! Sure, we know that the various Indian nations that stood in the way of American expansionism were given a low-down, dirty deal of disease-ridden blankets, broken treaties, and desolate reservations. Sure, we took plenty of land from Mexico, and we are aware of how badly the Asians who helped build the railroads were treated when they got into the game.

We know all of that, and we have been told all of that, and we need to never forget any of that. Selective memory is always a form of cowardice. But we also need to recognize that we are still a new people in perpetual remaking, a social species that is part European, part African, part American Indian, and part Asian, both in terms of blood and ways of being in the world. Those elements, however, have long since become versions of a fresh culture because the circumstances and the influences have remade everyone. For all of our enormous variety, we Americans are so easy for others to recognize that the idea of some kind of overwhelming alienation is a bad joke told over and over. We share too much, no matter what that sharing has cost us.

A story I often tell goes like this: If Louis Farrakhan and Patrick Buchanan took a plane to Ireland, arguing furiously with each other until they arrived in Dublin, the Irish, upon hearing them and watching them move, would say to one another the same thing that the Africans would, if the two men then continued their trip by going on to Ghana—"Surely two Americans there." European or African, people always notice the thing that crosses the gulf, just as we, upon looking at a piece of fluff like *Spice World*, immediately realize that all of those characters from England—white, black, and Asian—are inarguably British. Each character, no matter the class or color, is representative of England. Something steps up over the ethnic fences, the occupations, and the class backgrounds. It affects the varieties of accent, the wit, the repartee, and all the rest. That kind of commonality is equally true of the people of this nation but in a more consequential way.

We Americans, like the people of any other country, are not all the same by any means. In a nation this large that would be impossible, even if we were not as we are. But since we are Americans, certain things guarantee enormous variations. There are far too many ingredients, too many different geographical influences, too many regional customs, too many accents, too many senses of humor, too many federal, state, and local political histories, too many relationships to natural wonder and to natural disaster for us to come out as if we were the victims of cultural precision engineering. But we do share, like Farrakhan and Buchanan, a number of things that make us immediately recognizable to those who remained in the lands and cultures that our forebears came from.

For example, our sense of the individual working with, and against, the community is distinct from any other in the world. It is the grand story of the age, the greatest success of the past 200 years, the vision (and the many factual examples) that hardly a person anywhere else can resist. That is why, whenever they get a chance to figure out how to bring it home their own way, people the world over try to become Americans. They seek their own variations on the drama of the solitary person struggling to find himself or herself—sometimes in a very costly way. Other people know that part of our charisma is that we exhibit a style that combines humorous arrogance with disguised or overstated seriousness that can also be seen as hilarious. The American believes—even for all of the conspiracy theories that have substantially replaced the myriad superstitions we brought here from all over the world—that you can get up and do it. Your pain can pay off. You, little man or little woman, can make the difference.

Cynicism, for the American, is just a way of saying that you have to prove to me that the best is still possible, that we can still deduce and sweat our way beyond the trouble piled up on our contemporary plate. Behind it all is a joy, a battered one perhaps, but a heroic joy nonetheless, that affirms the *possibility*—not the guarantee—of moving on up to higher ground. It is what I call "tragic optimism."

That particular spirit is the result of Americans always trying to figure out what works best at the moment, because ours is a tradition of perpetually improvising our identity. We exist in the society exactly the way that our government exists on the page: Everything is up for further interpretation, for further definition, for new experiments. In the very best and the very worst sense of the words, we are a fashion-oriented people always looking for something that has an attractive quality yet adds an unexpected freshness to our perspective. We want something that doesn't seem handed down for the umpteenth time.

Of course, that puts us at the risk of being manipulated by novelty, of being overly impressed by elements that are more surprising on the surface than substantial. But it is equally true that we have made the scientific method something that works in the realm of society as well as aesthetics and governmental policy. These attitudes, whether rendered and considered in a profound or trivial way, are things that we share and that we make both the best and worst of, regardless of where in this nation we come from.

That is the basis of what I'm after in my novel *Don't the Moon Look Lonesome,* which will arrive for approval or dismissal in April 2000. (It was this forthcoming book that my *Forbes ASAP* editor, Michael S. Malone, got wind of and asked me to use as the basis for this "Big Issue" essay.) What I wanted to do in my novel was show, in an unpredictable manner, that we Americans are variations on, and unique composites of, one another. No matter where we come from, our American reality will eventually speak.

I also wanted to move free of the segregation so prevalent in American fiction, with people writing only of their own ethnic groups or sexes because they are not supposed to know that much about any other kind of life in this country. Beyond those things, I was interested in a tale that would expose my main character to many types of Americans, of different classes, educational levels, and cultural styles.

Finally, I wanted to take a risk and see just what my knowledge of life in this country could or could not do. So I chose to make the lead character, Carla, a white woman of Norwegian American heritage from South Dakota. This took me immediately across the taboo lines of race and sex. As the well-educated and vain daughter of a college teacher of classics and history, Carla personally knows something of the Indians and of the vast spaces of the plains, so much in contrast to what she encounters when she moves to New York to become a jazz singer.

Her pioneer heritage and her urban experience, rife with all manner of complexities, are what Carla has to handle. Both, for completely different reasons, can make the individual feel either insignificant or part of something mightily overwhelming. One has big, empty plains; the other overcrowding. Carla's narcissism has to do battle with understanding other people as they exist *apart* from what she expects and wants them to be. As a white person intent on becoming a first-class jazz singer, she has to address the Negro, discovering that there are many, many different kinds, just as there are many different kinds of other people.

What she discovers, over and over, is that the human quality defined within the American context speaks across all the lines, forcing her—and us, if we are free or brave enough—to recognize the bright, the gray, the dark sides of ourselves in whatever direction we turn.

That human quality, always ready for battle and perhaps too naive to consider the odds, is what makes us Americans the supreme social improvisers of all time. That is why the central metaphor of *Don't the Moon Look Lonesome* is jazz. Though Carla is a singer, jazz is, primarily, the indigenous instrumental music in which the individual and the collective constantly redefine themselves through improvisation. As instrumentalists, jazz musicians provide an extraordinary metaphor for the relationship between human beings and technology, the human being and the machine, which is what an instrument is.

This, in fact, is so true to our culture at large that it is part of our ethos. We see, for instance, in movie after movie, the American hero or heroine becoming part detective and part improviser. He or she must deduce what the trouble is and often invent a solution, something in which individual imagination and technology become a force of human bravery and affirmation. While that ethos is so often reduced to pulp brutality and indefensible carnage in our dubious popular culture, it is still, when the coarseness is scraped away, the essence of just what we are as Americans.

This American essence travels the distance, from sea to shining sea, and inspires the rest of the world as much as it does us whenever we take the time to recognize just what kind of people we are—the most freely human the world has ever known. That is the point of *Don't the Moon Look Lonesome,* which, if I'm lucky, might stir up just the kind of democratic commotion any writer who loves the tragic optimism of this country would want. As with all else in this nation, we'll see.

TOM PETERS

—>·◆·<—

Please . . . I just need some quiet time

TOM PETERS *is the best-selling business author of all time. His books include* The Circle of Innovation, The Pursuit of Wow! *and* In Search of Excellence.

JULY 19, 1999. Cape Poge, Martha's Vineyard. My new house is in the shadow—literally—of the old Cape Poge lighthouse. As far away from organized American society as one can get. End of the world. More or less. Access only across the beach by four-wheel drive with deflated tires. No electricity. (We do have solar panels.) No phone, sporadic cellular reception. We are isolated by design.

Circa 2009: Driving home. On the freeway. When I arrive, the front door will magically open, and the interior "environment" will be as I wish it. The microwave will have automatically zapped whatever. The refrigerator will have informed NetGrocer.com that I'm out of the skim milk my Suzanne Somers diet calls for. Etc. Etc. (Some Valley geeks already have this crap.)

I read *Forbes ASAP.* I believe that in 25 years the computer will be smarter than me. My human role called into question.

But there I am. At 5:15 A.M. On Cape Poge Bay. Rowing my Steve Kaulback Adirondack Guide Boat. Waters glassy. My prow slices the surface. I disturb several diving cormorants. I am transfixed. I am in touch. I am human. I am not on I-280 in Silicon Valley. Stuck amidst 28-year-old millionaires in a traffic jam. I have—can you believe it?—thoughts.

I want to see. To be fresh. I want to matter. To do that I need to be at Cape Poge. Or I need to be on my farm, 1,300 acres, at the north end of the Metowee Valley in West Tinmouth, Vermont.

But the info revolution has pursued me to West Tinmouth, which is why I spend more and more time at Cape Poge. But at least I can watch the Canadian geese do breathtaking landings on my farm pond in West Tinmouth. Which distracts me momentarily from the chatter of the two fax machines and the emails pouring in to one of the six computers on "the farm."

The more convergence converges on me, the more I need LOTSA space. To think. To exist. To make a difference.

Maybe the "infotech"/Microsoft/Web/Cisco revolution will spawn a counterrevolution. Not Hippie II. Not back to nature. But a quest for space. I used to have a quote on the wall of my office. As I recall, the authority was Judge Louis Brandeis. The quote: "The right to be left alone—the most comprehensive of all rights and the right most valued by civilized man."

The right to be left alone is—the right to think. Oh God. How I need to be a-w-a-y. To have s-p-a-c-e. To reflect. The world—call it convergence—is closing in on us. All of us. And I believe that my/our number-one requirement is—SPACE.

"Convergence." The topic of this year's Big Issue. The people over at *ASAP* have asked me to write for this annual issue ever since they launched the idea three years ago. I am flattered. But I almost missed participating in this issue. Why? Because I could not get my psyche around Convergence.

You see, I'm a Divergence kinda guy. I want to walk a different path. I find that increasingly hard to do as convergence converges. Maybe it's my "seminal event," i.e., *In Search of Excellence.* You see, that "event" was born of naïveté. And Divergence. My pal Bob Waterman and I went out in search of joints that worked. We found an abiding concern for people that went beyond lip service. A passion for listening to customers.

The point: The Book was a product of space. Of naïveté. Of a Fresh Look. I have a fetish about "fresh looks." I think Steve Jobs is a Classic Fresh Look Guy. So, too, Charlie Schwab. And Marc Andreessen. And damn few others. I don't know Steve J's tricks. But I bet he has some. I bet he needs and gets space. Somehow.

Convergence. GOOD STUFF. (Whatever it is.) Space. BETTER

STUFF. The opportunity to be human. To think. At Cape Poge. At 5:15 A.M. In a Steve Kaulback Adirondack Guide Boat. Great stuff. Trust me. Or, please, at least think about it.

RICHARD DAWKINS

Snake Oil and Holy Water

Illogical thinking is the only thing joining science and religion together

RICHARD DAWKINS *is the Charles Simonyi Professor of the Public Understanding of Science at the University of Oxford. His books include* The Selfish Gene *and* Unweaving the Rainbow: Science, Delusion, and the Appetite for Wonder.

ARE SCIENCE AND religion converging? No.

There are modern scientists whose words sound religious but whose beliefs, on close examination, turn out to be identical to those of other scientists who call themselves atheists. Ursula Goodenough's lyrical book, *The Sacred Depths of Nature,* is sold as a religious book, is endorsed by theologians on the back cover, and its chapters are liberally laced with prayers and devotional meditations.

Yet, by the book's own account, Goodenough does not believe in any sort of supreme being, does not believe in any sort of life after death. By any normal understanding of the English language, she is no more religious than I am. She shares with other atheistic scientists a feeling of awe at the majesty of the universe and the intricate complexity of life. Indeed, the jacket copy for her book—the message that science does not "point to an existence that is bleak, devoid of meaning, pointless," but on the contrary "can be a wellspring of solace and hope"—would have been equally suitable for my book, *Unweaving the Rainbow,* or Carl Sagan's *Pale Blue Dot.* If that is religion, then I am a deeply religious man. But it isn't. And I'm not. As far as I can tell, my "atheistic" views are identical to Ursula's "religious" ones. One of us is misusing the English language, and I don't think it's me.

Goodenough happens to be a biologist, but this kind of neo-Deistic pseudoreligion is more often associated with physicists. In Stephen Hawking's case, I hasten to insist, the accusation is unjust. His much-quoted phrase, "the mind of God," no more indicates belief in God than my saying, "God knows!" as a way of indicating that I don't. I suspect the same of Einstein invoking "dear Lord" to personify the laws of physics. Paul Davies, however, adopted Hawking's phrase as the title of a book that went on to earn the Templeton Prize for Progress in Religion, the most lucrative prize in the world today, prestigious enough to be presented in Westminster Abbey. The philosopher Daniel Dennett once remarked to me in Faustian vein: "Richard, if ever you fall on hard times . . . "

If you count Einstein and Hawking as religious, if you allow the cosmic awe of Goodenough, Davies, Sagan, and me as true religion, then religion and science have indeed merged, especially when you factor in such atheistic priests as Don Cupitt and many university chaplains. But if the term *religion* is allowed such a flabbily elastic definition, what word is left for conventional religion, religion as the ordinary person in the pew or on the prayer mat understands it to-day—indeed, as any intellectual would have understood it in previous centuries, when intellectuals were religious like everybody else?

If *God* is a synonym for the deepest principles of physics, what word is left for a hypothetical being who answers prayers, intervenes to save cancer patients or helps evolution over difficult jumps, for-gives sins or dies for them? If we are allowed to relabel scientific awe as a religious impulse, the case goes through on the nod. You have redefined science as religion, so it's hardly surprising if they turn out to "converge."

Another kind of marriage has been alleged between modern physics and Eastern mysticism. The argument goes as follows: Quantum me-chanics, that brilliantly successful flagship theory of modern science, is deeply mysterious and hard to understand. Eastern mystics have always been deeply mysterious and hard to understand. Therefore, Eastern mystics must have been talking about quantum theory all along.

Similar mileage is made of Heisenberg's uncertainty principle ("Aren't we all, in a very real sense, uncertain?"), fuzzy logic ("Yes, it's okay for you to be fuzzy, too"), chaos and complexity theory (the but-terfly effect, the Platonic, hidden beauty of the Mandelbrot Set—you name it, somebody has mysticized it and turned it into dollars). You can buy any number of books on "quantum healing," not to mention quantum psychology, quantum responsibility, quantum morality, quantum immortality, and quantum theology. I haven't found a book on quantum feminism, quantum financial management, or Afroquantum theory, but give it time.

The whole dippy business is ably exposed by the physicist Victor Stenger in his book, *The Unconscious Quantum*, from which the following gem is taken. In a lecture on "Afrocentric healing," the psychiatrist Patricia Newton said that traditional healers "are able to tap that other realm of negative entropy—that superquantum velocity and frequency of electromagnetic energy—and bring them as conduits down to our level. It's not magic. It's not mumbo jumbo. You will see the dawn of the 21st century, the new medical quantum physics really distributing these energies and what they are doing."

Sorry, but mumbo jumbo is precisely what it is. Not African mumbo jumbo but pseudoscientific mumbo jumbo, down to the trademark misuse of the word *energy*. It is also religion, masquerading as science in a cloying love feast of bogus convergence.

In 1996 the Vatican, fresh from its magnanimous reconciliation with Galileo, a mere 350 years after his death, publicly announced that evolution had been promoted from tentative hypothesis to accepted theory of science. This is less dramatic than many American Protestants think it is, for the Roman Catholic Church has never been noted for biblical literalism—on the contrary, it has treated the Bible with suspicion, as something close to a subversive document, needing to be carefully filtered through priests rather than given raw to congregations. The pope's recent message on evolution has, nevertheless, been hailed as another example of late-20th-century convergence between science and religion.

Responses to the pope's message exhibited liberal intellectuals at their worst, falling over themselves in their eagerness to concede to religion its own magisterium, of equal importance to that of science, but not opposed to it. Such agnostic conciliation is, once again, easy to mistake for a genuine meeting of minds.

At its most naive, this appeasement policy partitions the intellectual territory into "how questions" (science) and "why questions" (religion). What are "why questions," and why should we feel entitled to think they deserve an answer? There may be some deep questions about the cosmos that are forever beyond science. The mistake is to think that they are therefore not beyond religion, too.

I once asked a distinguished astronomer, a fellow of my college, to explain the big bang theory to me. He did so to the best of his (and my) ability, and I then asked what it was about the fundamental laws of physics that made the spontaneous origin of space and time possible. "Ah," he smiled, "now we move beyond the realm of science. This is where I have to hand you over to our good friend, the chaplain." But why the chaplain? Why not the gardener or the chef? Of course chaplains, unlike chefs and gardeners, claim to have some insight into ultimate questions. But what reason have we ever been given for taking their claims seriously? Once again, I suspect that my friend, the professor of astronomy, was using the Einstein/Hawking trick of letting "God" stand for "That which we don't understand." It would be a harmless trick if it were not continually misunderstood by those hungry to misunderstand it. In any case, optimists among scientists, of whom I am one, will insist, "That which we don't understand" means only "That which we don't yet understand." Science is still working on the problem. We don't know where, or even whether, we ultimately shall be brought up short.

Agnostic conciliation, which is the decent liberal bending over backward to concede as much as possible to anybody who shouts loud enough, reaches ludicrous lengths in the following common piece of sloppy thinking. It goes roughly like this: You can't prove a negative (so far so good). Science has no way to disprove the existence of a supreme being (this is strictly true). Therefore, belief or disbelief in a supreme being is a matter of pure, individual inclination, and both are therefore equally deserving of respectful attention! When you say it like that, the fallacy is almost self-evident; we hardly need spell out the reductio ad absurdum. As my colleague, the physical chemist Peter Atkins, puts it, we must be equally agnostic about the theory that there is a teapot in orbit around the planet Pluto. We can't disprove it. But that doesn't mean the theory that there is a teapot is on level terms with the theory that there *isn't*.

Now, if it be retorted that there actually are reasons X, Y, and Z for finding a supreme being more plausible than a teapot, then X, Y, and Z should be spelled out—because, if legitimate, they are proper scientific arguments that should be evaluated. Don't protect them from scrutiny behind a screen of agnostic tolerance. If religious arguments are actually better than Atkins' teapot theory, let us hear the case. Otherwise, let those who call themselves agnostic with respect to religion add that they are equally agnostic about orbiting teapots. At the same time, modern theists might acknowledge that, when it comes to Baal and the golden calf, Thor and Wotan, Poseidon and Apollo, Mithras and Ammon Ra, they are actually atheists. We are all atheists about most of the gods that humanity has ever believed in. Some of us just go one god further.

In any case, the belief that religion and science occupy separate magisteria is dishonest. It founders on the undeniable fact that religions still make claims about the world that on analysis turn out to be scientific claims. Moreover, religious apologists try to have it both ways. When talking to intellectuals, they carefully keep off science's turf, safe inside the separate and invulnerable religious magisterium. But when talking to a nonintellectual mass audience, they make wanton use of miracle stories—which are blatant intrusions into scientific territory.

The Virgin Birth, the Resurrection, the raising of Lazarus, even the Old Testament miracles, all are freely used for religious propaganda, and they are very effective with an audience of unsophisticates and children. Every one of these miracles amounts to a violation of the normal running of the natural world. Theologians should make a choice. You can claim your own magisterium, separate from science's but still deserving of respect. But in that case, you must renounce miracles. Or you can keep your Lourdes and your miracles and enjoy their huge recruiting potential among the uneducated. But then you must kiss goodbye to separate magisteria and your high-minded aspiration to converge with science.

The desire to have it both ways is not surprising in a good propagandist. What is surprising is the readiness of liberal agnostics to go along with it, and their readiness to write off, as simplistic, insensitive extremists, those of us with the temerity to blow the whistle. The whistle-blowers are accused of imagining an outdated caricature of religion in which God has a long white beard and lives in a physical place called heaven. Nowadays, we are told, religion has moved on. Heaven is not a physical place, and God does not have a physical body where a beard might sit. Well, yes, admirable: separate magisteria, real convergence. But the doctrine of the Assumption was defined as an Article of Faith by Pope Pius XII as recently as November 1, 1950, and is binding on all Catholics. It clearly states that the body of Mary was taken into heaven and reunited with her soul. What can that mean, if not that heaven is a physical place containing bodies? To repeat, this is not a quaint and obsolete tradition with just a purely symbolic significance. It has officially, and recently, been declared to be literally true.

Convergence? Only when it suits. To an honest judge, the alleged marriage between religion and science is a shallow, empty, spin-doctored sham.

PAUL DAVIES

➤◆◄

At the Crossroads

Two of the world's greatest institutions
take a step closer to each other

PAUL DAVIES, *Australia's best-known scientist, has published more than 100 research papers in the fields of cosmology, gravitation, and quantum field theory. He was described by the* Washington Times *as "the best science writer on either side of the Atlantic." His recent book is* The Fifth Miracle: The Search for the Origin and Meaning of Life.

AMONG HIS MORE MEMORABLE aphorisms, Albert Einstein's oft-quoted phrase, "Science without religion is lame; religion without science is blind," stands out as the most intriguing. Einstein was not a conventionally religious man, but he often spoke of a deep reverence for nature, a "cosmic religious feeling," guiding him in his quest to unravel the secrets of the universe. Many other scientists share Einstein's deep sense of awe for nature's mathematical elegance and sheer breathtaking ingenuity. For some, their research takes on the form of a spiritual quest.

High-profile scientists such as Stephen Hawking, Stephen Jay Gould, and Richard Dawkins are increasingly willing to pronounce on God and the meaning of life. Although these celebrities normally present themselves as atheists, some of their lesser-known colleagues are happy to declare religious beliefs and even go so far as to become theologians. The Anglican priest John Polkinghorne, for example, was formerly professor of mathematical physics at the University of Cambridge in England. In Berkeley, Robert John Russell holds degrees in both physics and divinity and runs the Center for Theology and the Natural Sciences, which fosters a dialogue between the two.

The new rapprochement between science and theology has no better illustration than the changing attitude toward Charles Darwin's theory of evolution. Even the pope has now given it his blessing. Theologians such as Ian Barbour feel perfectly comfortable with the idea that life has evolved over billions of years by accidental mutations subjected to the sieve of natural selection. Barbour regards the cumulative changes of gradual evolution as God's method of creation over time.

Nor does the big bang theory of the origin of the universe any longer pose a problem for theology. Hawking earned notoriety by suggesting that his theory of the cosmic birth left God with nothing to do, since quantum physics provides a natural explanation for how the universe originated from nothing. But Hawking's tease was based on a popular misconception of the Christian concept of creation ex nihilo. It does not mean God suddenly brought the universe into existence but rather that God held in place the natural order of things, timelessly.

The source of the confusion goes back to the nature of time itself. By the fifth century St. Augustine proclaimed that "the world was made, not in time, but simultaneously with time." In other words, God is the creator not only of matter but of time as well. This is more or less the picture of the big bang as derived from Einstein's general theory of relativity and the laws of quantum physics. The big bang represents not just the sudden appearance of matter in a burst of energy but also the origin of space and time. There was no time before the big bang.

Nonscientists are often startled to learn that the arcane equations of theoretical physics can inspire a type of religious fervor among scientists. Yet it may not be as strange as it first appears, for history reveals that science is the child of theology. Seventeenth-century European thought was dominated by monotheism, according to which God imposed order on nature as part of a rational plan. And because man was made in God's image, human beings might be able to comprehend the great cosmic plan. Early physicists such as Galileo, Kepler, and Newton thought their scientific investigations unveiled God's handiwork, enabling man to glimpse the mind of God. The term *natural theology* was used by those who sought evidence for God in the processes of nature, in contrast to divine revelation.

In the 18th century, science and theology began to part company, especially following the publication of Darwin's *On the Origin of Species* in 1859. Today most scientists would not deem their work to have any theological component whatsoever. But even the stoutest atheist among them unwittingly retains the view that nature is rationally ordered and intelligible. It wouldn't be possible to be a scientist without accepting the rational intelligibility of the universe as an act of faith. And *faith* is the right word. Science cannot prove that nature *has* to be this way. Yet many scientists assume that nature conforms to a design or scheme of some sort, even if they are coy about admitting it.

Part of the reason for the recent convergence of science and religion is the dazzling pace of scientific advance. For centuries, such topics as the birth of the universe, the origin of life, the nature of time and consciousness, and the final destiny of the cosmos lay outside the scope of scientific inquiry. But today they form part of mainstream scientific research. Scientists find themselves tackling questions that once were the exclusive preserve of priests and mystics. Inevitably they have been forced to confront the deep issues of existence raised by these questions, such as why the world is logical and rational, and where the laws of nature come from. Strictly speaking, these are not scientific questions but metaphysical ones. The scientist must take the laws of nature as given and get on with the job. But some scientists are not content to accept the existence of an ordered universe as a package that just happens to be. They ask what the world might be like if the laws were different, or there were no laws. Would life and consciousness still flourish? Would anyone be around to observe them?

Remarkably, it is possible to investigate such questions using mathematical modeling. How different would the universe be if protons were a tad heavier, or if space had four dimensions rather than three? What if the big bang had been a little bigger? Physicists have studied these topics and, as a general rule, find that the situation in the real universe is rather special. If things were only fractionally different, then stars like the sun would not exist and carbon-based life would be unlikely to arise. British cosmologist Fred Hoyle thought the laws of physics seemed so contrived that he proclaimed the universe "a put-up job."

Does this fine-tuning imply that the cosmos was designed with conscious organisms in mind? Few scientists are prepared to put that sort of theological spin on it. Some retreat instead to the cosmic absurdity theory, shrugging aside the felicitous numerical relationships as accidents. They add wryly that if the "coincidences" were not satisfied, we would not be here to worry about them. The trouble with this "so what?" approach is that it's contradictory: The essence of scientific belief is that nature is neither arbitrary nor absurd, that there are valid reasons for the way things are. Cosmic absurdity theorists assert that there is no explanation for why particular laws are as they are. They ask us to accept that the rational structure of nature as revealed by science has no moorings, implying that the universe is ultimately absurd.

Another, somewhat more considered, explanation is the lottery theory. It holds that there is not just one universe but an enormous collection, with each universe differing in the form of its laws. Since life depends on the "right" laws and conditions, it is clear that only a very tiny fraction of these many universes will permit observers. Those beings will marvel at how organized and propitious their particular universe seems, and how well it suits the emergence of life and mind. But actually they are just the winners in a vast and meaningless cosmic lottery.

A serious objection to the lottery theory is that it fails to meet the Occam's razor test, which says that, all else being equal, one should choose the simplest explanation for the facts. Invoking an infinity of unseen universes just to explain features of the universe we do see seems like overkill. Lottery theorists retort that unseen universes are better than an unseen God, but actually both explanations are equivalent in this regard. What we are trying to explain is how one particular, rather special universe is picked out from an infinity of also-ran contenders. The lottery theory amounts to little more than theism dressed in science's clothing.

It is conceivable that the fine-tuning riddle can be solved by introducing an element of design into nature, without resorting to the rather crass image of an omniscient God inspecting a colossal shopping list of alternative universes. Although *design* is a loaded term, there have been attempts to put the concept on a sound mathematical footing. After all, Darwin's theory provides a physical mechanism that designs organisms to fit niches. Maybe the laws of physics incorporate design principles too.

A new branch of science known as complexity theory seeks to identify the universal mathematical principles that govern the emergence of complex organization in chemical mixtures, star clusters, turbulent fluids, and life itself. This research hints that certain physical systems possess inherent self-organizing qualities and can leap spontaneously from random chaos to elaborate and coherent organized states.

The convergence of science and religion has not been wholly one-sided. For their part, theologians have begun to see science as a welcome illuminating influence. In popular religion, God is often portrayed as a sort of cosmic magician who creates the universe in a series of gigantic miracles and then prods it fitfully from time to time. Scholarly theologians, however, long ago abandoned this image of God as a miracle-working superbeing, derisively dubbing it "the God-of-the-gaps." The phrase stems from the notion that although science can explain most of how the world works, it still leaves gaps that require supernatural plugs. For example, scientists remain baffled by the puzzle of how the first living thing formed from lifeless chemicals: Perhaps the initial step required a miracle? But this position is a dangerous one for theologians, lest the mystery be explained by a future scientific discovery. It also gives the impression that as scientists explain the mysteries of the cosmos, God gets squeezed out of more gaps. Better to accept that the laws of nature apply unfailingly and seek God as the architect rather than the violator of them.

In this vein, some theologians prefer to regard God not so much as "a being" but rather as being itself—or, to use the words of Paul Tillich, "the ground of being." Describing God as the rational ground in which the laws of the universe are rooted meshes well with science, which is founded on the assumption that the orderly operation of nature is guaranteed. The modern image of a "hands-off" deity who sustains but does not meddle with nature removes the head-to-head conflict with science, but it leaves God rather remote and abstract. Most worshipers still seek comfort by believing in a personal God who answers prayers and maybe even intervenes in history. Fundamental to the Christian faith is a belief that God took on human flesh in the person of Jesus Christ. If Christianity is to retain the Incarnation as its defining doctrine, this is one miracle that appears to be nonnegotiable.

It would be wrong to give the impression that science and religion will one day merge. After all, science is founded on skepticism and challenge while conventional religion demands unquestioning faith. But these two great systems of thought can meet happily in the middle ground. Many scholars are convinced we've entered a new phase of scientific maturity in which scientists no longer ridicule people's genuine spiritual hunger but seek instead to address the deep issues of meaning and purpose in a more constructive way.

KURT VONNEGUT

The Trouble with Reunions

War, genocide, famine, plagues . . . and so it goes

KURT VONNEGUT *is the legendary author of 13 novels, including the recent* Timequake. *Before becoming a writer, he worked as a police reporter in Chicago and in public relations for General Electric.*

WHEN I WAS a graduate student in the anthropology department of the University of Chicago immediately following the Second World War, the only job opportunities on the departmental bulletin board were in the South Pacific. There, this country had taken over the trusteeship of many islands previously overseen by the Japanese. To send in anthropologists after the United States Marines to learn the customs and hopes and dreams of the aborigines, never our enemies, was a strikingly wise and humane thing for our government to do.

I did not go from the South Side of Chicago to the island of Yap, say, with its enormous stone money, but perforce immersed myself and my family in the customs of the General Electric Company in Schenectady, New York, instead.

I can nonetheless celebrate my fellow anthropologists' contributions to my country's generally respectful trusteeship for the native societies of Yap, Truk, Ponape, and Kosrae in the South Pacific. Our oversight ended in 1986, with the founding of a wholly sovereign nation: the Federated States of Micronesia.

I note, too, that this is a rare instance of a mutually respectful coming together of unlike societies with strikingly unlike cultures, one overwhelmingly powerful, the other pitifully weak.

When the British took over the island of Tasmania in 1803, for instance, they didn't bother to learn anything at all about the aborigines, their language, their religion, or whatever. They simply drove them into hiding—where they were bound to starve to death. The last native Tasmanian to die, a woman, was until recently on exhibit in a museum in Hobart. The Brits had no need of the typically sympathetic and chickenhearted advice of a cultural anthropologist. All they needed was a stand for the skeleton.

Hitler didn't even need that, when deciding what to do about the unlike culture of Jews in Europe. His problem was where to put the ashes. When the Turks got rid of 2 million unlike Armenians in their midst during World War I, they did what the Serbs did to the unlike Kosovars just this spring. They drove them out of their homes, and many, many died of exposure, or, like the last of the Tasmanian aborigines, starved to death.

The sound bite that justified what was done to the Tasmanians by the Brits, or to the aborigines of the whole Western Hemisphere by Europeans, or to Jews by Nazis, or to Kosovars by Serbs, was this: "They are not Christians." Never mind the landgrab going on. But in the United States, as I was growing up, the sound bite for the people with whom we could never converge, the sort of subhumans we wished weren't even on the same planet with us, was this: "Communists!"

Converge with Communists? Never! Better dead than Red.

And what I remember now, appropriately enough on Memorial Day, is another day in May in 1945. I was one of a bunch of American prisoners of war who had been turned loose in farmland somewhere south of the ruins of Dresden, in what would become the Soviet Union's zone of occupation. But the Red Army had yet to show up. So every conceivable sort of survivor of the war was bleakly adrift and bewildered in the area—including concentration camp victims, Gypsies, lunatics, German soldiers still carrying weapons—which was a big mistake—and on and on.

A German soldier, upon learning I was American, said to me, "Now you will have to fight them." He meant the Communists.

I was then 22, a private first class with three years of college as a

chemist, a retired rifleman. I had yet to become a cultural anthropologist, but I was already thinking like one, believing no culture, with
the exception of Nazism, was utterly contemptible. It was, moreover,
only natural for me to be politically ecumenical at that point, with the
Red Army about to sweep us up.

So I said this to him: "No. We will become a little more like them,
and they will become a little more like us." If Hitler had been put on
display instead of buried, incidentally, that would have been okay with
me.

What I meant back then was that we would adopt some of their
country's *avowed* ideals, with respect to a fair economic shake for
working stiffs and their families, and they would adopt our *avowed*
love of freedom of speech and all that.

If an African American had been there, he might have protested
that, back home in "the Land of the Free," he couldn't even vote,
couldn't sit wherever he liked in a bus, couldn't get served in most eating places, could use only certain public toilets and drinking fountains, and so on. (I am *white*, by the way.)

If a native of the Ukraine had been there, he would surely have
pointed out that millions of his people had been deliberately starved
to death by his government in "the Workers' Paradise."

Whatever! I already knew all that. I simply thought it would be nice
for all concerned, and still feel that way, if the Communists' most humane *stated* aspirations and ours *converged*. Who was to say, with the
passage of time, that those aspirations might not stop being a lot of
horse crap in both countries, or at least in one? Stranger things had
happened.

Yes—and in the intervening 55 years, Americans of color, not without a struggle, have in fact won civil rights once reserved for white
people. Moreover, they can no longer be barred from certain restaurants and hotels and public toilets and drinking fountains and parts of
buses—and white mobs can no longer string them up with impunity,
and so on.

And while there is no longer a Soviet Union, the people in what was
once the heart of it, Russia, whom we are still prepared to nuke,
should push come to shove, are so free as individuals, saying whatever
they damn please, going wherever they damn please, getting money
however they damn please, spending it any way they damn please,

that they might as well be living under an enforced Bill of Rights of our Constitution. As in the United States, they can even be gangsters and racketeers.

As for taking good care of ordinary working stiffs and their families, giving them work to do day after day, paying them enough so that they can afford food and shelter and medical services, and their kids can get decent educations—that costs money, and Russia is so poorly equipped, technologically, institutionally, professionally, and spiritually, to sell anything in a high tech global free market that it can't pay its own people anything for anything.

In the Soviet Union's closed economy, currency worthless to the outside world could still buy essential goods and services at home. Workers there used to say, "We pretend to work, and they pretend to pay us," but they actually did work and had enough to eat, and places to live, and health care, no matter how lousy. That's all over now. *Merde.*

In my own country, we still, as always, have enormous pockets of abject poverty, millions of Americans as badly off as anybody in Lekhovskoye or Ostashkov. But no longer have politicians and minor political parties any say-so. And our corporate executives with stock options, already free to help themselves from treasuries greater than those of any nation formerly part of the Communist bloc, are now rewarded by Wall Street as well for laying off employees. *Merde* again.

I was in Leipzig last October, a city in the former Communist nation that had recently converged with the free-market Germany to the west. The situation was virtually unique in history, so far as I know, since two societies that were identical racially, and spoke the same language, and had inherited the same history from before the end of the Second World War, were coming together with radically different cultures with respect to individual freedoms and what was to be done with money.

Cultural anthropologists, or at least people who thought like them—and there can be no such politicians—should have been called upon for advice on how reunification for the East Germans might have been less meanly ridiculous. One matter that might have been better understood and somehow dealt with, it seems to me, was the contempt, or worse, so many West Germans felt for those in the East—long before reunification.

There was high unemployment in the former East Germany last October. Unprofitable factories had been closed. Young people were untrained for jobs in a microchip megalopolis. And yet there were luxury shops such as one sees in Monte Carlo. And I said to a Leipzig journalist who was interviewing me, "Where are the satirists and cabaret comedians who should be jeering at such a sinister result?"

And he said this to me: "Don't you remember? We killed all our Jews."

TOM WOLFE

———⇒◆⇐———

Digibabble, Fairy Dust, and the Human Anthill

What do a Jesuit priest, a Canadian communications theorist, and Darwin II all have in common?

TOM WOLFE *has chronicled American popular culture for more than three decades. His best-selling books include* The Electric Kool-Aid Acid Test, The Right Stuff, The Bonfire of the Vanities, *and* A Man in Full. *His next novel is about collegiate life.*

The scene was the Suntory Museum, Osaka, Japan, in an auditorium so postmodern it made your teeth vibrate. In the audience were hundreds of Japanese art students. The occasion was the opening of a show of the work of four of the greatest American illustrators of the 20th century: Seymour Chwast, Paul Davis, Milton Glaser, and James McMullan, the core of New York's fabled Push Pin Studio. The show was titled *Push Pin and Beyond: The Celebrated Studio That Transformed Graphic Design.* Up on the stage, aglow with global fame, the Americans had every reason to feel terrific about themselves.

Seated facing them was an interpreter. The Suntory's director began his introduction in Japanese, then paused for the interpreter's English translation:

"Our guests today are a group of American artists from the Manual Age."

Now the director was speaking again, but his American guests were no longer listening. They were too busy trying to process his opening line. *The Manual Age . . . The Manual Age . . .* The phrase ricocheted about inside their skulls . . . bounced off their pyramids of Betz, whistled through their corpora callosa, and lodged in the Broca's and Wernicke's areas of their brains.

All at once they got it. The hundreds of young Japanese staring at them from the auditorium seats saw them not as visionaries on the cutting edge . . . but as woolly old mammoths who had somehow wandered into the Suntory Museum from out of the mists of a Pliocene past . . . a lineup of relics unaccountably still living, still breathing, left over from . . . *the Manual Age!*

Marvelous. I wish I had known Japanese and could have talked to all those students as they scrutinized the primeval spectacle before them. They were children of the dawn of—need one spell it out?—the Digital Age. Manual, "free hand" illustrations? How brave of those old men to have persevered, having so little to work with. Here and now in the Digital Age illustrators used—what else?—the digital computer. Creating images from scratch? What a quaint old term, "from scratch," and what a quaint old notion. . . . In the Digital Age, illustrators "morphed" existing pictures into altered forms on the digital screen. The very concept of postmodernity was based on the universal use of the digital computer . . . whether one was morphing illustrations or synthesizing music or sending rocket probes into space or achieving, on the Internet, instantaneous communication and information retrieval among people all over the globe. The world had shrunk, shrink-wrapped in an electronic membrane. No person on earth was more than six mouse clicks away from any other. The Digital Age was fast rendering national boundaries and city limits and other old geographical notions obsolete. Likewise, regional markets, labor pools, and industries. The world was now unified . . . online. There remained only one "region," and its name was the Digital Universe.

Out of that fond belief has come the concept of convergence.

Or perhaps I should say out of that *faith,* since the origin of the concept is religious; Roman Catholic, to be specific. The term itself, *convergence,* as we are using it in these pages, was coined by a Jesuit priest, Pierre Teilhard de Chardin. Another ardent Roman Catholic, Marshall McLuhan, broadcast the message throughout the intellectual world and gave the Digital Universe its first and most memorable name: "the global village." Thousands of dot.com dreamers are now busy amplifying the message without the faintest idea where it came from.

Teilhard de Chardin—usually referred to by the first part of his last name, Teilhard, pronounced TAY-yar—was one of those geniuses who, in Nietzsche's phrase (and as in Nietzsche's case), was doomed to be understood only after his death. Teilhard died in 1955. It has taken the current Web mania, nearly half a century later, for this romantic figure's theories to catch fire. Born in 1881, he was the second son among 11 children in the family of one of the richest landowners in France's Auvergne region. As a young man he experienced three passionate callings: the priesthood, science, and Paris. He was the sort of worldly priest European hostesses at the turn of the century died for: tall, dark, and handsome, and aristocratic on top of that, with beautifully tailored black clerical suits and masculinity to burn. His athletic body and ruddy complexion he came by honestly, from the outdoor life he led as a paleontologist in archeological digs all over the world. And the way that hard, lean, weathered face of his would break into a confidential smile when he met a pretty woman—by all accounts, every other woman in *le monde* swore she would be the one to separate this glamorous Jesuit from his vows.

For Teilhard also had glamour to burn, three kinds of it. At the age of 32 he had been the French star of the most sensational archeological find of all time, the Piltdown man, the so-called missing link in the evolution of ape to man, in a dig near Lewes, England, led by the Englishman Charles Dawson. One year later, when the First World War broke out, Teilhard refused the chance to serve as a chaplain in favor of going to the front as a stretcher bearer rescuing the wounded in the midst of combat. He was decorated for bravery in that worst-of-all-infantry-wars' bloodiest battles: Ypres, Artois, Verdun, Villers-Cotterêts, and the Marne. Meantime, in the lulls between battles he had begun writing the treatise with which he hoped to unify all of science and all of religion, all of matter and all of spirit, heralding God's plan to turn all the world, from inert rock to humankind, into a single sublime Holy Spirit.

"With the evolution of Man," he wrote, "a new law of Nature has come into force—that of convergence." Biological evolution had created step one, "expansive convergence." Now, in the 20th century, by means of technology, God was creating "compressive convergence." Thanks to technology, "the hitherto scattered" species *Homo sapiens* was being united by a single "nervous system for humanity," a "living membrane," a single "stupendous thinking machine," a unified consciousness that would cover the earth like "a thinking skin," a "noö-sphere," to use Teilhard's favorite neologism. And just what technology was going to bring about this convergence, this noösphere? On this point, in later years, Teilhard was quite specific: radio, television, the telephone, and "those astonishing electronic computers, pulsating with signals at the rate of hundreds of thousands a second."

One can think whatever one wants about Teilhard's theology, but no one can deny his stunning prescience. When he died in 1955, television was in its infancy and there was no such thing as a computer you could buy ready-made. Computers were huge, hellishly expensive, made-to-order machines as big as a suburban living room and bristling with vacuum tubes that gave off an unbearable heat. Since the microchip and the microprocessor had not yet been invented, no one was even speculating about a personal computer in every home, much less about combining the personal computer with the telephone to create an entirely new medium of communication. Half a century ago, only Teilhard foresaw what is now known as the Internet.

What Teilhard's superiors in the Society of Jesus and the church hierarchy thought about it all in the 1920s, however, was not much. The plain fact was that Teilhard accepted the Darwinian theory of evolution. He argued that biological evolution had been nothing more than God's first step in an infinitely grander design. Nevertheless, he accepted it. When Teilhard had first felt his call to the priesthood, it had been during the intellectually liberal papacy of Leo XIII. But by the 1920s the pendulum had swung back within the church, and evolutionism was not acceptable in any guise. At this point began the central dilemma, the great sorrow—the tragedy, I am tempted to say—of this remarkable man's life. A priest was not allowed to put anything into public print without his superiors' approval. Teilhard's dilemma was precisely the fact that science and religion were not unified. As a scientist, he could not bear to disregard scientific truth; and in his opinion, as a man who had devoted decades to paleontology, the theory of evolution was indisputably correct. At the same time he could not envision a life lived outside of the church.

God knew there were plenty of women who were busy envisioning it for him. Teilhard's longest, closest, tenderest relationship was with an American sculptress named Lucile Swan. Lovely little Mrs. Swan was in her late 30s and had arrived in Peking in 1929 on the China leg of a world tour aimed at diluting the bitterness of her recent breakup with her husband. Teilhard was in town officially to engage in some major archeological digs in China and had only recently played a part in discovering the second great "missing link," the Peking man. In fact, the church had exiled him from Europe for fear he would ply his evolutionism among priests and other intellectuals. Lucile Swan couldn't get over him. He was the right age, 48, a celebrated scientist, a war hero, and the most gorgeous white man in Peking. The crowning touch of glamour was his brave, doomed relationship with his own church. She had him over to her house daily "for tea." In addition to her charms, which were many, she seems also to have offered an argument aimed at teasing him out of the shell of celibacy. In effect, the church was forsaking him because he had founded his own new religion. Correct? Since it was his religion, couldn't he have his priests do anything he wanted them to do? When she was away, he wrote her letters of great tenderness and longing. "For the very reason that you are such a treasure to me, dear Lucile," he wrote at one point, "I ask you not to build too much of your life on me. . . . Remember, whatever sweetness I force myself not to give you, I do in order to be worthy of you."

The final three decades of his life played out with the same unvarying frustration. He completed half a dozen books, including his great work, *The Phenomenon of Man.* The church allowed him to publish none of it and kept him in perpetual exile from Europe and his beloved Paris. His only pleasure and ease came from the generosity of women, who remained attracted to him even in his old age. In 1953, two years before his death, he suffered one especially cruel blow. It was discovered that the Piltdown man had been, in fact, a colossal hoax pulled off by Charles Dawson, who had hidden various doctored ape and human bones like Easter eggs for Teilhard and others to find. He was in an acute state of depression when he died of a cerebral hemorrhage at the age of 74, still in exile. His final abode was a dim little room in the Hotel Fourteen on East 60th Street in Manhattan, with a single window looking out on a filthy air shaft comprised, in part, of a blank exterior wall of the Copacabana nightclub.

The All-in-One Global Village

Not a word of his great masterwork had ever been published, and yet Teilhard had enjoyed a certain shady eminence for years. Some of his manuscripts had circulated among his fellow Jesuits, *sub rosa, sotto voce,* in a Jesuit *samizdat.* In Canada he was a frequent topic of conversation at St. Michael's, the Roman Catholic college of the University of Toronto. Immediately following his death, his Paris secretary, Jeanne Mortier, to whom he had left his papers, began publishing his writings in a steady stream, including *The Phenomenon of Man.* No one paid closer attention to this gusher of Teilhardiana than a 44-year-old St. Michael's teaching fellow named Marshall McLuhan, who taught English literature. McLuhan was already something of a campus star at the University of Toronto when Teilhard died. He had dreamed up an extracurricular seminar on popular culture and was drawing packed houses as he held forth on topics such as the use of sex in advertising, a discourse that had led to his first book, *The Mechanical Bride,* in 1951. He was a tall, slender man, handsome in a lairdly Scottish way, who played the droll don to a "T," popping off deadpan three-liners—not one-liners but three-liners—people couldn't forget.

One time I asked him how it was that Pierre Trudeau managed to stay in power as prime minister through all the twists and turns of Canadian politics. Without even the twitch of a smile, McLuhan responded, "It's simple. He has a French name, he thinks like an Englishman, and he looks like an Indian. We all feel very guilty about the Indians here in Canada."

Another time I was in San Francisco doing stories on both McLuhan and topless restaurants, each of which was a new phenomenon. So I got the bright idea of taking the great communications theorist to a topless restaurant called the Off Broadway. Neither of us had ever seen such a thing. Here were scores of businessmen in drab suits skulking at tables in the dark as spotlights followed the waitresses, each of whom had astounding silicone-enlarged breasts and wore nothing but high heels, a G-string, and rouge on her nipples. Frankly, I was shocked and speechless. Not McLuhan.

"Very interesting," he said.

"What is, Marshall?"

He nodded at the waitresses. "They're wearing . . . us."

"What do you mean, Marshall?"

He said it very slowly, to make sure I got it:

"They're . . . putting . . . us . . . on."

But the three-liners and the pop culture seminar were nothing compared to what came next, in the wake of Teilhard's death: namely, McLuhanism.

McLuhanism was Marshall's synthesis of the ideas of two men. One was his fellow Canadian, the economic historian Harold Innis, who had written two books arguing that new technologies were primal, fundamental forces steering human history. The other was Teilhard. McLuhan was scrupulous about crediting scholars who had influenced him, so much so that he described his first book of communications theory, *The Gutenberg Galaxy*, as "a footnote to the work of Harold Innis."

In the case of Teilhard, however, he was caught in a bind. McLuhan's "global village" was nothing other than Teilhard's "noösphere," but the church had declared Teilhard's work heterodox, and McLuhan was not merely a Roman Catholic, he was a convert. He had been raised as a Baptist but had converted to Catholicism while in England studying at Cambridge during the 1930s, the palmy days of England's great Catholic literary intellectuals, G. K. Chesterton and Hilaire Belloc. Like most converts, he was highly devout. So in his own writings he mentioned neither Teilhard nor the two-step theory of evolution that was the foundation of Teilhard's worldview. Only a single reference, a mere *obiter dictum*, attached any religious significance whatsoever to the global village: "The Christian concept of the mystical body—all men as members of the body of Christ—this becomes technologically a fact under electronic conditions."

I don't have the slightest doubt that what fascinated him about television was the possibility it might help make real Teilhard's dream of the Christian unity of all souls on earth. At the same time, he was well aware that he was publishing his major works, *The Gutenberg Galaxy* (1962) and *Understanding Media* (1964), at a moment when even the slightest whiff of religiosity was taboo, if he cared to command the stage in the intellectual community. And that, I assure you, he did care to do. His father had been an obscure insurance and real estate salesman, but his mother, Elsie, had been an actress who toured Canada giving dramatic readings, and he had inherited her love of the limelight. So he presented his theory in entirely secular terms, arguing that a new, dominant medium such as television altered human consciousness by literally changing what he called the central nervous system's "sensory balance." For reasons that were never clear to me—although I did question him on the subject—McLuhan regarded television as not a visual but an "aural and tactile" medium that was thrusting the new television generation back into what he termed a "tribal" frame of mind. These are matters that today fall under the purview of neuroscience, the study of the brain and the central nervous system. Neuroscience has made spectacular progress over the past 25 years and is now the hottest field in science and, for that matter, in all of academia. But neuroscientists are not even remotely close to being able to determine something such as the effect of television upon one individual, much less an entire generation.

That didn't hold back McLuhan, or the spread of McLuhanism, for a second. He successfully established the concept that new media such as television have the power to alter the human mind and thereby history itself. He died in 1980 at the age of 69 after a series of strokes, more than a decade before the creation of the Internet. Dear God—if only he were alive today! What heaven the present moment would have been for him! How he would have loved the Web! What a shimmering Oz he would have turned his global village into!

But by 1980 he had spawned swarms of believers who were ready to take over where he left off. It is they, entirely secular souls, who dream up our *fin de siècle* notions of convergence for the Digital Age, never realizing for a moment that their ideas are founded upon Teilhard's and McLuhan's faith in the power of electronic technology to alter the human mind and unite all souls in a seamless Christian web, the All-in-One. Today you can pick up any organ of the digital press, those magazines for dot.com lizards that have been spawned thick as shad since 1993, and close your eyes and riffle through the pages and stab your forefinger and come across evangelical prose that sounds like a hallelujah! for the ideas of Teilhard or McLuhan or both.

I did just that, and in *Wired* magazine my finger landed on the name Danny Hillis, the man credited with pioneering the concept of massively parallel computers, who writes, "Telephony, computers, and CD-ROMs are all specialized mechanisms we've built to bind us together. Now evolution takes place in microseconds. . . . We're taking off. We're at that point analogous to when single-celled organisms were turning into multicelled organisms. We are amoebas and we can't figure out what the hell this thing is that we're creating. . . . We are not evolution's ultimate product. There's something coming after us, and I imagine it is something wonderful. But we may never be able to comprehend it, any more than a caterpillar can comprehend turning into a butterfly."

Teilhard seemed to think the phase-two technological evolution of man might take a century or more. But you will note that Hillis has it reduced to microseconds. Compared to Hillis, Bill Gates of Microsoft seems positively tentative and cautious as he rhapsodizes in *The Road Ahead:* "We are watching something historic happen, and it will affect the world seismically." He's "thrilled" by "squinting into the future and catching that first revealing hint of revolutionary possibilities." He feels "incredibly lucky" to be playing a part "in the beginning of an epochal change . . . "

We can only appreciate Gates' self-restraint when we take a stab at the pages of the September 1998 issue of *Upside* magazine and come across its editor in chief, Richard L. Brandt, revealing just how epochally revolutionary Gates' Microsoft really is: "I expect to see the overthrow of the U.S. government in my lifetime. But it won't come from revolutionaries or armed conflict. It won't be a quick-and-bloody coup; it will be a gradual takeover. . . . Microsoft is gradually taking over everything. But I'm not suggesting that Microsoft will be the upstart that will gradually make the U.S. government obsolete. The culprit is more obvious. It's the Internet, damn it. The Internet is a global phenomenon on a scale we've never witnessed."

In less able hands such speculations quickly degenerate into what all who follow the digital press have become accustomed to: Digibabble. All of our digifuturists, even the best, suffer from what the philosopher Joseph Levine calls "the explanatory gap." There is never an explanation of just why or how such vast changes, such evolutionary and revolutionary great leaps forward, are going to take place. McLuhan at least recognized the problem and went to the trouble of offering a neuroscientific hypothesis, his theory of how various media alter the human nervous system by changing the "sensory balance." Everyone after him has succumbed to what is known as the "Web-mind fallacy," the purely magical assumption that as the Web, the Internet, spreads over the globe, the human mind expands with it. Magical beliefs are leaps of logic based on proximity or resemblance. Many primitive tribes have associated the waving of the crops or tall grass in the wind with the rain that follows. During a drought the tribesmen get together and create harmonic waves with their bodies in the belief that it is the waving that brings on the rain. Anthropologists have posited these tribal hulas as the origin of dance. Similarly, we have the current magical Web euphoria. A computer is a computer, and the human brain is a computer. Therefore, a computer is a brain, too, and if we get a sufficient number of them, millions, billions, operating all over the world, in a single seamless Web, we will have a superbrain that converges on a plane far above such old-fashioned concerns as nationalism and racial and ethnic competition.

I hate to be the one who brings this news to the tribe, to the magic Digikingdom, but the simple truth is that the Web, the Internet, does one thing. It speeds up the retrieval and dissemination of information, messages, and images, partially eliminating such chores as going outdoors to the mailbox or the adult bookstore, or having to pick up the phone to get ahold of your stockbroker or some buddies to shoot the breeze with. That one thing the Internet does, and only that. All the rest is Digibabble.

May I log on to the past for a moment? Ever since the 1830s, people in the Western Hemisphere have been told that technology was making the world smaller, the assumption being that only good could come of the shrinkage. When the railroad locomotive first came into use, in the 1830s, people marveled and said it made the world smaller by bringing widely separated populations closer together. When the telephone was invented, and the transoceanic cable and the telegraph and the radio and the automobile and the airplane and the television and the fax, people marveled and said it all over again, many times. But if these inventions, remarkable as they surely are, have improved the human mind or reduced the human beast's zeal for banding together with his blood brethren against other human beasts, it has escaped my notice. One hundred and seventy years after the introduction of the locomotive, the Balkans today are a cluster of virulent spores more bloody-minded than ever. The former Soviet Union is now 15 nations split up along ethnic bloodlines. The very zeitgeist of the end of the 20th century is summed up in the cry, "Back to blood!" The thin crust of nationhoods the British established in Asia and Africa at the zenith of their imperial might has vanished, and it is the tribes of old that rule. What has made national boundaries obsolete

in so much of eastern Europe, Africa, and Asia? Not the Internet but
the tribes. What have the breathtaking advances in communications
technology done for the human mind? Beats me. SAT scores among
the top tenth of high school students in the United States, that fraction who are prime candidates for higher education in any period, are
lower today than they were in the early 1960s. Believe, if you wish,
that computers and the Internet in the classroom will change all that,
but I assure you it is sheer Digibabble.

The Little People

Since so many theories of convergence were magical assumptions
about the human mind in the Digital Age, notions that had no neuroscientific foundation whatsoever, I wondered what was going on in
neuroscience that might bear upon the subject. This quickly led me
back to neuroscience's most extraordinary figure, Edward O. Wilson.
Three years ago the first Big Issue of *Forbes ASAP* asked the question,
"What will be the most important development in technology over the
next 10 years?" My nomination was brain imaging, the recording of
brain activity on-screen in real time. And why? Specifically because I
saw brain imaging as a means, eventually, of testing Edward O. Wilson's arresting theories of the brain and human behavior. I dubbed
him "Darwin II," for two reasons. He is a painfully devout Darwin-
ist—more about that in a moment—and his influence as a scientist
and an interpreter of the human condition is as great as Charles Darwin's was a century ago.

Wilson's own life is a good argument for his thesis, which is that
among humans, no less than among racehorses, inbred traits will
trump upbringing and environment every time. In its bare outlines his
childhood biography reads like a case history for the sort of boy who
today winds up as the subject of a tabloid headline: DISSED DORK
SNIPERS JOCKS. He was born in Alabama to a farmer's daughter
and a railroad engineer's son who became an accountant and an alco-
holic. His parents separated when Wilson was 7 years old and he was
sent off to the Gulf Coast Military Academy. A chaotic childhood was
to follow. His father worked for the federal Rural Electrification Administration, which kept reassigning him to different locations, from
the Deep South to Washington, D.C., and back again, so that in 11

years Wilson attended 14 different public schools. He grew up shy and introverted and liked the company only of other loners, preferably those who shared his enthusiasm for collecting insects. For years he was a skinny runt, and then for years after that he was a beanpole. But no matter what ectomorphic shape he took and no matter what school he went to, his life had one great center of gravity: He could be stuck anywhere on God's green earth and he would always be the smartest person in his class. That remained true after he graduated with a bachelor's degree and a master's in biology from the University of Alabama and became a doctoral candidate and then a teacher of biology at Harvard for the next half century. He remained the best in his class every inch of the way. Seething Harvard savant after seething Harvard savant, including one Nobel laureate, has seen his reputation eclipsed by this terribly reserved, terribly polite Alabamian, Edward O. Wilson.

Wilson's field within the discipline of biology was zoology; and within zoology, entomology, the study of insects; and within entomology, myrmecology, the study of ants. Year after year he studied his ants, from Massachusetts to the wilds of Suriname. He made major discoveries about ants, concerning, for example, their system of communicating via the scent of sticky chemical substances known as pheromones—all this to great applause in the world of myrmecology, considerable applause in the world of entomology, fair-to-middling applause in the world of zoology, and polite applause in the vast world of biology generally. The consensus was that quiet Ed Wilson was doing precisely what quiet Ed Wilson had been born to do, namely, study ants, and God bless him. Apparently none of them realized that Wilson had experienced that moment of blazing revelation all scientists dream of having. It is known as the "Aha!" phenomenon.

In 1971 Wilson began publishing his now-famous sociobiology trilogy. Volume one, *The Insect Societies,* was a grand picture of the complex social structure of insect colonies in general, starring the ants, of course. The applause was well nigh universal, even among Harvard faculty members who kept their envy and resentment on a hair trigger. So far Ed Wilson had not tipped his hand.

The Insect Societies spelled out in great detail just how extraordinarily diverse and finely calibrated the career paths and social rankings of insects were. A single ant queen gave birth to a million offspring in an astonishing variety of sizes, with each ant fated for a particular career. Forager ants went out to find and bring back food. Big army ants went forth as marauders, "the Huns and Tartars of the insect world," slaughtering other ant colonies, eating their dead victims, and even bringing back captured ant larvae to feed the colony. Still other ants went forth as herdsmen, going up tree trunks and capturing mealybugs and caterpillars, milking them for the viscous ooze they egested (more food), and driving them down into the underground colony for the night, i.e., to the stables. Livestock!

But what steered the bugs into their various, highly specialized callings? Nobody trained them, and they did not learn by observation. They were born, and they went to work. The answer, as every entomologist knew, was genetics, the codes imprinted (or hardwired, to use another metaphor) at birth. So what, if anything, did this have to do with humans, who in advanced societies typically spent 12 or 13 years, and often much longer, going to school, taking aptitude tests, talking to job counselors, before deciding upon a career?

The answer, Wilson knew, was to be found in the jungles of a Caribbean island. Fifteen years earlier, in 1956, he had been a freshly minted Harvard biology instructor accompanying his first graduate student, Stuart Altmann, to Cayo Santiago, known among zoologists as "monkey island," off the coast of Puerto Rico. Altmann was studying rhesus macaque monkeys in their own habitat. This was four years before Jane Goodall began studying chimpanzees in the wild in East Africa. Wilson, as he put it later in his autobiography, was bowled over by the monkeys' "sophisticated and often brutal world of dominance orders, alliances, kinship bonds, territorial disputes, threats and displays, and unnerving intrigues." In the evenings, teacher and student, both in their 20s, talked about the possibility of finding common characteristics among social animals, even among those as outwardly different as ants and rhesus macaques. They decided they would have to ignore glib surface comparisons and find deep principles, statistically demonstrable principles. Altmann already had a name for such a discipline, "sociobiology," which would cover all animals that lived within social orders, from insects to primates. Wilson thought about that—

Aha!

—human beings were primates, too. It took him 19 years and excursions into such esoteric and highly statistical disciplines as population biology and allometry ("relative growth of a part in relation to an entire organism") to work it out to the point of a compelling synthesis grounded in detailed observation, in the wild and in the laboratory, and set forth in terms of precise measurements. *The Insect Societies* had been merely the groundwork. In 1975 he published the central thesis itself: *Sociobiology: The New Synthesis*. Not, as everyone in the world of biology noticed, *A* new synthesis but *The* new synthesis. *The* with a capital *T*.

In the book's final chapter, the now famous Chapter 27, he announced that man and all of man's works were the products of deep patterns running throughout the story of evolution, from ants one tenth of an inch long to the species *Homo sapiens*. Among *Homo sapiens*, the division of roles and work assignments between men and women, the division of labor between the rulers and the ruled, between the great pioneers and the lifelong drudges, could not be explained by such superficial, external approaches as history, economics, sociology, or anthropology. Only sociobiology, firmly grounded in genetics and the Darwinian theory of evolution, could do the job.

During the furor that followed, Wilson compressed his theory into one sentence during an interview. Every human brain, he said, is born not as a blank slate waiting to be filled in by experience but as "an exposed negative waiting to be slipped into developer fluid." The negative might be developed well or it might be developed poorly, but all you were going to get was what was already on the negative at birth.

In one of the most remarkable displays of wounded Marxist chauvinism in American academic history (and there have been many), two of Wilson's well-known colleagues at Harvard's Museum of Comparative Zoology, paleontologist Stephen Jay Gould and geneticist Richard Lewontin, joined a group of radical activists called Science for the People to form what can only be called an "antiseptic squad." The goal, judging by their public statements, was to demonize Wilson as a reactionary eugenicist, a Nazi in embryo, and exterminate sociobiology as an approach to the study of human behavior. After three months of organizing, the cadre opened its campaign with a letter, signed by 15 faculty members and students in the Boston area, to the leading American organ of intellectual etiquette and deviation sniffing, the *New York Review of Books*. Theories like Wilson's, they charged, "tend to provide a genetic justification of the *status quo* and of existing privileges for certain groups according to class, race, or sex." In the past, vile Wilson-like intellectual poisons had "provided an important basis for the enactment of sterilization laws . . . and also for the eugenics policies which led to the establishment of gas chambers in Nazi Germany." The campaign went on for years. Protesters picketed Wilson's sociobiology class at Harvard (and the university and the faculty kept mum and did nothing). Members of INCAR, the International Committee Against Racism, a group known for its violent confrontations, stormed the annual meeting of the American Association for the Advancement of Science in Washington and commandeered the podium just before Wilson was supposed to speak. One goony seized the microphone and delivered a diatribe against Wilson while the others jeered and held up signs with swastikas—whereupon a woman positioned behind Wilson poured a carafe of ice water, cubes and all, over his head, and the entire antiseptic squad joined in the chorus: "You're all wet! You're all wet! You're all wet!"

The long smear campaign against Edward O. Wilson was one of the most sickening episodes in American academic history—and it could not have backfired more completely. As Freud once said, "Many enemies, much honor." Overnight, Ed Wilson became the most famous biologist in the United States. He was soon adorned with the usual ribbons of celebrity: appearances on the *Today Show*, the *Dick Cavett Show*, *Good Morning America*, and the covers of *Time* and the *New York Times Magazine* . . . while Gould and Lewontin seethed . . . and seethed . . . and contemplated their likely place in the history of science in the 20th century: a footnote or two down in the ibid. thickets of the biographies of Edward Osborne Wilson.

In 1977 Wilson won the National Medal for Science. In 1979 he won the Pulitzer Prize for nonfiction for the third volume of his sociobiology trilogy, *On Human Nature*. Eleven years later he and his fellow myrmecologist, Bert Hölldobler, published a massive (7½ pounds), highly technical work, *The Ants*, meant as the last word on these industrious creatures who had played such a big part in Wilson's career. The book won the two men Pulitzer Prizes. It was Wilson's second.

His smashing success revived Darwinism in a big way. Sociobiology had presented evolution as the ultimate theory, the convergence of all knowledge. Darwinists had been with us always, of course, ever since

the days of the great man himself. But in the 20th century the Darwin-
ist story of human life—natural selection, sexual selection, survival of
the fittest, and the rest of it—had been overshadowed by the Freudian
and Marxist stories. Marx said social class determined a human being's
destiny; Freud said it was the Oedipal drama within the family. Both
were forces external to the newborn infant. Darwinists, Wilson foremost among them, turned all that upside down and proclaimed that the
genes the infant was born with determined his destiny.

A field called evolutionary psychology became all the rage, attract-
ing many young biologists and philosophers who enjoyed the naughty
and delicious thrill of being Darwinian fundamentalists. The influence of genes was absolute. Free will among humans, no less than
among ants, was an illusion. The "soul" and the "mind" were illusions,
too, and so was the very notion of a "self." The quotation marks began
spreading like dermatitis over all the commonsense beliefs about human nature. The new breed, the fundamentalists, hesitated to use
Wilson's term, sociobiology, because there was always the danger that
the antiseptic squads, the Goulds and the Lewontins and the INCAR
goonies and goonettes, might come gitchoo. But all the bright new
fundamentalists were Ed Wilson's offspring, nevertheless.

They soon ran into a problem that Wilson had largely finessed by offering only the broadest strokes. Darwin's theory provided a wonder-
fully elegant story of how the human beast evolved from a single cell in
the primordial ooze and became the fittest beast on earth—but offered precious little to account for what man had created once he
reached the level of the wheel, the shoe, and the toothbrush. Somehow
the story of man's evolution from the apes had not set the stage for what
came next. Religions, ideologies, scholarly disciplines, aesthetic experiences such as art, music, literature, and the movies, technological
wonders such as the Brooklyn Bridge and breaking the bonds of
Earth's gravity with spaceships, not to mention the ability to create
words and grammars and record such extraordinary accomplish-
ments—there was nothing even remotely homologous to be found
among gorillas, chimpanzees, or any other beasts. So was it really just
Darwinian evolution? Anthropologists had always chalked such things
up to culture. But it had to be Darwinian evolution! Genetics had to be
the answer! Otherwise, fundamentalism did not mean much.

In 1976, a year after Wilson had lit up the sky with *Sociobiology:*

The New Synthesis, a British zoologist and Darwinian fundamentalist, Richard Dawkins, published a book called *The Selfish Gene* in which he announced the discovery of memes. Memes were viruses in the form of ideas, slogans, tunes, styles, images, doctrines, anything with sufficient attractiveness or catchiness to infect the brain—infect, like virus, became part of the subject's earnest, wannabescientific terminology—after which they operated like genes, passing along what had been naively thought of as the creations of culture.

Dawkins' memes definitely infected the fundamentalists, in any event. The literature of Memeland began pouring out: Daniel C. Dennett's *Darwin's Dangerous Idea,* William H. Calvin's *How Brains Think,* Steven Pinker's *How the Mind Works,* Robert Wright's *The Moral Animal,* and, recently, *The Meme Machine* by Susan Blackmore (with a foreword by Richard Dawkins), and on and on. Dawkins has many devout followers precisely because his memes are seen as the missing link in Darwinism as a theory, a theoretical discovery every bit as important as the skull of the Peking man. One of Bill Gates' epigones at Microsoft, Charles Simonyi, was so impressed with Dawkins and his memes and their historic place on the scientific frontier, he endowed a chair at Oxford University titled the Charles Simonyi Professor of the Public Understanding of Science and installed Dawkins in it. This makes Dawkins the postmodern equivalent of the Archbishop of Canterbury. Dawkins is now Archbishop of Darwinian Fundamentalism and Hierophant of the Memes.

There turns out to be one serious problem with memes, however. They don't exist. A neurophysiologist can use the most powerful and sophisticated brain imaging now available—three-dimensional electroencephalography, the functional MRI, the PET scan, the PET reporter gene/PET reporter probe, which can cause genes in the brain to light up on a screen when they are being used—a neurophysiologist can try all these instruments and still not find a meme. The Darwinian fundamentalists, like fundamentalists in any area, are ready for such an obvious objection. They will explain that memes operate in a way analogous to genes, i.e., through natural selection and survival of the fittest memes. But in science, unfortunately, "analogous to" just won't do. The tribal hula is analogous to the waving of a wheat field in the wind before the rain, too. Here the explanatory gap becomes enormous. Even though some of the fundamentalists have scientific credentials, not one even hazards a guess as to how, in physiological, neural terms, the meme "infection" is supposed to take place. Although no scientist, McLuhan at least offered a neuroscientific hypothesis for McLuhanism.

So our fundamentalists find themselves in the awkward position of being like those Englishmen in the year 1000 who believed quite literally in the little people, the fairies, trolls, and elves. To them, Jack Frost was not merely a twee personification of winter weather. Jack Frost was one of the little people, an elf who made your fingers cold, froze the tip of your nose like an icicle, and left the ground too hard to plow. You couldn't see him, but he was there. Thus also with memes. Memes are little people who sprinkle fairy dust on genes to enable them to pass along so-called cultural information to succeeding generations in a proper Darwinian way.

Wilson, who has a lot to answer for, transmitted more than fairy dust to his progeny, however. He gave them the urge to be popular. After all, he was a serious scientist who had become a celebrity. Not only that, he had made the best-seller lists. As they say in scholarly circles, much of his work has been really quite accessible. But there is accessible . . . and there is cute. The fundamentalists have developed the habit of cozying up to the reader or, as they are likely to put it, "cozying up." When they are courting the book-buying public, they use quotation marks as friendly winks. They are quick to use the second person singular in order to make you ("you") feel right at home ("right at home") and italicized words to make sure you *get it* and lots of conversational contractions so you *won't* feel intimidated by a lot of big words such as "algorithms," which *you're* not likely to tolerate unless *there's* some way to bring you closer to your wise friend, the author, by a just-between-us-pals approach. Simple, *I'd* say! One fundamentalist book begins with the statement that "intelligence is what you use when you don't know what to do (an apt description of my present predicament as I attempt to write about intelligence). If you're good at finding the one right answer to life's multiple-choice questions, you're *smart*. But there's more to being *intelligent*—a creative aspect, whereby you invent something new 'on the fly'" (*How Brains Think* by William H. Calvin, who also came up with a marvelously loopy synonym for fairy dust: "Darwinian soft-wiring").

The Match Game

Meantime, as far as Darwin II himself is concerned, he has nice things to say about Dawkins and his Neuro Pop brood, and he wishes them well in their study of the little people, the memes, but he is far too savvy to buy the idea himself. He theorizes about something called "culturgens," which sound suspiciously like memes, but then goes on to speak of the possibility of a "gene-culture coevolution." I am convinced that in his heart Edward O. Wilson believes just as strongly as Dawkins in Darwinian fundamentalism. I am sure he believes just as absolutely in the idea that human beings, for all of their extraordinary works, consist solely of matter and water, of strings of molecules containing DNA that are connected to a chemical analog computer known as the brain, a mechanism that creates such illusions as "free will" and . . . "me." But Darwin II is patient, and he is a scientist. He is not going to engage in any such sci-fi as meme theory. To test meme theory it would be necessary first to fill in two vast Saharas in the field of brain research: memory and consciousness itself. Memory has largely defied detailed neural analysis, and consciousness has proven totally baffling. No one can even define it. Anesthesiologists who administer drugs and gases to turn their patients' consciousness off before surgery have no idea why they work. Until memory and consciousness are understood, meme theory will remain what it is today: amateur night.

But Wilson is convinced that in time the entire physics and chemistry, the entire neurobiology of the brain and the central nervous system will be known, just as the 100,000-or-so genes are now being identified and located one by one in the Human Genome Project. When the process is completed, he believes, then all knowledge of living things will converge . . . under the umbrella of biology. All mental activity, from using allometry to enjoying music, will be understood in biological terms.

He actually said as much a quarter of a century ago in the opening paragraph of *Sociobiology*'s incendiary Chapter 27. The humanities and social sciences, he said, would "shrink to specialized branches of biology." Such venerable genres as history, biography, and the novel would become "the research protocols," i.e., preliminary reports of the study of human evolution. Anthropology and sociology would disappear as separate disciplines and be subsumed by "the sociobiology of a single primate species," *Homo sapiens*. There was so much else in Chapter 27 to outrage the conventional wisdom of the Goulds and the Lewontins of the academic world that they didn't pay much attention to this convergence of all human disciplines and literary pursuits.

But in 1998 Wilson spelled it out at length and so clearly that no one inside or outside of academia could fail to get the point. He published an entire book on the subject, *Consilience*, which immediately became a best-seller, despite the theoretical nature of the material. The term "consilience" was an obsolete word referring to the coming together, the confluence, of different branches of knowledge.

The ruckus *Consilience* kicked up spread far beyond the fields of biology and evolutionism. *Consilience* was a stick in the eye of every novelist, every historian, every biographer, every social scientist—every intellectual of any stripe, come to think of it. They were all about to be downsized, if not terminated, in a vast intellectual merger. The counterattack began. Jeremy Bernstein, writing in *Commentary*, drew first blood with a review titled "E. O. Wilson's Theory of Everything." It began, "It is not uncommon for people approaching the outer shores of middle age to go slightly dotty." Oh, Lord, another theory of everything from the dotty professor. This became an intellectual drumbeat—"just another theory of everything"—and Wilson saw himself tried and hanged on a charge of *hubris*.

As for me, despite the prospect of becoming a mere research protocol drudge for evolutionism, I am willing to wait for the evidence. I am skeptical, but like Wilson, I am willing to wait. If Wilson is right, what interests me is not so much what happens when all knowledge flows together as what people will do with it once every nanometer and every action and reaction of the human brain has been calibrated and made manifest in predictable statistical formulas. I can't help thinking of our children of the dawn, the art students we last saw in the Suntory Museum, Osaka, Japan. Not only will they be able to morph illustrations on the digital computer, they will also be able to predict, with breathtaking accuracy, the effect that certain types of illustrations will have on certain types of brains. But, of course, the illustrators' targets will be able to dial up the same formulas and information and diagnose the effect that any illustration, any commercial, any speech, any flirtation, any bill, any coo has been crafted to produce. Life will become one incessant, colossal round of the match game or liar's poker or one-finger-two-finger or rock-paper-scissors.

Something tells me, mere research protocol drudge though I may be, that I will love it all, cherish it, press it to my bosom. For I already have a working title, *The Human Comedy*, and I promise you, you will laugh your head off . . . your head and that damnable, unfathomable chemical analog computer inside of it, too.

MICHAEL S. MALONE

—◆—

Pixie's Last Lesson
Some things in life can be taught only by the dying

MICHAEL S. MALONE, *editor of* Forbes ASAP, *is a business and technology writer who has covered Silicon Valley for more than 20 years. His books include* Infinite Loop, The Big Score, *and* Going Public.

Appropriately, Pixie died while I was at a meeting discussing the future of the Internet. I missed her departure from this world by minutes. She was stretched out on the bathroom floor next to her bowl of water and untouched plate of food. Her body was still limp and warm.

Thankfully, it hadn't been a lonely death. My wife and youngest son had spent the morning holding and petting and talking softly to her. They had left briefly to pick up my oldest son from school when I returned and found her. Even in death, Pixie looked beautiful. At 18, she was an old cat but looked half her age—and the bath at the vet, which had probably given her the fatal heart attack, made her look even younger.

I picked her up and cradled her in my arms, the way I had every night of her life, and carried her around the house. Six thousand nights. Since she was a kitten named Scoundrel. Since she had moved in with us from the house next door, with its endless parties and drug dealers. Since she had played with a black widow spider and had been left to lie near death for a week.

Now, almost two decades later, long after she'd outlived most of the creatures and even some of the people who had bedeviled her, death came for Pixie after just four days of illness. It was the kind of gentle departure that often comes to the very old. Our 96-year-old neighbor, at whose house Pixie was known as Lady, had time to say goodbye to her friends before slipping away. My grandmother, visiting one of my aunts, went to bed early, and in the morning my cousin found her lying in bed, her clothes neatly folded on a chair, her arms carefully folded across her chest.

Even while Pixie was ill, I was editing an essay by a technology futurist. In it, he predicted that, thanks to the relentless pace of technological innovation, people would soon begin loading the electrical grid of their own brains onto computer disks. Encoded literally as ghosts in the machine, their brains could be upgraded quickly with new languages and libraries of knowledge, linked directly to the world via the Internet, and, of course, regularly copied and debugged. As stunning as this prediction was, what made it even more disquieting was the futurist's absolute confidence that human beings would happily surrender their corporeal selves for a chance at digital immortality.

He wasn't alone in hearing the faint echo of living heartbeats emanating from the silvery surface of a silicon chip. Others are looking at the Internet, with its hundreds of millions of networked personal computers and servers, and seeing a digital leviathan, a metaorganism about to shake itself to awareness. At MIT, they are debating whether turning off a new robot constitutes an act of murder. Onscreen, as the new *Star Wars* draws millions to a technocatechism, director George Lucas expresses real regret that, for now, he still has to work with human actors.

On the wall above my oldest son's bed is a poster of all the Pokémon characters—a menagerie of 150 creatures, some mutations of others, all designed by Japanese animators. Pokémon isn't just a comic book but a trading-card set, stuffed animals, a videogame, and a television show whose throbbing graphics were once accused of causing seizures. And if that weren't enough, you can buy a special cable and link your Pokémon-playing Game Boy to your friend's and discover additional "pocket monsters" together.

In this alternative consumer universe, little Pikachu and its horde of confederates aren't just cartoons but the first multimedia creatures, rounded out not by flesh and bone but by multiple formats. And that makes them infinitely more intriguing than any real animal. Perhaps that was why I often saw my oldest son, 8, reach out and absently stroke Pixie's ears but then turn and focus on the figures gamboling across the little LCD screen of his Game Boy.

The Magnificent Chip?

Today we are all dreaming the ultimate dream—immortality. No doubt it is because science has entered the game, and for 400 years now, wherever science has played, it has won. Disease, time, space, even God himself, have retreated before the relentless march of the scientific method. Physicists now speak triumphantly of the Theory of Everything, the imminent empirical proof of superstring theory and the knitting together of the five basic forces into the pentagram of all existence. So when biologists confidently announce that human beings will soon live to 150, who are we to doubt? One hundred fifty isn't immortality, but you might be able to see it from there.

Moreover, we already have, literally at our fingertips, proof that technology can do just what it claims. Medusa conferred a form of immortality by turning passersby into undying stone. Solid-state physics, the most influential science of this closing century, does much the same thing, and its unruly stepchild, semiconductor technology, grows 100 million tiny crystalline statues every day. The integrated circuit, especially its evolved form, the microprocessor, is as close to an immortal creature as God or man has yet devised. Left literally to its own devices, and barring a power surge, a chip will outlive the oldest bristlecone pine. Only cosmic rays, hurtling across the universe, can really harm it. Encase it in diamond (which we will), adapt it to derive power from the stars (which we will), and fling it into space (which we already do), and it will likely still be muttering its Boolean thoughts, a billion a second, as the cosmos goes black.

The chip is immortal because it is magnificently elemental. It was Gordon Moore, the man who helped invent the chip, who first pointed out that the integrated circuit is made from the most plentiful and enduring things on Earth: silicon sand, oxygen, water, and heat. Fire, water, earth, and air; Anaximenes redux—the theories of the Greek scientist-philosophers made manifest by immigrant vestals of the Gorgon, dressed in clean-room bunny suits.

We can't help but look at these tiny wonders and feel both admiration and fear. We are in awe of the microprocessor because it presents an impossible balance between complexity of design and singleness of purpose. Set before it a vast problem and it will chase the solution, at an unimaginable speed, until the end of time. We console ourselves with the conclusion that this makes chips mere idiot savants, but at 400 million calculations per second for thousands of years, this is a kind of divine idiocy before which we can only stand in wonderment.

That wonderment is also why we fear the chip. We sense that it is leaving us behind. A gigahertz processor experiences in less than a second the equivalent of all the thoughts we have in a lifetime. And there will soon be 100 billion such processors. And a trillion other chips—more than all of the mammals, including man, on Earth. And chips are social creatures. Take a few hundred microprocessors, add a few thousand support chips for memory and communications, hook them together, and you have a supercomputer capable of sophisticated speech recognition, robotic control, even the building of other chips. In 20 more years there will be as many silicon gates in one of these computers as there are neurons in the human brain. Link a computer via a broadband Internet to millions of other computers, large and small, around the world, and the great cyberhomunculus rears its silicon and fiber head.

But you have only to look at the empty heart of a computer to realize that terra incognita will be a cold, empty place. Chase immortality down an optical fiber and you may find endless existence—at the cost of everything else.

It's not that we haven't been warned many times. The first warning came 400 years ago, literally on the morning the modern world was created. Tucked into the pages of the book that gave us the scientific revolution, *The Advancement of Learning,* there is a tiny phrase that may prove the most important and enduring admonition ever given. This revolution, Francis Bacon said, must be "for the uses of life." Since he was also a consummate politician and one of the greatest of all essayists, we can assume this was not a throwaway line. The Lord Chancellor meant what he said, and he meant it both ways: Science must always work to improve life and always be at the service of living things.

Bacon wasn't alone. Two hundred years ago, Mary Shelley tried to warn us again. The real monster in *Frankenstein* is not the poor, tragic creature—though, tellingly, here in this century we've convinced ourselves it is—but the doctor himself. He is a man of science and genius who sets out to find the secret of life so that, a Modern Prometheus, he can bestow the gift of immortality on mankind. How fitting that the story should reach its climax in the frozen Arctic.

The third, and perhaps final, warning about technology and immortality came from the anthropologist Loren Eiseley. Eiseley is (or was) justly celebrated for the powerful imagery in his essays: the snout rising up from the primordial ooze to sniff fresh air, the Neanderthal man walking down a crowded city street, the cave filled with millions of daddy longlegs—and most famously, the "star thrower," the solitary figure flinging beached and stranded starfish back into the waves.

But in Eiseley's greatest essay, the opposite is true: The images are unforgettable precisely because they are unexceptional. Eiseley finds himself on a beach, sitting under a beached boat. There, his thoughts cast back 30 years to the death of his father, a once powerful, vital man reduced at the end to little more than a shadow. Eiseley is paralyzed with his sorrow. Just then, he discovers he is not alone. He sees the tiny, excited face of a fox pup—"alone in a dread universe" but not afraid.

"He innocently selected what I think was a chicken bone from an untidy pile of splintered rubbish and shook it at me invitingly. There was a vast and playful humor in his face . . . the wide-eyed innocent fox inviting me to play, with the innate courtesy of its two forepaws placed appealingly together, along with a mock shake of the head. The universe was swinging in some fantastic fashion around to present its face, and the face was so small that the universe itself was laughing."

Deciding it is "not a time for human dignity," Eiseley arranges his own forepaws together, then leans forward, picks up a bone in his teeth and shakes it. The "puppy whimpered with ill-concealed excitement." Soon they are rolling around together, laughing and barking.

It is that gesture by the fox, the two cinnabar paws poised together in expectation, that redeems and saves Eiseley's life. The middle-aged scientist knows he can now go on. He can accept his father's death and ultimately his own. Life has once again closed the circle. The Innocent Fox, at the start of its own brief arc, is ready to play.

The message of all of Eiseley's essays is that nature is surpassingly strange. That this strangeness is our link with all living things. And that buried at the heart of this strangeness, perhaps forever unknowable, is our purpose.

Strangeness colors all of life, across the panorama of species, from beginning to end. It was there when I closed my father's eyes and when I watched my infant sons open theirs. It's there in the movements of the raccoon who rules my yard by night, and the Cooper's hawk who hunts the same yard by day. It's there in the indifferent brutality of the scorpion in my oldest son's terrarium. And in the endless wakefulness of the goldfish who tirelessly circles in a glass tank nearby.

Most of all, it was there in Pixie. The same cat who always kept a careful distance from the mischievous hands of our boys also managed to appear within the frame of every photograph we took of them. The same creature who would meet me at night with the wild look of a killer and who would torture a mouse until it finally succumbed to trauma and shock, also stayed on the bed with my wife during her second, horrifying pregnancy—creakily limping outside only when forced to do so.

Strange but True

Thanks to technology, we can pretend the animals are still around, only safely packaged, controlled, and edited. We can turn on the Discovery Channel and watch, in the comfort of the living room, exotic animals we would never normally encounter. We can see them at the zoo. Or dissect them on the computer. Better yet, we can invent our own, like the legions of Pokémon, all of them odd but never strange. Always anthropomorphic, they can never live their lives without us. Only our pets remain, and in my son's absentminded gesture of patting Pixie's head, then turning back to the computer screen, I fear I saw the future all too well.

Once we lived embedded in the world of living things different from us. It was scary and exhilarating and instructional. In the animals around us, we found a definition of life and even, if only for an instant, thought we caught a glimpse of God passing by. We were within life, if only because we had no choice.

We now have that choice. And despite the warnings, we are turning away to a new partner. A partner that is perfectly knowable, perfectly predictable, and never dies. R2D2 has already replaced Lassie.

The sexiest woman on television is a Borg. And as we are now turning, soon we will be running, then racing with our arms outstretched toward that distant point of convergence with our machines, that frozen place where thoughts are singular and forever.

But we are not there yet. If we are lucky, we may never get there. And if and when we realize the futility of the chase, we will find ourselves alone . . . and rediscover that we are the strangest creatures of all.

We buried Pixie beneath the holly tree. It may be the oldest holly tree in California, probably brought as a seedling from Maryland during the Civil War. I dug the hole alone. Then my little family gathered as I lowered Pixie's tiny, blanket-wrapped body. My wife and children cried. My voice caught as I said a few words. Then we went back to our cell phones and computers and video games.

Unselfconsciously, through a precise combination of claws and purrs, flirtation and denial, Pixie taught my boys to be better human beings—and me a better parent. No video game and no intelligent agent/expert will ever do that. Those are the most important lessons of all, and those are the ones we are about to lose.

We cannot learn the big things from our machines, from our special effects, because they are not strange. At best, they are merely very precise mirrors.

When all that is left is reflections of ourselves, who will tell us what matters? Who will teach us how to live? And most of all, who will show us how to die?

CZESLAW MILOSZ

———⟫⬧⟪———

To a Hazel Tree

Born in Lithuania in 1911, CZESLAW MILOSZ witnessed the turmoil of early 20th-century Europe. Awarded the Nobel Prize for Literature in 1980, he has been called one of the greatest poets of our time.

You do not recognize me, but it's me, the same one

Who used to cut your brown shoots, so straight

And so swift in their running to the sun, for his bows.

You grew large, your shade is huge, you send up leafstalks again and again.

It's a pity I am not that boy any more.

Now I could cut for myself only a stick, for you see, I walk with a cane.

I love your brown bark, with a whitish tinge, of a true hazel color.

I am glad that some oaks and ashes survived, but I rejoice seeing you, as always magical, with the pearls of your nuts, with generations of squirrels that have danced in you.

This is something of a Heraclitean meditation, when I
stand here,

Remembering my bygone self and life as it was, but also
as it could have been.

Nothing lasts, but everything lasts: a great stability.

And I try to place in it my destiny.

Which, in truth, I did not want to accept.

I was happy with my bow, stalking at the edge of a fairy tale.

What happened to me later deserves no more than a shrug;

It is only biography i.e. fiction.

POST-SCRIPTUM

Biography or fiction or a long dream.

White clouds set in layers on a fragment of the sky
between the brightness of birches.

Yellow and rusty vineyards in the approaching dusk.

For a short time I was a servant and wanderer.

Released, I come back by a never taken road.

Szetejnie, Lithuania, and Napa Valley, California, Autumn 1997

————

Translated by the author and Robert Hass

WHAT IS TRUE
IN THE DIGITAL AGE

Rodes Fishburne

A s the years passed, it became apparent that the *Big Issue* was mirroring the public's fascination with technology, acting as a ghostly conscience to our appetite for limitless innovation and endless wealth. Each *Big Issue* in turn—the digital revolution, work, time, convergence—resembled an anthropological exploration into our daily lives.

The fifth *Big Issue* turned a mirror on the process itself. In terms of scope and audacity, it was the biggest issue yet: What is True? The idea arose from a January brainstorming meeting. The Nasdaq was then at an all-time high; technology was no longer a cult but a full-blown religion; and even the doubting Thomases were starting to doubt themselves. The euphoria surrounding the Internet and the stock market seemed as if it might keep going forever.

Yet, we knew in our hearts that this period of time wasn't real. Or rather, real but not realistic. Secretly we knew we were trapped in a strange and unreliable confabulation. And it was not just the events of the day that seemed untrue: Reality itself seemed mercilessly manipulated by technology.

We asked ourselves: How do you live in a world in which everything and everyone is viewed through the screen of technology? Then we challenged our writers to address what they find true, authentic, and enduring in an age of radical and continuous change.

As always, they surprised us. Some, like John Updike, rejected our distinction between trueness and truth. Others, like Pat Conroy, struck at the heart of the matter by writing about matters strictly emotional. Still others, like Elmore Leonard, magically toyed with the truth by using a newspaper headline to create a fictional character before our eyes.

In five years the *Big Issue* has gone from being a whimsical idea to hosting some of the most provocative writing in magazine publishing. Two hundred and fifty of the world's finest writers have written almost half a million words on their way toward understanding who we are and how we live in one of the most interesting and ephemeral periods of human history. Have they succeeded? You be the judge.

PAT CONROY

———>◆<———

My Heart's Content

Thirty years of one man's truth are up for reconsideration

PAT CONROY'S *novels include* The Prince of Tides, The Great
Santini, The Lords of Discipline, *and* Beach Music. *He lives
on Fripp Island, South Carolina. This essay is from his forthcoming book,* My Losing Season.

The true things always ambush me on the road and take me by surprise when I am drifting down the light of placid days, careless
about flanks and rearguard actions. I was not looking for a true thing
to come upon me in the state of New Jersey. Nothing has ever happened to me in New Jersey. But came it did, and it came to stay.

In the past four years I have been interviewing my teammates on
the 1966–67 basketball team at the Citadel for a book I'm writing. For
the most part, this has been like buying back a part of my past that I
had mislaid or shut out of my life. At first I thought I was writing about
being young and frisky and able to run up and down a court all day
long, but lately I realized I came to this book because I needed to
come to grips with being middle-aged and having ripened into a gray-
haired man you could not trust to handle the ball on a fast break.

When I visited my old teammate Al Kroboth's house in New Jersey, I spent the first hours quizzing him about his memories of games
and practices and the screams of coaches that had echoed in field
houses more than 30 years before. Al had been a splendid forward-
center for the Citadel; at 6 feet 5 inches and carrying 220 pounds, he
played with indefatigable energy and enthusiasm. For most of his senior year, he led the nation in field-goal percentage, with UCLA center

Lew Alcindor hot on his trail. Al was a battler and a brawler and a scrapper from the day he first stepped in as a Green Weenie as a sophomore to the day he graduated. After we talked basketball, we came to a subject I dreaded to bring up with Al, but which lay between us and would not lie still.

"Al, you know I was a draft dodger and antiwar demonstrator."

"That's what I heard, Conroy," Al said. "I have nothing against what you did, but I did what I thought was right."

"Tell me about Vietnam, big Al. Tell me what happened to you," I said.

On his seventh mission as a navigator in an A-6 for Major Leonard Robertson, Al was getting ready to deliver their payload when the fighter-bomber was hit by enemy fire. Though Al has no memory of it, he punched out somewhere in the middle of the ill-fated dive and lost consciousness. He doesn't know if he was unconscious for six hours or six days, nor does he know what happened to Major Robertson (whose name is engraved on the Wall in Washington and on the MIA bracelet Al wears).

When Al awoke, he couldn't move. A Viet Cong soldier held an AK-47 to his head. His back and his neck were broken, and he had shattered his left scapula in the fall. When he was well enough to get to his feet (he still can't recall how much time had passed), two armed Viet Cong led Al from the jungles of South Vietnam to a prison in Hanoi. The journey took three months. Al Kroboth walked barefooted through the most impassable terrain in Vietnam, and he did it sometimes in the dead of night. He bathed when it rained, and he slept in bomb craters with his two Viet Cong captors. As they moved farther north, infections began to erupt on his body, and his legs were covered with leeches picked up while crossing the rice paddies.

At the very time of Al's walk, I had a small role in organizing the only antiwar demonstration ever held in Beaufort, South Carolina, the home of Parris Island and the Marine Corps Air Station. In a Marine Corps town at that time, it was difficult to come up with a quorum of people who had even minor disagreements about the Vietnam War. But my small group managed to attract a crowd of about 150 to Beaufort's waterfront. With my mother and my wife on either side of me, we listened to the featured speaker, Dr. Howard Levy, suggest to the very few young enlisted marines present that if they get sent to

Vietnam, here's how they can help end this war: Roll a grenade under your officer's bunk when he's asleep in his tent. It's called fragging and is becoming more and more popular with the ground troops who know this war is bullshit. I was enraged by the suggestion. At that very moment my father, a marine officer, was asleep in Vietnam. But in 1972, at the age of 27, I thought I was serving America's interests by pointing out what massive flaws and miscalculations and corruptions had led her to conduct a ground war in Southeast Asia.

In the meantime, Al and his captors had finally arrived in the North, and the Viet Cong traded him to North Vietnamese soldiers for the final leg of the trip to Hanoi. Many times when they stopped to rest for the night, the local villagers tried to kill him. His captors wired his hands behind his back at night, so he trained himself to sleep in the center of huts when the villagers began sticking knives and bayonets into the thin walls. Following the U.S. air raids, old women would come into the huts to excrete on him and yank out hunks of his hair. After the nightmare journey of his walk north, Al was relieved when his guards finally delivered him to the POW camp in Hanoi and the cell door locked behind him.

It was at the camp that Al began to die. He threw up every meal he ate and before long was misidentified as the oldest American soldier in the prison because his appearance was so gaunt and skeletal. But the extraordinary camaraderie among fellow prisoners that sprang up in all the POW camps caught fire in Al, and did so in time to save his life.

When I was demonstrating in America against Nixon and the Christmas bombings in Hanoi, Al and his fellow prisoners were holding hands under the full fury of those bombings, singing "God Bless America." It was those bombs that convinced Hanoi they would do well to release the American POWs, including my college teammate. When he told me about the C-141 landing in Hanoi to pick up the prisoners, Al said he felt no emotion, none at all, until he saw the giant American flag painted on the plane's tail. I stopped writing as Al wept over the memory of that flag on that plane, on that morning, during that time in the life of America.

It was that same long night, after listening to Al's story, that I began to make judgments about how I had conducted myself during the Vietnam War. In the darkness of the sleeping Kroboth household, lying in the third-floor guest bedroom, I began to assess my role as a citizen in the '60s, when my country called my name and I shot her the bird. Unlike the stupid boys who wrapped themselves in Viet Cong flags and burned the American one, I knew how to demonstrate against the war without flirting with treason or astonishingly bad taste. I had come directly from the warrior culture of this country and I knew how to act. But in the 25 years that have passed since South Vietnam fell, I have immersed myself in the study of totalitarianism during the unspeakable century we just left behind. I have questioned survivors of Auschwitz and Bergen-Belsen, talked to Italians who told me tales of the Nazi occupation, French partisans who had counted German tanks in the forests of Normandy, and officers who survived the Bataan Death March. I quiz journalists returning from wars in Bosnia, the Sudan, the Congo, Angola, Indonesia, Guatemala, San Salvador, Chile, Northern Ireland, Algeria. As I lay sleepless, I realized I'd done all this research to better understand my country. I now revere words like democracy, freedom, the right to vote, and the grandeur of the extraordinary vision of the founding fathers. Do I see America's flaws? Of course. But I now can honor her basic, incorruptible virtues, the ones that let me walk the streets screaming my ass off that my country had no idea what it was doing in South Vietnam. My country let me scream to my heart's content—the same country that produced both Al Kroboth and me.

Now, at this moment in New Jersey, I come to a conclusion about my actions as a young man when Vietnam was a dirty word to me. I wish I'd led a platoon of marines in Vietnam. I would like to think I would have trained my troops well and that the Viet Cong would have had their hands full if they entered a firefight with us. From the day of my birth, I was programmed to enter the Marine Corps. I was the son of a marine fighter pilot, and I had grown up on marine bases where I had watched the men of the corps perform simulated war games in the forests of my childhood. That a novelist and poet bloomed darkly in the house of Santini strikes me as a remarkable irony. My mother and father had raised me to be an Al Kroboth, and during the Vietnam era they watched in horror as I metamorphosed into another breed of fanatic entirely. I understand now that I should have protested the war after my return from Vietnam, after I had done my duty for my country. I have come to a conclusion about my country that I knew then in my bones but lacked the courage to act on: America is good enough to die for even when she is wrong.

I looked for some conclusion, a summation of this trip to my teammate's house. I wanted to come to the single right thing, a true thing that I may not like but that I could live with. After hearing Al Kroboth's story of his walk across Vietnam and his brutal imprisonment in the North, I found myself passing harrowing, remorseless judgment on myself. I had not turned out to be the man I had once envisioned myself to be. I thought I would be the kind of man that America could point to and say, "There. That's the guy. That's the one who got it right. The whole package. The one I can depend on." It had never once occurred to me that I would find myself in the position I did on that night in Al Kroboth's house in Roselle, New Jersey: an American coward spending the night with an American hero.

ELMORE LEONARD

—⟩◆⟨—

McHeard Is the Word

The next novel is just a headline away

ELMORE LEONARD *has written more than 30 novels, including* Bandits, Touch, Freaky Deaky, Killshot, Get Shorty, Out of Sight, Cuba Libre, *and, more recently,* Pagan Babies. *He and his wife live in a suburb of Detroit, Michigan. His next novel may very well have George McHeard III in a supporting role.*

LAST APRIL I RECEIVED a newspaper clipping from a Mr. Harris Oswalt of Mobile, Alabama, saying, "I am a big fan of yours and thought this article so amazing that you could write a book about it."

The headline from the *Birmingham News* tells the story: "21-Year-Old Shooting Victim Leaves Behind 16 Children."

On April 3 a young man named George McHeard III was sitting in his Chevrolet Impala in the parking lot of an apartment complex in Pratt City, a suburb of Birmingham, Alabama. At about 5:45 P.M., according to police, a masked gunman walked up to the car and shot McHeard three times at point-blank range, killing him instantly.

The mothers of the children turned out to be at least nine young women from different parts of the city. LaDrea Campbell, mother of George's 8-month-old daughter, LaShundrea, said, "I didn't plan for him to leave."

Audrey Williams, George's mother, said that he began siring children shortly after he turned 14. She had often asked his girlfriends "not to have babies for my son." But her pleas, for the most part, were ignored. George's mom went on to say, "He loved his children and took care of them, bought them whatever they needed," essentials like milk, clothing, and diapers.

For all 16 kids? How could George afford it?

According to Audrey, whose nickname for George was Punchie, her son made his living as a self-employed car salesman, an independent dealer who sold all makes and models, not off a lot but from their home in Ensley Highlands. Audrey said he loved cars so much he named two of his daughters Mercedes and Infiniti.

She also mentioned that during the week leading up to her son's death, he was unusually quiet.

It's doubtful I would want to build an entire novel around George and his kids, as Harris Oswalt suggests in his note. But I would be tempted to use George in a supporting role just to see him in action and hear him talk: George coming on with sweet talk, street talk, always confident. The fact that you might not believe a word George says is beside the point; I don't make judgments about my people. You'll see that George lives by his wits, but isn't very bright. He struts through a world of his own, a little Big Daddy in a gray area of activity, playing the role of provider. My books thrive on gray areas, where truth is not seen in a clear light but can be interpreted and turned inside out to suit a character's needs.

One fictional scenario that might be drawn from the news story: George was involved in a hustle of some kind, perhaps in his role as a car salesman; the deal went bust and George got popped. Robbery did not appear to be a motive.

I hear his mother saying, "Punchie, the Lord helps those who help themselves." And George has to agree. "Yes, indeed, the Lord has shown me the way to take care of my kids. Was like getting hit by lightning. I mean it was getting hit by lightning."

You'll see what he's talking about in the following treatment of how a fictional character based on the real George might stumble into one of life's gray areas to find temporary happiness.

Here's George McHeard III, at age 12, thinking, What kind of stupid, old-man name is George? He's wanting to change it to Jamal or Ju-wan, until his mama tells him the original George, his grampa, had come to Alabama from Jamaica; least it's what she heard. Little George says, "Yeah . . . ?" thinking of Bob Marley and Lady Saw, hearing reggae in his head. Never mind the great Eddie Kendricks of the

Temptations was from Ensley, where they live, that Motown jive was old. George bops his head to reggae, and in two years has grown out his dreadlocks and taken up ganja, going around now as George III, the Reggae Kid, has quit school, and gone to work for Homeboys Catering. Never mind Domino's and Pizza Hut. They're too scared of drive-bys and armed robberies to make deliveries in Ensley and the projects. "LET YOUR HOMEBOYS DO THE DRIVING" is the slogan where George works. He picks up orders and delivers 'em anywhere. A cute girl answers the door, George makes his eyes soft and says in his Jamaican lilt, "Sweet chile, ride with me to the country." His first two children are conceived at the same time, the twins, Toni and Tawni, over by Bayview Lake. His daddy writes from McKean Correctional, "You just a boy. What you doing making babies?"

By the time he's 18, George has a dozen kids living in hoods from Pratt City to Bessemer, and the cute mamas who loved his locks and Rasta way of speaking are getting on his ass, one saying cold pizza and food stamps don't make it, baby; another saying a child needs shoes, a child needs toys, and a child's mama needs a few things, too, *mon*— giving him back his island sound with an edge.

George will tell you it isn't easy being loved by so many women.

He hooks up with an ex-con named Cochise Patterson, from around here but staying in Detroit, the stolen car capital of the world, and George's burden is eased some. Cochise boosts cars on order, has a boy drive them down, and George sells them in the projects—any luxury car you want, 10 Gs—mostly to entry-level drug sellers. George sees his role in a somewhat dark gray area: He doesn't steal the cars himself or see them being stolen, does he? No, all he does is sell 'em to people who don't care where they come from.

Here, an event that actually happened, two years before the real George McHeard met his end in the parking lot, is used to turn the plot.

On April 8, 1998, a Force 5 tornado swept across three Alabama counties, touched down on Birmingham's west side, and tore several neighborhoods to pieces. One of the hardest hit was Pratt City.

And here's 19-year-old George on that day, only minutes before the tornado rips through. He's delivering, free of charge, a Lexus with gold trim to Cochise's brother, Andre Patterson, released from prison up north and now dealing drugs from his great-grandma's home on

Miles Avenue in Pratt City. The granny is this little wisp of a woman, barely able to hold the door against the wind, who lets George into the kitchen and disappears. He finds Andre unconcerned with the weather; something else is troubling him.

"You hear? Cochise got his parole violated account of a dirty urine and he's back in the slam, has to finish his time. Man, two more years."

The news comes as a shock to George; he sees himself out of business. The only consolation is the tip Andre offers for delivering the car.

"Some fine blow. Sell it and buy toys for the kids." Andre looks up then, puzzled. "What's that noise?"

"Sounds like a train coming," George says.

As the roof is ripped from the house, George will remember the terrible sound screaming in his head as he's slammed against the wall, and then the dead silence as he picks himself up. The refrigerator has flattened Andre, who's lying dead. George looks around, sees money all over the place—currency, 20s, 50s, 100s, dope money Andre's hid away and the tornado finds—like a sign coming in the crash of lightning, the Lord helping those who help themselves, and George does. By the time he's collected the bills in a plastic bag, a hundred Gs easy, he hears the granny's plaintive cries for help.

Here are the storm damage photographs clipped from the *Birmingham News:* one of George the hero coming out of what's left of the house, the granny cradled in his arms; another one eight days later, George shaking hands with President Clinton, who has stopped off in Pratt City to commiserate and promise some federal aid.

Here are George and his mom at their house in Ensley handing out toys to his kids, to Toni and Tawni, to Charmaine, Coretta, George Junior, his second set of twins (Jamal and Ju-wan), Mercedes, Infiniti, LaDonna (they call her Peaches), Robert Marley, little 2-year-old Ziggy, Rochelle (they call her Shell), Tanisha, Martin Luther, and the last one so far, his baby girl LaShundrea, here with her mama—the only mama who came—on account of she's nursing. George is saying to a child, "No, honey, that's Tanisha's doll. You play with your doll and let Tanisha play with hers."

George is now living in the grayest gray area of his life. What's he supposed to do with the money but spend it? Give it to the police? "Oh, here some drug money I happen to find in a friend of mine's house." The house is gone and any trace that the money was there.

Give it to Andre's brother in the joint? Why? It ain't his. How would he even know about any money there? George doesn't consider the granny an heir—that nice old woman taking drug money? He does buy expensive gifts for the mamas, has to, the only way to keep 'em off his back for a time; and buys himself a Chevy so nobody will think he has money. Still, people notice things and they talk, especially the mamas. Damn.

Here's George, 21 now, picking up the phone to hear Cochise Patterson's voice saying, "Hey, Dog. I call to tell you I got my release."

George does not want to talk to this man, but he can act, sound cool when he has to. "You back in business?"

"Pretty soon. Listen, you know that picture was in the paper, you saving my old granny from the tornado? Yeah, different ones sent me the picture," Cochise says, "and I been keeping it the two years since. Was the day you dropped off the car, huh? You can see it all busted up in the picture. Lexus with the gold trim."

"Yeah, was the same day. Man, I'm sorry about Andre."

"He tell you anything before he died?"

"The man was already gone."

"He give you anything?"

"Some blow. I sold it."

"Was in that bag you carrying in the picture?"

"That was your granny's things she wanted."

"See, I talk to Andre just before. Tell him my parole been violated. We talking, he happen to mention he laid off six keys, must've been right before you got there."

"Yeah . . . ?"

"Cleared a hundred fourteen thousand."

"Never saw it. I walk in, man, a tornado hits the house—"

"See, what I hear's you been spending money."

"What I made off the blow, yeah."

"Like around a hundred thousand?"

"Come on, man, if it's gone was the tornado took it."

"You afraid to talk to me?"

"I am talking to you."

"How about to my face?"

"Tell me when you be down."

"I'm here, Dog. Saint Charles Villa Apartments. Get in your Chev-rolet and come on over."

About 5:45 that afternoon George is sitting in his car in the apart-ment parking lot. He sees Cochise Patterson come out of the building some distance away, the man too far off yet to recognize, though George can tell by his size and the way he walks it's Cochise, coming across the pavement now, something wrong with his face. No, some-thing on his face, covering it, the man liking to goof around. George grins.

He calls out, "Yo, man, you think it's Holloween?"

According to the *Birmingham News* story, during George's funeral, a brawl erupted involving three of the children's mothers.

CHARLES MANN

>—◦—<

All the World's a Bootleg

Sure, information wants to be free,
but does it want to be high quality?

CHARLES C. MANN *is the author of* The Aspirin Wars: Money, Medicine, and 100 Years of Rampant Competition *and* At Large: The Strange Case of the World's Biggest Internet Invasion.

KURT COBAIN AND William Shakespeare are rarely mentioned in the same breath, but the Bard of Avon's name forced itself into my brain when I was downloading some Nirvana for a 12-year-old I know. It happened early this year, when a friend came for dinner, his daughter in tow. I was telling them about Napster—this was before the music-sharing site appeared on the cover of *Newsweek,* when a few people on the planet still hadn't heard of it. Suddenly my friend's daughter, who had been silently absorbed in her Discman, noticed our existence. "You mean," she said, "you can download *any song you want?*"

Because I make my living from copyright, I'd been careful about Napster, downloading only music that I already owned on compact disc. Legally, this was probably still infringement, but I didn't think the musicians would mind. But now I was in a social quandary.

The girl was wearing a Kurt Cobain T-shirt. Her school backpack bore a Nirvana decal. She was listening to *Nevermind,* the group's second CD. No special genius was required to predict what she would like to download from Napster. But I don't own any Nirvana CDs, and so couldn't help her without violating my compact with myself.

A few minutes later, she was at my computer, searching for Kurt Cobain under my guilty instruction.

To keep the dinner party going, I eventually promised that I would burn her a CD of Nirvana songs—which is where William Shakespeare came in. Several of the Nirvana songs on Napster were live recordings of extremely poor sound quality, the vocals barely audible through audience noise. I assumed that these were bootlegged recordings, which by definition are hard to come by. I labeled the files "bootleg-rare." And I added them to the CD as lagniappe.

Napster allows each member of the "Napster community" to search other members' hard drives for particular songs. My live bootlegs attracted enormous, even rabid interest—they were uploaded by dozens of people, who in turn passed them on to many others. Each time I went on Napster and searched for Nirvana I saw them on other people's machines. Not only did this further add to my guilt, it made me wonder what I had on my machine. Bootlegs are always in demand, but why were these particular bootlegs so special? Investigating, I discovered to my chagrin that these recordings were not bootlegs at all but songs from a perfectly ordinary live album that had been ineptly converted to digital form by enthusiastic but technically unsophisticated Nirvana fans. I had inadvertently reinvented them as precious bootlegs and passed them on to Kurt Cobain aficionados hungry for any unheard notes from the master.

Not paying attention to copyright, in other words, had led me to act like a little engine of misinformation, spraying inaccurately labeled bits around the Internet. Which recalled to mind the many early editions of William Shakespeare.

Shakespeare's works are known entirely from badly printed quartos and folios, none of which were authorized by the playwright, and no two of which are identical. *Romeo and Juliet,* to cite one example, appeared in three disparate quarto editions—all anonymous, each different from its fellows—before first appearing under Shakespeare's name in the *First Folio* of 1623. The *First Folio's* editors complained that the earlier editions of Shakespeare were nothing but "stolen, and surreptitious copies, maimed, and deformed by the frauds and stealths of [the] injurious imposters, that exposed them" to the public. But the *Folio* editors published their edition seven years after the playwright's death, and there is no evidence that they had previously consulted him. Indeed, according to Steven Urkowitz of the City College of New York, these editors—or someone else—rewrote 400 lines of *King Lear*, altering character, theme, and plot.

Many of the other plays fared no better. As a result, there is no master copy of Shakespeare's work that can be compared with variants. The original, if it exists, has been swamped by mislabeled, badly produced junk copies. Shakespeare may be the English language's most celebrated dramatist, but nobody knows what he actually wrote.

Shakespeare was no anomaly. During the 16th and 17th centuries, according to Adrian Johns' *The Nature of the Book* (1998), new printing technologies appeared in Britain as the government-sponsored publishers' cartel was slowly losing its control over the book industry. It became vastly easier and cheaper to produce and distribute books—and there were no effective controls or regulation of the industry. (Copyright was invented a century later.) A period of bibliogonic chaos ensued. Anyone could—and did—print almost anything. When popular new texts appeared, they were instantly pirated by other printers and pamphleteers. Publishers felt no compunction about respecting the text, so the new, unauthorized versions were reedited (why not try a happy ending on *Lear*, which might then sell better?), misattributed (why not say it was written by the local aristocrat, who might then buy out the edition?), and dotted with errors (why pay for proofreading, when nobody else is doing it?). The result, Johns argues, "was an explosion of uncertainty." No one knew which, if any, text represented an author's intent; readers couldn't be certain if their copies of the *Principia Mathematica* truly presented Newton's laws. "Knowledge," Johns writes, "appeared and disappeared daily, with alarming transience."

The parallels to Napster—and to Gnutella, Scour, and other file-sharing software—are obvious and alarming. The Internet, a new technology, has greatly increased the opportunity for people to become publishers, producing and disseminating works more easily and cheaply than ever before. Like their 17th-century predecessors, many of these new "publishers" are simply republishing extant material. Much of the republication is not authorized; a considerable portion is characterized by errors, reediting, and misattribution. The same is true for the music on the Net. Despite the recording industry's complaints about the "perfect digital copies" on services like Napster, many song files are truncated, incorrectly labeled, and badly recorded (that is, badly translated into digital form). Even I, with my limited knowledge of Nirvana's oeuvre, could tell when one of the band's songs was cut off in the middle—and a lot of what I downloaded for my friend's daughter was like that.

I was seeing an information-age corollary to the physicists' famed uncertainty principle. Coined by Werner Heisenberg in 1926, the principle in one of its variants states that the more readily one can ascertain a subatomic particle's exact position, the less one can be sure of its precise momentum. The TCP/IP equivalent: The more readily a piece of information can be found on the Net, the less one can be sure of its accuracy.

Consider the Evolution Control Committee, an avant-garde music ensemble in Columbus, Ohio, which earlier this year trumpeted its invention of "Napster Bombs." In 1998 the group sampled Dan Rather as he delivered disaster news and spliced up his words into a disjointed litany of catastrophe, all played against a thudding beat taken from the rock band AC/DC. The group called the resulting song "Rocked by Rape," a phrase that Rather was made to deliver as a sort of chorus ("Rock, rock, rocked by rape / Rock, rock, rocked by rape / rock, rock, rocked by rape / Sex, drugs, and—rocked by rape"). After the parodic rap was reviewed in *Spin* magazine last February, CBS threatened the group's distributor with "appropriate action." Fearing litigation, the distributor pulled the song. In response, the Evolution Control Committee made the song available on Napster under a variety of other artists' names: Nirvana, Beck, the Grateful Dead, the artist formerly known as Prince. It was downloaded more than 500 times. The single most popular version was labeled "Nirvana— Rocked by Rape (bootleg-rare)."

I was not the only person messing with Kurt Cobain's legacy.

In the 18th century, Britain came up with a device to help authenticate texts: copyright. Although today copyright is mainly treated as a means to reward creators—or castigated as a scam that lets big media companies lock up culture—it has a second, rarely mentioned function: affixing the form of works of art and science. As copyright became more firmly established, texts became more firmly established. To this day the muddle around Shakespeare is so unrelieved that new, different editions of the play continue to be published, each quite different from the other. Although Dickens wrote at a time—the mid-19th century—of widespread piracy, one edition of his novels is much like the next, except for trivial differences in punctuation and spelling. By the mid-20th century, when Beckett had written *Waiting for Godot,* the author could control every comma—indeed, the playwright shut down productions that strayed too far from his rigidly specified stage directions.

Today we face what might be called the Cobain Conundrum. In the past, Nirvana's music was as a rule available in a single authorized version from a single source: the local record store. Licitly or not, the band's recordings can now be obtained in dozens of new ways: Napster, Wrapster, Napigator, Gnutella, Scour Exchange, CuteMX, iMesh, eCircles, FileSwap, MediaShare, MP123, NetBrilliant, OnShare . . . did I mention IRC? Each of these makes Nirvana available to everyone at next to no cost—but the average quality of Cobain's music is significantly decreased (if, in fact, you're actually getting Cobain's music, and not the parodic mayhem of the Evolution Control Committee). As piracy makes the cost of information fall toward zero, its obtainability becomes inversely proportional to its value. Infinite access = infinite mess.

The closest thing I can imagine to a solution is for musicians to fix their music in some tangible, immutable form that can only be played on special, authorized machines. I've even thought of a name for it: the "compact disc."

To me, and probably to most members of my generation, the cost and delayed gratification of CD acquisition doesn't seem a terrible price to pay for the assurance of quality and fidelity. To my friend's daughter, and apparently to most members of her generation, opting for free, immediate access to whatever passes for a "copy" is a no-brainer. The trend is clear. And who knows? Maybe I'll learn to enjoy collecting radically different versions of my favorite artists' works.

MICHAEL WOLFF

—⋙◆⋘—

Got It?

Inside technology's inner circle is a lot of talk . . . and attitude

MICHAEL WOLFF *is the media columnist for* New York *magazine. He is the author of* Burn Rate, *a best-seller.*

EARLY ON, I was attracted to the technology business because I really thought it represented an inner circle of understanding. No, that is not true. What attracted me was the distance of most people I knew from this inner circle.

The distinction between those who "got it" and those who "didn't get it" was the compelling thing.

"Getting it" was an accurate way to describe this inner circle of understanding, because it was like getting a joke. It was a riff: That is, there was no real knowledge that you had to possess, no scientific truth to be known. Getting it was closer to a religious truth or cultural truth. It was an insider's thing. It was more about attitude and affect and lingo. Were you hip enough?

It was also about knowing the right people.

The first person I knew who suggested that there was such a truth and that it could distinguish you from other people who didn't know or accept this truth was Louis Rossetto. "He just doesn't get it," Louis would say, shaking his head in disgust when almost anybody disagreed with him. *Wired,* the magazine he founded, was based on this notion that certain people understood something profound, while most did not. Reading *Wired,* of course, might help you understand what you were missing out on and how to enter the inner circle. Perhaps the true king of getting it, though, the standard-bearer of tech cool, and of disdain for those who were not tech cool, was Steve Jobs. All the cockiness and arrogance and presumption to come in the '90s was in his image.

Getting it was certainly the prize of the '90s. Not since the '60s had the world divided so cleanly between the hip and the square, between those who could talk the talk and walk the walk and those who were hopelessly flat-footed.

At the first technology conference I ever went to, in late 1991, I heard statements that were mesmerizing in their absolutism, in their verbal forcefulness, in their aphoristic neatness: "Everything is changing, and change is good." "Speed is the key to understanding information; speed changes the meaning of information." "The speed of the message is the message." "Information wants to be, needs to be, would be free." "Technology makes the weak strong."

It was an authority thing. The question was: Do you get the fact that power was passing to different people, that new cats were taking over? Except this wasn't a political or class upheaval. Indeed, the weird and novel thing was that this cultural revolution was cast in technological, and, by extension, business terms.

The full question was: Do you get it that the world has become a disintermediated and disaggregated place? In other words, this inner circle of understanding wasn't, when you parsed it, about human potential or the rights of man or any historical imperative. It was about the supply chain—it was about distribution. "Our goal," software guys would say, "is to achieve ubiquity."

It was an extraordinarily powerful business advantage to be able to represent yourself as being in the inner circle. Later in the digital revolution, it became very common for a headhunter to describe a job candidate as "getting it." ("Don't worry—he gets it.") Having gotten it, you were of course more valuable than—and of enormous value to—people who had not gotten it.

In the beginning, when I first started to hear people explain this vision of how networks were going to alter the way people communicate and relate to one another, and how they would buy things, it was a little like how it must have felt in the '30s to be an agitated student first hearing Marxist philosophy. Here was a new point of view that seemed to explain everything. It was the big picture. Comprehensive. Global. Here was a coherent theory of modern life. What's more, it didn't leave room for anyone else's point of view. That made it especially powerful. You either understood or not. You were either part of the solution or part of the problem. You were either the future or the ash heap.

There weren't a lot of people who could stand up to this intellectual aggressiveness and verbal abuse. I wish I could communicate, however guilty I feel about it now, the sheer joy of sitting in meetings with well-established businessmen representing billions of dollars of assets and multimillion-dollar profit streams and being able not only to high-hand them because I got it and they didn't, but also to be able to actually humble them, to flagrantly condescend to them, to treat them like children. On the basis of this attitude, this knowingness, hundreds of billions of dollars have traded hands.

Few places were more fascinated by the "getting it/not getting it" polarity than the media business, partly because it was in the throes of its own transition: The fat and easy audience of the '60s and '70s had gone away. And partly because the media business had missed out on the early cable and wireless profits. Not understanding this technology—and letting other entrepreneurs build the cable and wireless business—had cost it big. The media players were deeply insecure about what they did not understand about technology. While those in the media business (old media) knew they were more and more dependent on the technology of distribution (new media), the media business was, by and large, still run by old guys who didn't use computers. It was a classic, top-down, secretary sort of business where, up until just recently, media guys were still saying, "Call my girl. . . . " Now if you didn't use the machines (and didn't really want to use the machines), you tended to believe anyone who claimed familiarity with them.

For a time, I sat in meetings at Time Warner, at which technologists came to pitch their products: search engines, HTML writers, TCP/IP pack packagers, you name it. On one side of the table sat the Time Inc.-ers, who were like supplicants, novices, even mendicants, in their willingness to do anything to get it. On the other side of the table sat the blasé, profoundly arrogant technologists and technology salesmen who got it. The Time guys, mostly, believed everything they heard. They were deferential to a fault. (They really listened to a mountain of crap.) The fact that virtually all of the technology that was being peddled at Time would be obsolete within a year, if not a few months, and that much of it didn't work to begin with, has never really been accounted for.

Another reason those in the old-media business fell so hopelessly for this tech talk was because much of the new lingo was adapted from the traditional concerns of the media industry. At some moment, 1990, give or take, the technology business had promoted itself into the information business. As it happened, this was only metaphorically true. Ones and zeros were information only in the way cells were human beings. Certainly, it was not information that delivered explanations, elucidations, or coherent representations (which came to be called a somewhat less interesting category: content). But as soon as the metaphor came alive (say what you want, the information superhighway was the metaphor that built the business, and it was the much-maligned vice president's turn of phrase) it had the effect of taking the information business from the real information business. The technology guys—mechanics, engineers, technicians, and a few marketing types—suddenly seemed to control the means of expression, or at least claimed to.

Then, in early 1996, Wall Street got it. The fundamental sales quality of the we-get-it-you-don't pitch—i.e., we're in the club, you're not—was of course part of its power. It was a sales line that financial promoters could use. "These guys are 22, and they really get it."

"Well, then, if they get it. . . . "

Such faith became the basis for dot-com company valuations.

Getting it became the currency of the New Economy. After 1996, a serious rearguard action began throughout the media industry between companies that were in the know and those that weren't, and between workers who got it and coworkers who didn't. Certainly, getting it was a good career move for many younger managers in the media business. Time Warner, for instance, had launched Pathfinder in late 1994. Depending on your view, either Pathfinder was run by a small group at Time Warner who got it and was subverted by a larger group who didn't, or it was run by a small group who didn't get it and who managed to silence the new breed who did.

At Rupert Murdoch's News Corp., in the early Internet days, guys who didn't get it thought they could acquire it, buying first Delphi Internet Services and then trying to create iGuide. News Corp. hired lots of people who, in theory, got it. But then, seemingly, they lost it, possibly because of their proximity to the people at News Corp. who didn't get it. Instead of getting it rubbing off on those who didn't get it, the opposite happened.

At Disney, Jake Winebaum, on the strength of being in the know, managed to rise out of Disney's little magazine group to become Michael Eisner's right hand as the master of one of the media business' most ambitious Internet strategies. But then, reportedly because Eisner didn't get it enough, Winebaum left, plunging Disney's Internet business, including Infoseek, into disarray. Conversely, I know many people in Silicon Valley who will tell you that, in fact, Winebaum never got it.

There was no company in the media business that did not find itself thoroughly confounded by the difficulties of getting it. Personally, I believe this is because there is mostly almost nothing to get. Getting it, I believe, is a conceit on the part of people who are overly enamored with what technology can do. It is a form of snobbery on the part of people who believe understanding technology is more important than it historically has been. But, at the same time, we should not underestimate the extent to which the myth of getting it is just an ordinary hustle. "You only make big money from people who are stupider than you" is one of the few down-to-earth maxims I've heard in the technology business.

It isn't, necessarily, that what was being said and sold by the people who claimed to get it was untrue. But it was true in the sense that astrology is often true. Things would change. Sure. Duh. And then . . . ?

I have yet to meet a new-media guy who has a much better idea about how to build an economically sustainable relationship with an audience than any old-media guy. Nor have I met anybody who knows how the new speeded-up media distribution paradigm will make people laugh more. On the other hand, I can hear certain people, people I know well, shaking their heads and saying, "You just don't get it." Gerald Levin, undoubtedly, would say that. When Time Warner announced it was merging with AOL, Levin said this was a merger about getting it. Time Warner got it. By implication, other media companies did not.

And, believe it, this is suddenly the big question haunting every media company. How majorly are they not getting it? Mostly, that depends on the share price.

But I believe that the AOL–Time Warner announcement actually marked the end of the getting it/not getting it cultural divide. Getting it, for better or worse, became an issue of corporate strategy, rather than elusive truth.

Not long ago, I heard this maxim applied to ABC and *Who Wants to Be a Millionaire.* The show worked, I was told by a fellow media critic, because "Regis Philbin gets it." Indeed. If Regis gets it, why would you want to?

IAN FRAZIER

Th-th-that's Not All, Folks

Even two-dimensional characters have three dimensions

IAN FRAZIER *is one of America's foremost humorists. He is a regular contributor to* Outside *and the* Atlantic Monthly. *His books include* Dating Your Mom *and the nonfiction best-seller* Great Plains. *His recent book,* On the Rez, *is an account of the modern-day Oglala Sioux.*

Gladiator *[the movie] is a big hit, but is it historically accurate? . . . How much of* Gladiator *is actually true?·*

—*Newsweek*, May 14, 2000

YES, THERE WAS an actual duck on which the well-known screen character was based. He did not have a name; around the poultry shed where he nested, he had only a number, like all the other black ducks, but today there are conflicting stories about what the number was. His original owner says it was 27, but that could be wrong. Everyone who knew him agrees that nobody on the farm ever called him "Daffy," and that some scriptwriter must have thought that up. The pig was based on a real pig named Porky Pig who lived on the farm and died in 1989. He wore the little narrow-brimmed hat and bow tie only on special occasions, and the rest of the time he just rooted around in the mud with the other pigs. The fact that the fictional version of him became famous did not affect him at all. The stutter was a complete fabrication added by Hollywood to make him more interesting. The real pig did not stutter and spoke rarely or never, depending on who you ask.

Elmer Fudd, a patent attorney and amateur sportsman from Covina, California, was the inspiration for the character of that name. Fudd served four terms as state senator, so much of his life is a matter of public record, easy to check. When you dig a little deeper into some of the stories about him, however, you find that a lot of fudging of the facts has been going on. For example, in his passion for hunting he did shoot at several of the animals, including the duck, on a number of occasions. But according to a veterinarian's report filed June 8, 1959, a blast fired by Fudd point-blank at the duck's face left No. 27 (or "Daffy") with bird-shot pellets embedded in the front of the skull, as well as a partially perforated eardrum on the left side. In the film version of this incident, the full force of the gun blast strikes the duck squarely on the bill, causing the bill to spin quickly around the duck's head for perhaps two dozen rotations and come to rest at the back of the duck's head rather than the front. According to the best information we have found so far, this did not occur.

Other accounts of the doings of Fudd and his cronies play similarly fast and loose with the truth. A case in point is the portrait of Fudd's cinematic colleague, Yosemite Sam (*sic*—no last name given). This character appears to have been closely modeled on a man named Robert "Yellowstone Bob" Skinner, a rancher and sometime stuntman in the Sacramento area 40-odd years ago, whom many local residents remember well. Like his cinematic counterpart, Skinner was short, had a long red mustache that drooped almost to his feet, wore big boots and an oversize brown cowboy hat, and carried two six-shooters. Also like the screen version, Skinner used to hop up and down when angry and fire both his pistols simultaneously into the ground on either side of him, kicking up lots of dust, while megaphone-shaped bursts of steam shot out of both his ears. All of those details we have been able to verify from people who were there. Many other aspects of his behavior as depicted on film, however, are apparently unsubstantiated. On screen, for example, when this character becomes annoyed at something one of the other characters has done, he often exclaims, "Ton-sarn that varmint!" Unfortunately, no one who knew Skinner remembers him ever saying such a thing. Several recalled that occasionally he used to say, "Oh, Christ, Audrey—now what?" (Audrey was Skinner's second wife.) Such inconsistencies the makers of the film apparently felt free to disregard.

Most troubling, from the point of view of real-life accuracy, is the character of the rabbit. His inappropriate name ("Bugs"? Why that, for a rabbit?) is just one of many questions still unresolved. To make matters more confusing, on screen he sometimes dresses as the duck or as a beautiful woman to fool the hunter (Fudd), while at other times he appears as a bullfighter, a newspaper reporter, a Viking maiden, or the conductor of a symphony orchestra. The viewer is left wondering: Who, exactly, is he?

Our findings show that the character of the rabbit was actually a composite portrait based on several backyard rabbits who lived in greater Los Angeles during the late 1930s and early 1940s. One of these rabbits had very long ears, another had large white feet, another had two big front upper incisors, another was constantly chewing on carrots, and so on. Trying to pin down which real rabbit is the source for which on-screen exploit, however, is no easy task. Here one enters a hall of mirrors where truths, half-truths, and total falsehoods mix and mingle in a kaleidoscopic whirl, as reality slips maddeningly out of reach. Most of the rabbits' neighbors and other witnesses who could be of help have moved away or died. The memories of those few who remain are quite vague, perhaps unavoidably so, perhaps for some other reason. If, as the movie version claims, the rabbit and the duck once accidentally burrowed (!) into a cave full of treasure belonging to a sultan and got into a fight with a muscular guard named Hassan, and then a genie shrunk the duck down to a tiny size, and the duck went running off into the distance holding a diamond bigger than himself and screaming in a tiny voice how rich he was, this alleged event left no tangible physical evidence that we could find. If one of the original rabbits on which the cinematic rabbit was supposedly based did, in fact, dress in a tuxedo and pass himself off as Leopold Stokowski and conduct a symphony orchestra and make one of the singers hold a note so long that the singer's face turned several colors, and the proscenium arch directly overhead began to crumble, and the cracks in the proscenium spread, and pieces began to fall down, and the whole auditorium eventually collapsed—where, then, is the documentation? Are there program notes of the concert, newspaper stories about the disaster at the concert hall, insurance appraisals of the damage, and so on?

Confronted with these questions, the studio has so far stonewalled. To date, its only response has been a terse two-line statement saying that, although hard proof of certain events may not be immediately available, at least they "could have" occurred. Sadly, "could have" is not good enough for those of us demanding factual accountability. Granted, the rabbit "could have" gone into outer space and prevented a small Martian with a strange accent from blowing up the Earth—the Earth is still here, after all. Careful observers, however, will withhold judgment until more evidence comes to light. Meanwhile, the misquotations, distortions, and deliberate misrepresentations of the facts as purveyed on-screen have already done a serious disservice to the people and animals from whose lives these facts were drawn. In fairness to everybody, reality can only be what really occurred, and nothing more. As responsible viewers and citizens, we must keep on the alert to make sure that the supposed "reality" offered by films and the media is, in fact, actually true.

CARL HIAASEN

———⟫•⟪———

Destruction Ensues

Mother nature won't be modeled

CARL HIAASEN *is an award winning journalist whose novels
include* Double Whammy, Skin Tight, *and, more recently,*
Sick Puppy. *He is also a columnist for the* Miami Herald.

E VERY SPRING, A SCIENTIST named William M. Gray gives a fear-
less prediction in advance of hurricane season. He guesses at the
number of tropical storms that will stir to life, the number of those
that will become hurricanes, and the number of those that will grow
into life-threatening juggernauts with winds of 110 mph and higher.

Weather watchers await Gray's annual warnings as avidly as Wall
Street anticipates Alan Greenspan's periodic conjectures about infla-
tion. Yet while a laconic grunt from Greenspan causes instant reper-
cussions in the stock markets, Gray's most harrowing forecasts have
no discernible impact on human behavior. Nobody panics. Nobody
flees to northern latitudes. Nobody unloads that vacation time-share
on the barrier island. What most people do, basically, is shrug.

Gray is a professor in the Department of Atmospheric Sciences at
Colorado State University. I'm no meteorologist, but I can state with
certitude that he will never be struck by a hurricane as long as he
hangs close to campus.

Fort Collins, where Gray lives, is a long way from the Florida Keys,
where I live. Tropical storms menace here regularly and, with all due
respect to Gray's talents, his predictions are no damn good to me.
Hurricanes do whatever they please.

The sober media attention devoted to Gray's forecast is bemusing because even when he's in the ballpark (which is often), the numbers are useless. Unless you're in the business of insuring coastal real estate, it doesn't really help to know if there will be five or 25 hurricanes whirling around the Atlantic basin any particular summer. We still won't be sure where they're headed until they get there and, most important, we still won't be able to steer them or stop them.

Whether or not a hurricane creams us depends on a multitude of capricious conditions, none of which we can influence. The warm Pacific currents of an El Niño play a role in a tropical storm's life, as do the chilly ripples of its La Niña counterpart. The amount of rainfall in western Africa is a key factor, as are the surface water temperatures of the Atlantic Ocean and Caribbean Sea. Even a front moving across the Great Plains can, believe it or not, affect the course of a hurricane 2,000 miles away.

In 1999, based on "global circulation features," Gray predicted a 54% probability that the Atlantic coast of the United States would be struck by an "intense" Category 3, 4, or 5 hurricane. That's like saying the upper deck at Busch Stadium has a good chance of getting plunked by a Mark McGwire homer sometime between April and October.

For purposes of storm preparation, defining the Atlantic coast as a target zone is worthless. It would be infinitely more useful to know which county or even which state was in line for a hurricane thumping, but Gray can't possibly tell you that months in advance. No mortal can.

Even after a tropical storm blooms into one of those rubescent, rotating icons on the Weather Channel, no one knows precisely where it will go. Meteorologists feed computers with real-time data from radar, satellites, oceanic buoys, and aircraft. The computers then deliver "models" of likely hurricane behavior, based on what previous storms have done.

True, the general path of a hurricane sometimes can be projected two days ahead of the worst winds, giving residents in possible landfall range enough time to evacuate or board up. Unquestionably, these warnings save lives. Yet despite the high tech forecasting wizardry, thousands of people still die in fierce, quirky storms such as Hurricane Mitch, which devastated Honduras in 1998.

To cope with cataclysms we cannot prevent, we hurl ourselves into scientific inquiry. Brilliant lifetimes are spent gathering facts about phenomena that will forever remain immune from human interference. We know vastly more than our grandparents did about hurricanes, tornadoes, volcanoes, and earthquakes, yet we are no closer to controlling them. All we can do is hunker down, or get the hell out of the way.

Despite all our new knowledge, we're as helpless as june bugs, dodging nature's boot heels. This is a fantastic, liberating truth. Hurricane season lasts from June 1 to November 30, and all we can do is keep an anxious eye on the heavens.

Once I met a Seminole medicine woman who had witnessed every hurricane of the past 95 years. Susie Jim Billie had grown up in a village without radio, television, or Doppler radar, yet the tribal elders always knew when a hurricane was coming. "Signs from the clouds," Susie Jim Billie explained.

As soon as the sky took on a certain hue, the Seminoles would swiftly construct a sturdy, low-cut shelter of cypress logs and palm fronds. There the villagers would ride out the ferocious weather. When I asked Susie Jim Billie how many members of her tribe died in those storms, she smiled.

Not one, she said.

The first major hurricane in my memory was Donna, which killed 364 people on a marathon rampage from the eastern Caribbean to Maine in September 1960. After smashing the Keys, Donna aimed for the Florida mainland. Western Broward County, where my family lived, lay directly in its path.

After my father shuttered the windows, we lighted candles, filled the bathtubs with drinking water, turned on the transistor radio, and waited out the storm. Forty years later, the drill is pretty much the same at my house. All the new science is dazzling, but the essential hurricane experience hasn't changed at all.

In my lifetime, the character of Florida has transformed from sleepy rural to manic urban, and most of the cherished places from my boyhood are unrecognizable today. Where the natural world hasn't been destroyed, it has been brutally diminished. That's why some of us celebrate the invincibility of hurricanes, magnificent monsters that won't let us forget our puny place in the natural order.

Thanks to satellite photography, we are now able to track a tropical weather system from its moment of birth. But so what? All we've bought ourselves is an extra week of high anxiety. Like the old Seminoles, we still don't know if a storm will hit us until a few hours before it does. That's not because the technology has failed but rather because the technology is futile. A hurricane can be explained but never stopped.

There's no question that William Gray and his Colorado State colleagues are adept at reading and interpreting long-range atmospheric patterns. Last year Gray guessed that 14 tropical storms would develop; there were 12. He said that nine would become hurricanes; eight did. He guessed that four of the hurricanes would swell into serious ass-kickers; five did.

As weather forecasting goes, it was an impressive performance. However, neither Gray nor any other meteorologist made the one measly prediction that would have been helpful to me and my neighbors. He did not predict a hurricane would hit the island where I live on the morning of October 15.

The previous night, my family and I went to bed believing that a pesky Category 1 intruder named Irene would scuff Key West and then skitter safely away, into the Gulf of Mexico. That was the course foreseen by three state-of-the-art computer models, and confidently relayed to us at 11 P.M. by weathermen on every local TV station. But when we awoke at dawn, Hurricane Irene was coming squarely up the Keys, barreling along Highway 1 like a runaway beer truck. The storm had changed direction overnight, making instant fools of the experts. We had no time to lock down the shutters.

Even pip-squeak hurricanes are gloriously frightening to experience. We watched with awe as the sky changed from porcelain blue to lead, and the waters of Florida Bay went from slick to froth. The hum of the wind rose by octaves as the storm shouldered across the islands. Tree limbs twisted and moaned and snapped. Torn by 90-mph gusts off the tall palms, coconuts became cannonballs. From out of nowhere, a battered blue canoe landed in the mangroves. Inside our home, doors shuddered and candle flames shimmied as the passing storm sucked heavily at the air.

But we were safe. Our house is made of concrete and sits on solid, immovable pilings. Like many old structures in the Keys, ours was designed to withstand powerful winds and the accompanying surge of high water.

Unfortunately, most Floridians are not so highly situated or well protected. Irene eventually crossed to the mainland, dumping so much water that parts of Miami-Dade, Broward, and Palm Beach Counties remained submerged for days. The dikes and canals that long ago had been gouged throughout the Everglades to prevent such flooding—to subdue nature, in other words—couldn't keep pace with the deluge. State water managers admitted that Irene was a surprise but said it was doubtful that even a dead-on forecast would have helped. The pump stations weren't strong enough, and the canals weren't wide enough. There was simply too much rain falling way too fast.

And you never heard such whining. Suburbanites were mad about the mistaken weather report and madder still about how long it was taking to drain their streets and lawns. No one in authority dared to point out that if fault was to be found, it lay with those who were doing the griping, the ones who chose to settle in the hemisphere's hottest hurricane corridor. Monster cyclones have been ambushing Florida with hellish winds and choking downpours for millions of years, long before sardine-can subdivisions, condo canyons, megamalls, theme parks, interstate highways, and humankind.

Call it optimism or arrogance, but 71% of Florida's 14 million residents reside in coastal counties. We are the problem. We live where we don't belong, on a humid, flat, low-lying peninsula that every summer becomes a bull's-eye for bad weather. And every day, heedless of William Gray, about 800 new settlers arrive to take their chances. Nature will screw with them eventually, as it screws with all Floridians.

Knowing what we know, we surely deserve what we get. Hurricanes are grandly indifferent to human folly. Our house has been raked two years in a row. By the time you read this, it will be the height of hurricane season, and we could have been hit again—not just by a brat like Irene but by an Andrew-size whopper.

For the record, William Gray has made the following prediction for 2000: Twelve tropical storms will blossom into eight hurricanes, four of which will brew winds of 110-plus miles per hour. He calculates the chance of one or more violent tempests making landfall along the East Coast at 52%.

The estimate is partly based on a high-altitude occurrence called the Quasi-Biennial Oscillation, which causes equatorial winds to reverse directions for 12 to 16 months at a stretch. As Gray explained (sort of): "This year, the Quasi-Biennial is expected to blow from the east, a direction not normally favorable to hurricane formation. However, this year the winds have failed to drop as low as we expected, somewhat neutralizing the effect."

He added that relatively balmy temperatures in North Atlantic waters signaled a robust "thermohaline circulation system," also known as the Atlantic conveyor belt. As the term implies, it's a natural delivery system for weather systems, often nasty ones. The bottom line is "above-average" odds that a jumbo hurricane will hammer the eastern coastline this year, although the likelihood is slightly less than it was in 1999.

I honestly don't feel any safer. On the other hand, it's pointless to lie awake fretting about the Quasi-Biennial Oscillation, which is happening 10 to 20 miles up in the stratosphere and is laughably beyond the powers of man. With such staggering impotence comes a cold gust of clarity. The choice is simple: to live in the path of these fabulous storms, or to live somewhere safe—say, Fort Collins, Colorado.

William Gray made his decision, and I've made mine. The next time I'm dodging coconuts in the Keys, he'll be calmly sorting satellite images in his office on the Front Range of the Rockies. Still, after 47 seasons in harm's way, I submit that the most valuable thing to be learned about hurricanes is not a statistical probability but a nerve-shredding, orifice-puckering truth:

All it takes is one.

———

RICHARD FORD

>=⊸⊷=

The Act of Contemplation

Life's extra buzz is hidden between what we say and do

RICHARD FORD *is the author of many books, including* The Sportswriter, *and a collection of short stories,* Rock Springs. *His book* Independence Day *was the first novel to win both the Pulitzer Prize for fiction and the PEN/Faulkner Award. His recent work,* A Multitude of Sins, *is a book of stories.*

SOMETHING ABOUT BEING alive must always have made us feel uncomfortable. It's not just the new millennium or virtual reality or stock option angst that is responsible. From their early existence, humans must have felt the disquieting sensation that just thinking, feeling, making sounds, and moving around—all the existential prerogatives—didn't quite express or sum up the whole experience of being alive. Being alive was more than just waking up of a morning ready to outwit a mastodon. And this eerie sensation—that life was somehow more, well . . . multilayered—evolved into an urge to express existence's dense weave and in the process corroborate life and ourselves. (I mean, either it was that, or else early man understood that those experiential categories—feeling, moving, etc.—actually did sum up all of life, and the result was such despair about the grinding finitude of existence that something more was needed to console or distract him. I, of course, suppose otherwise.)

Among the many recognitions one takes away from a visit to the caves at Lascaux, where long-ago humans drew pictures of themselves and the creatures they met, is that the urge to represent self and scene responds to a need to designate as true this very complicated fact and nature of human existence.

Nearer our own day, a painting by Picasso or by Fairfield Porter asserts, among other things, that yes, what we thought was so about life is so: These pictured objects, evoked emotions, these represented people—they're all actually out there in the world. And in the world they look, sound, and make us feel in ways that these paintings demonstrate, provoke, or simulate. Plus, by their discordant variety, these paintings interpret that aspect of worldly existence we sense but can't easily find a correlative for—the sensation that existing comes to more than its enumerable parts.

This extra sensation, of course, can be thought of as one kind of contact with the unknown. And describing or credibly representing the unknown challenges anyone. Some minds it drives to drink, some to the practice of law, some to religion, others even to Ph.D.s in recondite subjects. The literary critic Lionel Trilling, for instance, referred to this difficult-to-describe *other* dimension to life as "the buzz of implication," which he felt accompanied life as we live it but disappeared once the present was lost.

Though for those driven merely to art (myself and Keats as well as Picasso and Porter), we often try to postulate that what our paintings and poems and stories deliver and certify is *truth*, which is understood to include not only the things we see and hear, and the extra "buzz" we only vaguely sense, but also the ancient primordial urge that inspires expression itself.

So, it's not just since we've had Web sites full of misinformation, or since the president found it difficult to define what *is* is. And if you think the world was a simpler, more manageable place before, say, World War I, or before the Industrial Revolution, and that truth was more readily findable back then, try reading Dickens or Hardy or George Eliot. Beam yourself back to the textile mills of Manchester, circa 1847. In Hardy's *The Mayor of Casterbridge,* for example, a young man sells (*sells!*) his wife to a sailor at a country fair, then goes on to become a successful small-time politician with a secret. What is the true nature of bad, Hardy asks us? How do we face ourselves? What is character?

These days, with TV and globalized culture, certain true parts of our existence on the planet are—unlike 10,000 years ago—more customarily and externally expressed. We can *see* ourselves wearing Nikes, drinking Cokes, committing murder, making love, being tried in court. And these new, visible evidences of ourselves, along with the less visible urges and anxieties they spring from—these complex truths—have relinquished their character as sacred unknowns and become something like bland facts. (If you doubt this, watch six episodes of *Cops,* end to end. There you will see real but anonymous, even generic, humans being pursued by uniformed but uniformly courteous policemen for committing crimes whose real, dastardly consequences somehow still fit into a 30-minute time slot just after the local news.)

We still sense the unease our ancestors experienced—the need for all of life to be expressed (including the not-quite-specifiable "buzzing" parts) and for our complex, discriminating selves to be substantiated. But with so many of our human qualities and urges being packaged and displayed like sitcoms, our experience of truth—whatever of it is not rendered as factual—is that it exists almost completely out of sight. And indeed, our dissatisfaction with our selves reduced to fact leads us in a hungry way to think of truth as residing *only* beyond the perimeters of what's certain—a suspicion that can perplex as easily as inspire us.

Sacred Texts

My favorite biblical injunction is from Hebrews, 11:1: "Faith is the evidence of things unseen." I, however, am not a god-believer but a secular, art-worshiping novelist, and for that reason I always substitute "imagination" where the Bible has "faith." I also feel certain that the "things" the Scripture refers to are truth. Thus, for me, imagination is the evidence of truth unseen. And in a holistic way, I'm convinced that truth is represented not just by what I eventually find and declare as fact, maxim, and rule, but that truth exists in the quest for truth itself: my imagination, my sense that there's more than meets the eye, my curiosity. These form the tissue of belief with which I try to connect myself to this immanent experience of existence I only dimly sense. To my mind then, truth for the Lascaux cave painters was evident not only in the fineness of their paintings but also in the scrupulous imagination necessary to translate the anxiety and discomfort of their existence into art. In essence, truth was their medium as well as their object.

That truth lies hidden is, of course, one of the bedrock principles of modernism, and a reason for treating literature and other art objects like sacred documents and talismans, and for treating artists as visionaries. Expressing truth was what T. S. Eliot was interested in when, in the "East Coker" section of the *Four Quartets,* he wrote that writing poems was "a raid on the inarticulate/With shabby equipment." Likewise it's what Antoine de Saint-Exupéry meant in *The Little Prince,* when he wrote, "It is only with the heart that one can see rightly. What is essential is invisible to the eye."

What these writers wished to express in a poem, or in a little magical tale, was, again, the part of existence we ordinarily don't have language for but are sure is there—the commodity (if you please) that satisfies our anxiety about life and certifies our own viability and existence in it. The truth.

The Space Between

"When do you put in the meaning?" a woman reader asked me once in a letter. I wrote her back quickly and said that the idea of meaning being plunked into a novel like a codfish into a cioppino wasn't the way I, at least, did it. Yet I did believe she was talking about truth (her "meaning") and wanted to know where truth was hiding in some book I'd written. Perhaps she'd been hoping it would be expressed in one or several clear maxims: "Happy families are all alike." Or "No man is punished twice for the same offense." Or "Two heads are better than one." (All these, of course, happen to be largely *un*true, which tells you something about much of "truth" that's written in stone: that its static relation to the changing nature of existence tends to vitiate absolute certainty.)

In my letter I told my lady reader that sometimes true things did turn up in novels—even my novels—in maxim form. "What more can you do for wayward strangers than to shelter them?" I wrote that in a book once and thought it was fresh and true, and felt very good about it. When I read it now, years after writing it, I see its limitations—its provisional trueness a product of my novel's artifice and its internal ethical system. I could also have stressed to my letter writer that the line I quoted was just the tip of an iceberg, and that the iceberg was the whole, complicated enterprise of my novel, and that this novel—not just one line in it—was both the medium and the evidence of truth's existence, and as such couldn't be paraphrased or boiled down to profit. Truth was an act of careful contemplation and writing, not just their product.

Truth in a novel, I told her, is usually found less overtly stated, almost as if greater simplicity, greater sententiousness robbed truth of its essence and thoroughness. Yet because our need to have life verified is real and constant, we develop ways to look longer and more carefully for truth. We take advantage, for instance, of our mind's peripheral vision, and we look in new places. "Between what I see and what I say/ Between what I say and what I keep silent . . . [is] poetry," the great Mexican Nobel laureate Octavio Paz wrote. For him, poetry means truth, and we experience it when we read a poem—that is, in the poem we hear the hum of important implication surrounding life, we pursue consolation, and our act certifies us. Of course, there is no literal "between," just as there's no anatomical inquiring "heart" in Saint-Exupéry. Writers make up their special, remote "places" to suggest that truth involves our relationship with the something sensed but not easily expressed, and that this something is rare and precious.

Somebody else will give you a different way of determining truth, of course. An attorney will say that truth resides not in whether his client did the crime but in a shadow of doubt that can be imagined (by a judge, a jury) as coloring the "facts." Truth to a surgeon lies in the range of anticipated possibility that an actual heart will stop, or a patient will survive a year or longer. Truth is expressible as fact; there's no doubt about it. The patient always dies, or lives. The distance from Detroit to Toledo stays the same. But truth also involves our lively contemplative relationship with what we sense to be actual but must work to find expression for. To know truth of all sorts requires, among other things, that we pay attention to as much as we can. And if the time has come when truth seems particularly elusive, maybe we're simply not paying attention closely enough.

ARTHUR MILLER

⊰⊶⊱

Fantastic Scoop

When the people who deliver the news don't want to hear it

ARTHUR MILLER *is a Pulitzer Prize–winning playwright whose most famous plays include* Death of a Salesman *and* The Crucible. *He was born in Brooklyn, New York, in 1926 and divides his time between Connecticut and Manhattan. His recent play is* The Ride Down Mount Morgan.

IT IS 1986, AND THE SOVIET UNION is immortal. My phone rings. The caller's voice seems so distant that I imagine the wind is carrying it. And, indeed, he says he is calling from Kirghizia. I am not sure where that is, but I recall hearing that it is a vast and nearly empty Soviet space somewhere along the Chinese border. The voice becomes clearer. He is a novelist I had met in Moscow a year or two earlier, Chingiz Aitmatov. He is inviting me to a writers' forum in a town called Issy-kul. I dread the thought of attending another Soviet gabfest designed to lull foreign writers into believing they are terribly important and beloved by the Soviet culture apparatus.

"This is not what you think," Aitmatov begins. "There will be no party supervision. Everyone will be free to say anything he wishes. We need you here. We have Peter Ustinov coming and Claude Simon, the French novelist, and James Baldwin. Please come!" There is something genuinely needful in his voice. I know of his problems with Soviet censorship and his reputation for independence.

What, I ask, is the purpose of the meeting?

"We want a new sort of dialogue with the West—a way of exchanging ideas freely, without political interference," he says. "Will you come?" That he was saying such things on an open phone line was itself remarkable, for his implication was that the party was not a truly marvelous institution.

Aitmatov's promise turned out to be true. When we arrived, there was, in fact, no inevitable pro forma party line pronouncement under the transparent disguise of some poet's lament about American racism or the cruelties of unemployment in London or New York. People were themselves, curious about one another and candid about their own difficulties with publishers and critics. There was a certain hyperexpectancy among the Soviet writers, a waiting-for-the-other-shoe-to-drop, due no doubt to this newly liberated system under which we were all operating. If it was still not altogether a relaxed, Western-style atmosphere, all agreed that for some as-yet-unknown reason, Gorbachev had taken a step toward simple candor—something unheard of before.

We had a fine couple of days at a health resort on the vast inland sea called Lake Issy-kul, had our first taste of mare's milk, visited people in their yurts, watched some fantastic horsemanship by both women and men, and had our first sleep on beds with blood pressure measuring devices attached. The air was clear and cold and the local people polite and happy to see us. Jimmy Baldwin, ailing and watched over by his brother, saw hope for the world in this new forthrightness that seemed to reflect some mysterious political change, and Ustinov's jokes were never smarter nor more insane. In brief, some sharp injection of oxygen into what would normally have been a routine international handshaking exercise had everybody a bit on edge, wondering what had happened on high to cause this remarkable change.

On the morning of our departure, a message was relayed by one of the Soviets that we were invited to meet with Chairman Gorbachev in Moscow that afternoon. This astonishing news even raised the eyebrows of Claude Simon, the rather dour French Nobelist (who earlier in the trip had admitted to my wife, Ingeborg Morath, that the prize had knocked him backward, since hardly anyone in or out of France read his books).

They arranged our group around a mile-long conference table high up in the central Communist Party headquarters skyscraper in the center of Moscow. We were—American, British, French, Italian, Ethiopian, and several other nationalities—all excited at the prospect of meeting the head of this mighty country.

Gorbachev rather strolled in, smiling and nodding to each of us as we were introduced, then took his place at the head of the table. We each had headphones plugged into outlets on the table connected to the various translators who were in some other room. Gorbachev had a couple of translators at each side but quite evidently no "assistant" to police what he might say. However he may have been primed for this meeting, he did seem to have read Baldwin's work and knew some of my titles as well as those of some of the other writers present.

I never take notes on such occasions, but after a few minutes it seemed obvious to me that we had not been summoned here to pass an hour's chat but to deliver a message to the world, and I began writing as fast I could in order to get an accurate rendering of what Gorbachev was saying, for what he was saying was momentous.

He said he believed that a change in substance had to begin inside the Soviet Union, as well as in its relations to other countries. This was a new age, unforeseen by Marx, who knew nothing of atomic power, electronics, or any of the other inventions that have transformed the post–World War II societies.

As he saw it, the main lesson was that it was useless to try to communicate by repeating old, outworn shibboleths and political formulations. We must work from realities, not textbooks or dogma, and those realities were unknown to 19th-century thinkers, including Marx, who was a genius, to be sure, but not a mystical prophet. The notion of a moribund dogma was repeated a number of times until Gorbachev seemed to be signaling that even standard Marxist certainties were now up for grabs.

I could hardly believe my ears. He went on in this vein for some 20 minutes. I wondered if I dared ask him if he thought of himself as a Marxist, and after much inner turmoil, I did so.

"I am a Marxist-Leninist, but not a Stalinist," he said. This remark, made in the headquarters of the Soviet Communist Party at that time, was the equivalent of a pope declaring he was a Christian but not a Catholic while standing in St. Peter's Square.

Arriving home, I told the story to my neighbor, Harrison Salisbury, a retired *New York Times* reporter who had spent a decade or so in

Moscow in the worst years of the Cold War, and who had invented the paper's op-ed page. He had gone to Vietnam for the *Times* at the height of the war and had himself photographed standing in front of a bombed-out hospital that the U.S. government had been denying existed.

Hearing my story, he was astounded and insisted I write up what I had heard. "This is a fantastic scoop," he declared, and he offered to send it immediately to the *Times* editors, who he was sure would snap it up.

I wrote what I had heard Gorbachev say, thankful for my extensive notes, and Salisbury immediately sent my manuscript to the *Times*, whose current editors he, of course, knew very well.

The *Times* refused to print my piece. Salisbury was astonished. He could only think they didn't believe what I had written. He then sent it to his friends at the *Washington Post* and received the same refusal.

Clearly, the American mind-set had been so calcified by nearly two decades of Cold War that it was simply not conceivable for the head of the Soviet Union to be speaking as I reported. I offered to ring up Claude Simon, James Baldwin, and any of the others who had been present to confirm my report, but nothing came of this. As far as two of the most powerful newspapers in the United States, and presumably the U.S. State Department, were concerned, the change Gorbachev clearly implied had not taken place in the most crucial element of world reality.

I now understood why Gorbachev had summoned this group of artists. He no doubt had been finding it impossible to penetrate the Western mind—at least its press and diplomatic representatives—with his new concept of what was real.

No one in 1986 could imagine the Soviet Union literally breaking into pieces, and I am reasonably sure that Gorbachev had no such expectation either. He seemed to imagine that the Communist Party could actually run the country while tolerating dissenting opinions and even allowing other competing parties to operate. He repeatedly told us that there was no single truth to be handed out like a dish of eggs, but a process by which truth might be discerned.

As it soon turned out, of course, the party's monopoly on power collapsed, bringing down the Soviet Union itself as soon as Gorbachev refused to use force against Czech and Hungarian dissidents. (In former times, they would have been promptly crushed.) My own guess was that when he spoke to us, he really believed it would be possible for the Communist Party's ruling power to be based on the consent of the people. But, in truth, the party's power was based largely on the military; when the army was leashed, the whole thing collapsed.

And so I open the papers now, ever since this experience, wondering what else is real but not reportable. What else does our fixed mindset find too incredible to print? Gorbachev's vision of reality led directly to the collapse of the Soviet Union, possibly the most important story of the 20th century, and it was, in effect, suppressed—not by some government censor but by men free to print just about anything.

What's the lesson here? I think it is that one has to endlessly reexamine what one is absolutely sure is beyond possibility.

STEPHEN E. AMBROSE

Old Soldiers Never Lie

History actually happens, but you can't trust the ones who make it

STEPHEN E. AMBROSE *is one of America's most eclectic historians and biographers. He is the author of best-selling books such as* Nixon, Undaunted Courage, *and* Citizen Soldiers. *His latest works are* Comrades: Brothers, Fathers, Heroes, Sons, Pals *and* Nothing Like It in the World: The Men Who Built the Transcontinental Railroad, 1865–1869.

NOTHING IS RELATIVE. What happened, happened. What didn't happen, didn't, and to assert it is to lie.

Historians are obsessed with what is true. They have to prove what really happened; in quoting someone, they must demonstrate that person really did speak or write those exact words.

The problem is that facts are never sufficient. They require interpretation. And interpretation makes us hostage to histories not yet written.

I used to tell my students that President Harry Truman was wrong to use the atomic bombs against the Japanese. I believed the Japanese were already ready, even eager, to surrender, as long as they could keep their emperor. I was wrong. New documents reveal that the Japanese intended to fight to the death. I realized that Truman was exactly right and that his decision saved uncounted American and Japanese lives.

Interpreting a lie is more difficult. It forces the historian to construct the realities of statesmanship with morality. The fact is that lies are sometimes necessary and can produce good or at least defensible outcomes, especially in statecraft. In two decades of interviewing Dwight Eisenhower, and in studying his writings and actions, I've caught him in only two lies. One was to Adolf Hitler: the deception about where he intended to invade France in June 1944. The other was to Nikita Khrushchev, in May 1960, on what Francis Gary Powers was doing flying over the Soviet Union in a U-2 spy plane. The first lie worked out just fine; the second one caused much harm. Otherwise, Eisenhower always tried to make his word his bond. He once told his cabinet, with Vice President Richard Nixon present, that if you got caught in a lie in Washington, D.C., don't try to cover up, because if you do you will be found out and punished.

Needless to say, Nixon didn't listen. He was not alone. Lyndon Baines Johnson told lies about Vietnam. William Clinton tells lies about his own life and actions. Like Nixon, they got caught and tried to cover up and could not. Which is why we remember Eisenhower with great fondness and regard him as one of our best 20th century presidents, while Johnson, Nixon, and Clinton are recalled with distaste and rank at the bottom of the list of presidents.

Such judgments may be modified over time. Lies can be overcome, or at least downplayed and even ignored. Achievements will partially eclipse the crimes.

Still, I'm convinced that telling the truth is better. Always. That rule holds for presidents and historians.

It is true, for example, that our first president was a slave owner, and our second president ignored the pleas of his wife to give full citizenship, including the vote, to women. But it is also true that George Washington was our leader in war and peace, that it is thanks to him, above all others, that we are a democracy, not a monarchy. It is further true that John Adams brought the New England states into the Revolutionary War and, when defeated in 1800 by Thomas Jefferson, obligingly yielded his presidential post, thus ensuring the staying power of democracy. It is also true that these two men, and their associates, in rebelling against the British Empire, were risking their lives and fortunes. Had the British captured them, they probably would have been taken to London, tried, found guilty, and then drawn and quartered. These are all facts, and they perpetually await our interpretation.

The lies are waiting out there, too, posing an even greater challenge. Douglas MacArthur lied his way out of his problems or to cover up mistakes, such as the Japanese destroying his bombers on December 7, 1941, as they sat lined up, wingtip to wingtip, on Clark Field in the Philippines. After MacArthur left the Philippines to go to Australia, Jonathan Wainwright took command in the islands. From the safety of Australia, MacArthur ordered Wainwright to fight on to the last bullet, then lead his men on a suicidal bayonet charge. Wainwright, with sick, starving men barely able to walk, much less charge, surrendered instead.

Wainwright spent the rest of the war in a Japanese POW camp. He refused extra rations and insisted on being treated like his fellow prisoners. When liberated in the summer of 1945, he became a hero: "Skinny" Wainwright. Army Chief of Staff George Marshall told MacArthur he wanted Wainwright recommended for the Medal of Honor. MacArthur said no, that Wainwright had disobeyed his attack orders. Marshall transferred Wainwright out of MacArthur's command and put him under his own, then recommended him for the Medal of Honor, which Wainwright received. At the surrender ceremony, on the battleship USS *Missouri*, MacArthur threw his arm around Wainwright's shoulders, said how splendid it was to see him again, then added that he was so glad he could get that Medal of Honor for Wainwright.

That lie probably didn't hurt anyone, except MacArthur, who, despite everything, was a great soldier. In interpreting his life, we must take into account the totality of these facts. Each generation gathers these facts, including those newly uncovered, of victories and failure, acts of decency and outright lies, and renders an interpretation for that time. Then, a few years later, we do it again.

Does that mean everything is relative? No. As I said, facts are facts. And both historians and their subjects should never forget that. A president or a general or a business leader or the chancellor of a university or anyone else in a leadership role, at least in my opinion, based on a lifetime of studying American leaders, will always do better to tell the truth and will always suffer by defending himself or herself, when caught in a lie, by asserting that "everything is relative." Facts are facts. Events really do happen. And if journalists don't encourage the truth, historians eventually will. Ask Dick Nixon. Meriwether Lewis and William Clark never lied to the American people. A later explorer, John C. Fremont, lied nearly always about his exploits. Which ones do we remember and honor today?

KAREN SOUTHWICK

—✦—

Circling Faith

Does God insist on unquestioning faith,
or is there room for doubt?

KAREN SOUTHWICK *is the executive editor of* Forbes ASAP.
She is the author of Silicon Gold Rush: The Next Generation
of High-Tech Stars Rewrites the Rules of Business *and* High
Noon: The Inside Story of Scott McNealy and the Rise of Sun
Microsystems. *Her latest book is* The Kingmakers: Venture
Capital and the Money behind the Net. *She is an active mem-
ber of the Mormon Church.*

THE YOUNG MISSIONARY was flushed and earnest as he related the
story: A team of scientists had located the mausoleum of Alexan-
der the Great. Inside they found the king's skeleton, perched on a
throne, surrounded by all the riches of the earth. The thing closest to
him was a tattered scroll; one bony finger pointed to a scripture from
Matthew in the New Testament: "For what is a man profited, if he
shall gain the whole world, and lose his own soul?"

An excellent illustration of the missionary's point: We're not after
the rewards of this earth but the rewards of spirituality and righteous
living. The only problem was, his story couldn't possibly have been
true. As I pointed out to him after his Sunday meeting speech, Alexan-
der the Great had lived more than 300 years before Christ, and the
New Testament hadn't even been compiled until several hundred
years after. The king would have had no knowledge of Christ, nor
could he have been entombed clutching the Bible.

"But my mission president told us!" the missionary protested. The implication: His mission president, his spiritual leader, would never mislead him, so the story had to be accurate.

I shook my head, marveling once more at the unquestioning acceptance of authority on the part of sincere believers. This young man, 21 years old, had spent the past two years of his life seeking to convince others of the truth of the gospel preached by the Church of Jesus Christ of Latter-day Saints, better known as the Mormons. He was devoted, caught up in a cause greater than himself.

But that skepticism, that shell of disbelief that we all must form about what is true and what isn't, had failed him. He was patently not stupid. His talk in church that day was articulate and thoughtful; his point well made with other examples besides the mistaken one. Still, he hadn't caught the obvious error.

The young missionary was enmeshed in a dilemma faced by many of us who are members of religions that dictate truths that cannot be verified by the senses alone. How far do you let faith and belief in spiritual authority carry you? When do you dare question that authority? And what are the consequences of either unquestioning obedience or overt skepticism?

As both a fifth-generation Mormon and a career journalist who practices critical thinking for a living, I often find myself torn by controversial church policies. As a woman, I have a passionate conviction about gender equality. But my church hews insistently to the notion of separate, traditional roles for women and men; these supposedly equal roles don't feel that way, at least to me.

Before the late 1970s, my church firmly stated that African Americans could not hold the priesthood, which is held by only men in its ranks and is the indisputable tool of power. All important decisions, and most of the smaller ones (except maybe what to serve for dinner at a church social) are made by the priesthood, meaning the men. And prior to 1978, meaning nonblack men.

Various theories were supplied to account for the withholding of the priesthood from black men: They had not been valiant enough in our premortal lives. The mark of Cain was a black skin, so those who bore it were unworthy. Other reasons were more practical: It would have been too difficult to attract converts, especially in the 19th century when the church was getting its start, if we fully embraced blacks as equals.

Troublesome as the issue was, most faithful Mormons, including my father, an avid supporter of civil rights who had a poster of Martin Luther King Jr. on our basement wall, swallowed hard and accepted the official position. To the church's credit, when it finally ended the practice, under the aegis of a "revelation from God," it did so whole-heartedly. African American men were immediately ordained to the priesthood and have been able, in some cases, to rise into important leadership roles. There was, however, never any adequate explanation as to why black men were unworthy of the priesthood one day, while the very same black men could be ordained the next day—except that, speaking through our spiritual authorities, God (defined as an "unchangeable being" in Mormon scripture) had suddenly changed his mind and ordered it so.

The issue of women and the priesthood continues to fester, especially since the church came out in opposition to the Equal Rights Amendment and then excommunicated an outspoken ERA advocate, Sonia Johnson, in 1979. Other religions are grappling with the role of women as well. The Southern Baptists recently stated that women cannot serve as pastors, although where this leaves women who have already been ordained to such a role has not been clarified. The Catholics are under increasing fire to expand their depleted priest-hood by opening it to women and/or to noncelibates of both genders.

The president and current prophet of the Mormon Church, Gordon B. Hinckley, has insisted in public forums that Mormon women "are happy" in their God-ordained separate roles. Yet I know many who are not happy. We struggle constantly with questions of self-worth: If a woman has leadership qualities, where does she exercise them? If a woman does not choose—or is not fortunate enough to participate in—marriage, childbearing, and motherhood, is she condemned in this life and the next?

Ironically, I found the most empathy for my struggle to remain a faithful member of the church and still true to my own inner, feminist voice among gay male members. In the late 1980s and early 1990s, I witnessed how a few courageous bishops (heads of Mormon congregations) in San Francisco reached out to gay Mormons to gather them into the fold. These men had doubts similar to mine about the "straight and narrow way" to salvation in the next life.

Although it does not claim doctrinal infallibility, Mormonism, like religions ranging from Islam to Catholicism, holds that its designated spiritual leader speaks for God. That makes it really difficult to argue with him, for then you are by implication arguing with God himself. But there is an apparent out. Most churches teach some form of free will or free agency. We are entitled to have our internal confirmation of anything that the prophet says, be it direction on blacks receiving the priesthood or in favor of "defense of marriage" legislation stating that marriage can exist only between a man and a woman.

So what if your internal confirmation clashes with your spiritual leader's position? This is religion's equivalent of catch-22, because the implication is, of course, that it must be you who's wrong. It couldn't possibly be the person speaking with the power and authority of God. It was that same conditioning that kept the young missionary from questioning his mission president's story.

Therein lies both the strength and the biggest challenge in organized religion: To an extent, you have to suspend your own "truth detector" in favor of following someone else's, someone who may not be willing to tell you exactly why he's going in a particular direction. "Take it on faith" is a common response to difficult questions like, "Why would God discriminate based on skin color or gender?" or "How can polygamy be sinful for one generation and not for the next?"

In the end, for me the greatest act of faith is not believing in outright miracles like resurrection into another life; rather, it's believing despite all the contradictions in this one. I tell myself that while God is perfect, the people who speak for him are not. So there may be problems in translation or interpretation of his will, allowing me some wiggle room to exercise my conscience.

Compared to the young missionary, though, that reasoning can leave me uncomfortably stuck on the fence. In a way, I envy him. For who is really better off? The one who burst his little bubble, or the one with the unwavering faith? I like to think that, in the long run, I am better off, that God prefers people who think critically and act righteously for themselves, not because someone tells them what to do. So I tell the truth as I see it. I really have no choice.

WILLIAM VOLLMAN

Upside Down and Backward

When all is false and dull, a flip of the lens
brings everything into focus

Journalist WILLIAM VOLLMAN *is the author of several highly acclaimed works of fiction, most recently* The Royal Family. *In 1997 he was awarded the PEN Center USA West Fiction Award for his book* The Atlas.

I

UPON THE SHALLOW CURVED BOWL within the camera obscura, the gray sea began to turn. It had been turning before, but until my pupils dilated I saw nothing but darkness. A circular railing protected me from falling into this living picture of organized daylight projected into that concavity. Came the Cliff House, out of focus because it was too near. I might have seen two lovers wandering hand and hand into the Musée Mecanique.

Then the great lens swiveled severely up and about, the beach now offering itself to my gaze, more lovely in similitude than it actually was: brown and silver, long and lonely, bordered by an unstable line of foam from the streaks of the blue-gray sea, which in their pale and silent motions were streaks of life, streaks of time. Beachwalkers got doubled by their reflections in the wet sand. Now the Seal Rocks went swimming by like hoary, barnacle-encrusted seashell-creatures. I saw a blurred bird. Then the lens tilted upward so that the boundary stretched between sea and sky.

The real world's horizon has haunted me, although I've looked at it for 40 years.

Shouldn't a walk upon San Francisco's Ocean Beach have felt more vivid than any projected image of it? But the focused transcendence of the display, set off by darkness, forced me to see. Every time I paid my dollar to enter the chamber on the ocean's edge, I lost myself in the contemplation of movement and space. Neither pacing nor selection was mine. My imagination had to follow the lens.

The camera obscura focused my attention on a certain scene, at a certain angle of view, at a certain tempo. Like it or not, that was how I had to look. I'd glimpse a seal, and then the picture had left the seal behind, and I found myself thinking more about the animal because I hadn't gotten to gaze at it as long as I wanted. But in compensation for the loss of the seal, here was the most marvelous wave I could ever remember . . . forgetting it immediately, I saw another marvelous wave.

When, at last, I stepped outside, back into the brilliant sea fog, I felt a greater awe for this world into which I could now venture almost as freely as did the great lens in its stately whirling. If I descended to the beach, the crunching of my heels in the wet sand was real enough, but I remained within a splendid dream. Anyone inside the camera obscura could see me. I was a part of that pure, pale music box world that my baby daughter could still perceive—she still embraced her own shadow; she waved goodbye to dogs and characters on television screens; all was real to her, and all new.

II

Sometimes my daughter grows heavy in my arms, and I'll set her down. Fearing that I might never pick her up again, she weeps in grief and terror. I hope to teach her faith in my constancy. As long as I live, I'll always love her. But her certainty of my solicitude, if I succeed in conveying it to her, will doubtless arrive alongside a certainty of the law of gravity. In time she'll simply think: Yes, that's Ocean Beach. It will be time for the camera obscura.

Freshness wilts. We arrive at a spuriously eternal kind of knowledge: When I open my fingers, the pen will always fall from my hand. I am alive; everything I see is familiar to me; therefore nothing new will disturb my activities. I will never die. These propositions are equally parochial. Knowledge proves them so.

But the strange thing about knowledge is that the more one knows, the more one must qualify perceived certainties, until everything oozes back into unfamiliarity. The poems of Mandelstam, the body of a lover, an Arctic landscape, these are composed of ingredients as basic as the chemical elements—Mandelstam must use the same letters of the alphabet as every other Russian!—and yet the words grow new; the world renews itself.

III

For several years, I made a regular pilgrimage to the camera obscura (it's closed now). After the first time I knew "how it would be," of course, and yet I wanted that strangeness. The fact that it became a familiar unfamiliarity did not detract from it a single jot. If anything, I was able to enjoy the delights of its world more intensely than ever.

I haven't felt the need to look into the camera obscura now for two decades. Lately this other world, the one outside the camera obscura, has come to seem so real and strange to me. Could that be because I finally believe in my own death? My profession as a journalist is occasionally dangerous. Many of my assignments require me to interview terrorists, travel to pariah nations and war zones, and other oddities.

I have seen some very sad things. I have almost died violently. I am ready to die at any time. My affairs are in order; all I fear is torture, and the secondary torture it would cause those who love me. Every day, I try to think about what I have seen in the world I perceive. The lens of my vocation has shown me the agony of a Cambodian woman whose entire family was beaten to death with shovels by the Khmer Rouge. The survivor, who had to watch, dwells alone with their screams. I don't want to forget her, or them, for the same reason that I prefer not to forget the intricate streak patterns of the ocean within the camera obscura. This is what is real. Those who live as though any part of the world does not exist lose some of their own existence. What is the dull boom of mortar fire far away across the border? Or the shit stench of Colombian refugees in a Red Cross compound. The great lens turns and turns.

I see a Tasmanian cloud peak; a Jamaican ghetto boy standing in no-man's-land making defiant gang signs, but the other side holds fire;

or the Burmese prostitute combing her hair into something as rich and dark as some tincture of shadows; she hooks her shimmery black tights over her feet. The great world whirls.

IV

How can it be that the first woman I ever loved is now dead of breast cancer, leaving three small children to grieve without comprehending? How can it be that my own dear child, whose birth I witnessed, was born only so that she will someday die? It is all such a mystery to me, and only by studying a lover's body, or an Arctic landscape, or gazing through other focusing lenses of strange knowledge, can I hope to see a little farther within that mystery.

I will never solve the mystery. I know that now. Could it really be explicated, except through the elliptical means of poetry, why we were born or why the camera obscura's ocean is quite literally marvelous? I would follow that rotating horizon in every direction if I could. I would make my own way, take my own time. I would fall into error many times, to be sure, but I would go my own way. For what purpose do we walk this earth? Nobody can tell me truly. I cannot tell myself.

V

Not only does the quest to the mystery require the skills of the hunter, the laborious patience of a hod carrier, and the faith of a saint, but murderers lie in wait along the path. Their names are Necessity, Egotism, Misconception, Distraction, and Censorship. And now they've crept into the camera obscura itself. Within that bowl on which the light of reality was projected, they've overpainted the blankness with their own spurious clouds and seagulls, whose garish falseness occludes the delicacy of the world I came to see. They've murdered my view. When I complain, they promise me that the imitation will soon be better than the real thing, and that I'll thank them in the end. Soon they'll seal off the aperture to the sky, the better to insert their own movies behind the lens. They'll allow me to choose the color of their ocean—"I preferred it when it was gray"—"Next week you'll be able to have a gray ocean, too! And you'll be able to make it stormy. . . . "

VI

In our country, the murder of reality has proceeded not without pleasure to the victims. We have spun the lens to so fast a velocity that only the most fluorescent patterns, and of only the greatest crudity, can register on the gazer's perception. Well, why not? People like bright colors.

After the hydrogen bomb, perhaps the most dangerous American invention is television.

VII

Dostoyevsky tells me that the only way to make meaning out of the suffering of others is to assume responsibility for it. If a man is murdered on the other side of the earth, then I stand guilty of that murder, for I am a human being just as the murderer is. What an insane principle! When I first read it, it terrified me, and I rejected it. I still reject it. But it hoards a strange purity. The soul must enter the camera obscura to read *The Brothers Karamazov*. Slowly, the soul's pupils dilate in that dreary, muddy, provincial 19th century darkness. It takes many pages and characters for Dostoyevsky to say what he needs to say. He is not to be rushed.

VIII

The lens whirls over a map of Afghanistan. We see points of light. These mark the sites where our cruise missiles have struck. Whom did we kill and why? No matter—the lens must move on. What do our new enemies say about us in their capital? Well, we can imagine—or more likely, we can't imagine—and it's time to move on.

Here is Kabul at night: headlights, lanterns within wheeled fruit stands, people in buses packed tightly together like the inmates of mass graves, turbaned Talibs sauntering down the street, lords of all they survey, everything dark and dim, then just dark with snow falling. Women in blue and black *burqas* are walking home. I hear the rattle of handcarts, and now it's darker and darker. My lens moves on. Have I "understood" Afghanistan? Not by a long shot. But at least I saw it. I didn't just watch it on CNN.

IX

"Do you think they're having a good time?" I ask the waitress at the Las Vegas Millennium Café. "Those people on the slot machines, when the payoff comes out, they don't even look . . ."

"Oh, they're always grouchy," she says.

"I feel sorry for them. How about you?"

"How about me what?"

"What do you think about it all?"

"I don't think anymore. I just work."

Are they weary because their experience is inauthentic? I doubt it. More likely, the illusion isn't good enough. The corporate logos that now crowd the camera obscura have changed shape and color too many times. They obscure the obscura.

X

An old lady in a Canadian Arctic town once told me what had happened on the day that television arrived: The children didn't go out to play. People stopped visiting one another. While she exaggerated the case, it did make me sad to come in from the frozen ocean and see the blue glow coming from windows, and not see any people. I have seen that same blue glow in California and everywhere else in the world.

If the camera obscura were ever reopened, with the lens set back to its thoughtful speed, and the great image bowl scrubbed blank again, we might well perceive that those who've been robbing and murdering reality have made the world into a very ugly place. (*Editor's note: Since this essay was written, it has reopened.*)

XI

The murderers can't yet murder me. Any place can be a camera obscura, and so I defy them. For you too. Just look around. From the 21st floor of the Century Hyatt in Shinjuku I see the moment when twilight has almost given way to full darkness, skeletons of light. Soon the velvety spread and moss-pad treetops will be gone, fading like the intermediate graynesses of the skyscrapers. For the moment, they're both still there, but what increasingly represents the entire world beyond my window is light alone. The red eyes of cars recede from me, and the yellow eyes of cars rush close. The skyscrapers are fast becoming hollow latticeworks of yellow light. Far away, on the very horizon, another city slowly pulses dark and bright, a ball of violet blue luminescence like some immensely powerful firefly.

Above everything, in the middle of the sky, I see a blinding white object, most vivid and strange because it excludes not only light but also texture. For a moment I cannot tell what it is. Finally I realize that it must be the reflection of my pillow, on which the bedside lamp is shining, projecting its starched whiteness to the edges of divinity.

JOE FIRMAGE

Cruising the Cosmos

Everything we know so far is in beta version

JOE FIRMAGE *cofounded and was CEO of USWeb. He resigned from his position as chief strategist in late 1999 to pursue his interest in 21st-century physics. He is now CEO of One Cosmos Network, a new-age Internet portal.*

A N AMAZING FEW YEARS of my life have brought me to this rest stop tonight. Skyline Boulevard traces the peaks of the hills that separate Silicon Valley from the Pacific Ocean. A few miles north of the Page Mill turnoff, a small lookout offers the view I seek. As I look through the windshield across the heart of our New Economy and wonder at the remarkable transformations of human affairs incubating around the Bay Area, I take a moment to reflect upon the past decade.

I became a millionaire at age 23, having invented a rather primitive, icon-based application construction system called Serius. In retrospect, it was a useful if incomplete start to an important idea, sort of like its name suggests.

In 1993, I became a vice president of the software company Novell, engaged in the genesis of what would later become the Internet revolution. After locking horns with some in the leadership there, I moved on and cofounded what would become the largest Internet consulting company in the world, USWeb.

The early days of the New Economy were wild ones for all of us in Silicon Valley. I was working with the brightest of my peers to help build a large, sustainable company and leading thousands of talented people toward a shared vision.

Then in early 1998—to my surprise—the pace of my life accelerated. I began to use the Internet to learn about issues beyond my immediate ken. Sparked by a very unusual experience in consciousness, I became acutely aware of the depth of the environmental and cultural challenges facing humanity. I watched as Asia's economies collapsed, sending people accustomed to using cell phones into the streets to protest. Because of my parents' long-standing campaign against nuclear arms, I worried that our world's diverse array of weapons of mass destruction might circulate among profiteers and terrorists via monetary—or now simply chat room—exchanges. I saw the idiotic wings of institutionalized religions around the globe continue their tradition of shooting instead of speaking.

Technology was not solving these problems. During this time I watched the Internet accelerate both sustainable and unsustainable growth within human culture. Consumerism was becoming more scalable than ever before. The global economy was heading toward something still shrouded in mirage.

My intuition screamed to me that the path humanity travels into the future depends on how we evolve the role of "ideotechnomics"—the ideologically informed, technologically empowered machinery of economics. A mouthful to say, but to me the concept of ideotechnomics describes the vital structure supporting modern civilization. What are our civilization's programmed purposes? What are its wastes? What are the consequences of a race for productivity between human beings and increasingly fast, forceful, and intelligent machines?

In this interesting time of my life, I returned to the study of subjects I'd left long before in college, and an awesome flash of realization awaited me. Staring at me from the pages of well-respected science journals were new ideas that fundamentally changed how we understood key principles within physics. Ideas that suggested scientists might soon learn of new phenomena that would unlock the limits of nature, make technology possible to cut human waste drastically, and create tools that could reprogram ideotechnomics into a better balance with the human spirit and organic life.

Stirring within me was the deep sense that I must speak loudly about these ideas. A missionlike instinct told me to break through intolerance and ignorance and speak out, as a few other courageous folks have already done. So, after many fitful nights weighing the consequences, I did.

Mind in the Sky

I was a typical Mormon boy raised in a promising middle-income family in a small suburb of Salt Lake City. I was blessed with an unusually complete childhood, filled with intellectual challenge and nourishing emotional support. My father planted me, at the age of 12, in front of the television one Sunday night and forced me to watch a new PBS series called *Cosmos*. It was awe-inspiringly beautiful. Actually, it was staggering and humbling. In the years that followed I would listen to the music of *Cosmos* until the vinyl record was scratched beyond use.

At home, I pondered questions like: Is there a God? What are the points of light in the heavens? Are there other planets like ours? Are there other beings asking the same questions? What is the cycle of birth and death about? Will I actually go to hell if I drink coffee, smoke a joint, or enjoy masturbation (uh, did I say that out loud)?

Effective as Mormonism is in establishing a sense of loving community, no seminary lecture could hold a candle to the awesome truths I saw in the nature of our cosmos. By age 15 my Sundays were spent outside the church.

I was able to buy my first telescope and SLR camera by pooling my lawn-mowing income with money from my parents. I spent countless nights outside, beyond the lights of the city, right eye glued to the wide-angle eyepiece, marveling at the galaxies, star clusters, and nebulae of deep space. Shortly after plunging into astronomy, I proudly gave my first astrophotography presentation to a monthly meeting of the Salt Lake Astronomical Society. My loving mother sneaked into the planetarium, in violation of her promised absence from my lecture, disguised as a vagrant in a blanket.

It took me two years to complete high school, and from there I enrolled in the University of Utah to study astrophysics. I did well in the core science disciplines—mathematics and physics—but it was a serendipitous request by my mother that focused me on another of my passions: software programming. My mother's small greeting card business needed a basic computerized accounting system, so I began to build one. I was astonished at the level of difficulty in coding for the modeless graphical windowing system of my new Macintosh computer, so after I finished coding the accounting software, I designed an easier way to build software applications. Five years later, in 1993, Novell was interested enough in my concepts to buy our small company, Serius, for $24 million.

From Serius . . . to Sirius?

One night three years ago I was reading several physics articles I'd discovered on the Web. The articles floated a new idea from several noted astrophysicists and mathematicians—the idea that inertia is a zero-point force of the vacuum of space.

You might ask, "I'm not sure what inertia is, and what the hell is a zero-point force?"

You are not alone in a lack of understanding about the nature of inertia. Physicists do not know why objects resist acceleration—why objects push back when pushed. They do not know for sure why your head snaps back when your car speeds up. Inertia "just is." Also, contrary to popular assumption, scientists don't understand the mechanism that causes matter to attract itself—the force of gravity that makes objects fall to the ground. To be sure, scientists have painstakingly measured the rates of fall and resistance, and so we can build all sorts of technology that work flawlessly within the equations of these everyday forces. But we do not know why these forces work the way they do.

It is also a fact that the dividing line science draws between the phenomena it either "permits" or "forbids" the laws of physics to address is based upon the scientists' incomplete understanding of the forces of inertia and gravity. Hmmm.

My mind was churning that night, three years ago. If the "vacuum of space" is actually something more like a "medium of energy" continuously jostling or accelerating all particles even at zero temperature, then we may be in for some amazing surprises in the 21st century. The possibilities for the reach of human life, and the qualities to which all sentient life-forms might ascend, could be astonishing—if it is possible to influence this medium of energy directly, if it is possible to engineer the so-called zero-point force.

The next morning I had the most astonishing experience of my life. As I was waking, either a vision or a visitor appeared in my bedroom. We shared a few interesting words, or thoughts, about space travel with each other. Some have said my experience was a rare internal event of consciousness, some have said it was the mind of another human meeting mine, some said I went nuts, others have said I met my future self, others say I was visited by an angel, still others say the visitor must have been an extraterrestrial—or the consciousness of one. Who knows?

But for me that morning punctuated a rising understanding of scientific breakthroughs that may be on the horizon.

Mystical experiences aside, as I seriously studied recent advances in zero-point energy research—even though they are not complete— I saw that we could think about the nature of matter, energy, force, space, and time quite differently than we do today. It is possible to consider these notions in more integrated and elegant mental visualizations, like the idea that space is an ocean of all-pervading force, with a beautiful yin-and-yang-like pattern of motion, in which all things—galaxies, suns, planets, and humans—are evolving beings sharing a common cosmic dance.

To the engineer in me, these visualizations suggest that we may soon discover a new class of electromagnetic circuits, circuits that depend upon a refined understanding of the medium we call space-time. If we can do this, we will be able to build technology to:

- Move vehicles through space without shooting matter out of a nozzle.
- Propel a spacecraft many times faster than the speed of light, without the occupants feeling an inertial kickback.
- Avoid the effect known as time dilation within the field of this new kind of practical interstellar propulsion system.
- Draw limitless quantities of energy directly from space, powering any kind of machine, at virtually no cost.

Of course, it's a rather big leap from a physics hypothesis to interstellar spacecraft, and intelligent people disagree on these questions. But these theories are clearly solid enough to motivate us to reconsider our presumptions. If we might voyage to other worlds, then other advanced life-forms certainly have already. There have been hundreds of thousands of sightings of unexplained aerospatial anomalies in the past half century. There are credible accounts with photographs or radar records. Similarly described sightings stretch back for thousands of years. They have been dismissed in large part because of the presumption that no life-form can ever figure out a way to control the forces of inertia and gravity—the very forces that modern science has yet to fully understand.

Eventually, the question of whether alien life-forms are buzzing around our planet will be settled as the gap narrows between the truths of second-millennium physics and the realities of third-millennium physics.

Indeed, something undeniable and profound is happening across many serious communities of thought. We are awakening to the possibility that generations alive today could become the extraterrestrials of other earths.

Sailing among the Stars

Believe me, I know the scenarios I'm talking about are mind-bending. Seeing how everything these days seems reduced to digits sliding across a Nasdaq ticker, a few deeper ideas are worthwhile to think about. Particularly ideas that suggest that humans weren't evolved simply to become Nielsen statistics or stock symbols. Particularly ideas that suggest we should drop our weapons and let them rust. Particularly ideas that motivate us to love and serve one another.

These kinds of ideas move us to reflect on some of the deepest mysteries of life, and the most basic of questions: What are we? Who are we? What is the purpose of our reality?

The faithful of the world's great religions believe that we have spirits. Scientists believe that we are biological forms made of chemical forms obeying the laws of physics. There are other labels than these that can transform our sense of who and what we really are, labels that are true to science and startlingly spiritual at once: I believe each of us is an individual living pattern within patterns within patterns of a universal lightlike force, experiencing itself through us. Everything in the cosmos is such an entity, individual beings integrating within larger beings, on scales likely having no spatial or temporal limits.

The next time you have an evening free, drive away from the city into the forests or fields of the countryside. Feel nature's wind gently run her fingers through your hair. Smell the scents from the soil that feeds and clothes you. Hear the music of the denizens of the night, singing as integral organs in the symphony of your life. Look up into a moonless night sky, and imagine yourself as a light-force being, evolving on the shore of our mother planet, a grand old being some of us call Gaia. Picture yourself standing on her 8,000-mile-wide, ever-resculpting organic body, her face turning as she revolves around the guardian Sun that warms and nourishes her and all of us . . . revolving around the center of the Milky Way, one of uncountable galaxies swimming across the cosmos.

And then imagine: What if we did discover a new kind of sailing vessel along the way from truth to reality? It's the kind of mental picture that, if held by a critical number of individuals, may nudge the compass needle of our ideotechnomic machine to the right side of the left.

Back at the rest stop, as I press the button on the console next to the shifter in my convertible, I look up into the night. The stars sweep into view as the canvas rises and folds back. The semiconductor-controlled, laser-driven CD sound system perfectly reproduces a symphony-hall experience of the music of *Cosmos,* through magnets hidden in the walls of this amazing land craft. As I stare into the heavens, I wonder when the day will come that we recognize a new truth, like light shining through our cosmic eggshell, as the path is shown enabling our young human family to take its next evolutionary step.

JOHN UPDIKE

———◆◇◆———

The Tried and Trēowe

Despite our maneuverings to the contrary
we will always be more animal than robot

JOHN UPDIKE *is one of America's most acclaimed writers. His work includes short stories, essays, nonfiction, and novels. He won Pulitzer Prizes for both* Rabbit Is Rich *and* Rabbit at Rest. *His most recent book is* Gertrude and Claudius. *He lives in Massachusetts and regularly contributes to the* New Yorker.

A WRITER OF FICTION, a professional liar, is paradoxically obsessed with what is true. A career in writing begins with a sense that what has already been written, by others, has not been quite true enough; however revered, it lacks the latest information, the newest slant. As the careerist ages, the wave slips on, and he finds himself paddling in the foam-studded aftermath, indifferent to more and more fads and celebrities, failing to "get" more and more jokes in *The New Yorker.* Still, for truth he has his humanity and the stretch of history his lengthening life now includes. Art does not belong only to the young; far from it. What does belong to the young is the future, and with it the confidence that your instincts will be vindicated by future developments. You know what is true in your bones.

Untrue often means simply outmoded—the pieties of your fathers, foremost. These pieties may be a Presbyterian faith or a Socialist atheism, or a loyalty to this or that established political party, or to labor unions, laissez-faire economics, the American flag, or the planet Earth. To the bearer of the new truth, the old issues are not even worth debating; they are beside the point. The new point is not easy to locate. Boredom and indifference are more readily felt than excitement. But excitement is the Geiger counter to the new true—for instance, the pleasure that youngsters effortlessly take in the manipulated digitized imagery of computer games and MTV videos. Millions find a bliss of sorts in losing themselves in the vastness of the Internet, a phantom creation that sublimates the bulky, dust-gathering contents of libraries and supermarkets into something impalpable and instantaneous. The Web is conjured like the genie of legend with a few strokes of the fingers, opening with a phrase or two a labyrinth littered with trash, pitted with chat rooms, at once fascinatingly extensive and intensely private. Communication is antiseptically cleansed of all the germs and awkwardness of even the most mannerly transaction with another human body.

A mass retreat into a richly populated privacy has occurred before: in the acts of reading and of going to the movies. Excitement lay in both for my generation. Those of us who were young in the 1950s pored over the sacred, crabbed texts of Yeats and Eliot, Joyce and Pound, and of more ancient magi like Shakespeare, Donne, Milton, Pope, Keats, Dickens, and Browning. Their magic was to be extracted drop by drop and mixed with our own, still unanalyzed elixirs. I have yet to be persuaded that the information revolution is anything but an exercise in reading and writing wherein evanescent and odorless PC screens take the place of durable, faintly fragrant paper and ink. As to the movies—who of my generation did not seek his innermost self within the glittering, surging, world picture that cinema presented to its rapt receivers in the semidark? What was worthwhile and true was somehow there, coded in Gary Cooper's pale-eyed deadpan and Esther Williams' underwater smile.

This question of the true arrives at the end of a century whose first decades saw the theories of relativity and quantum mechanics undermine our intuitive grasp of matter. The subatomic microcosm and the outer space populated by receding galaxies both became impossibly strange, even as evidence relentlessly accumulated for the accuracy of the scientific world picture.

Materialism explains nearly everything now; only we, in our inner sense of ourselves, at the center of our ambitions and emotions, remain immaterial. In between preposterous cosmic immensities and madly multiple and elusive particles, human beings still seek to make sense of their lives. The unit of truth, at least for a fiction writer, is the human animal, belonging to the species Homo sapiens, unchanged for at least 100,000 years. A Cro-Magnon man, properly shaved, dressed, and educated, could be the CEO of a cutting-edge software company. He could be the man sharing your seat on the commuter train. He has our intelligence and physical appearance; the culture of Cro-Magnon times—its cave paintings and ritual mutilations and altars of aurochs' skulls—catered to the same species as does contemporary culture, with its rock concerts and art museums and book reviews by Michiko Kakutani. Evolution moves more slowly than history, and much slower than the technology of recent centuries; surely sociobiology, surprisingly maligned in some scientific quarters, performs a useful service in investigating what traits are innate and which are acquired. What kind of cultural software can our evolved hard-wiring support? Fiction, in its groping way, is drawn to those moments of discomfort when society asks more than its individual members can, or wish to, provide. Ordinary people experiencing friction on the page is what warms our hands and hearts as we write.

One of the casualties of the electronic age is, perhaps, a sense of history, in its cyclical repetitions and organically gradual progress. To minds conditioned by the rapid electronic reflexes of the computer and its allied entertainments, the end of the world is a flicker away, around the corner, and the significant past happened just yesterday. Compared to virtual reality, actual reality is sluggish. The patient virtues of the rural village make a hard sell even in the year of a presidential campaign. But is every novelty around us really unprecedented and radically transformative? Was not bioengineering, for instance, carried on by the prehistoric New World farmers who developed corn out of wild maize, and by the hunting and sheepherding tribesmen who tamed and split the wild wolf into the astonishing variety of breeds of dog? Can family values, so-called, and the morality of social interdependence, be banished by a tap of the DELETE button, or do they sturdily spring from our basic biological makeup, which includes an instinctive, self-serving decency? Is our sense of the true foisted upon us by disintegrating tyrannies of the air, or does it spring from the ineluctable necessity of our creative selves? The root sense of the word, from the old English *trēowe*, is not "not false" but "faithful." The fair maiden will be true to her knight; he will stay true to his principles. Amid so much electronic clutter and chatter in this disheveled, oversupplied, desperately commercial world, the human organism compels us to remain faithful to truth or else fall into ill health and spiritual discordancy. Freed by technology from exercise, we re-embrace it for the body's sake; freed by science from the fear of a wrathful God, we seek the peace, the relief from competitive striving, that religion brings.

Freud defined happiness as the relief of tension. To be human is to be in the tense condition of a death-foreseeing, consciously libidinous animal. No other earthly creature suffers such a capacity for thought, such a complexity of envisioned but frustrated possibilities, such a troubling ability to question the tribal and biological imperatives.

So conflicted and ingenious a creature makes an endlessly interesting focus for the meditations of fiction. It seems to me true that Homo sapiens will never settle into any utopia so complacently as to relax all its conflicts and erase all its perversity-breeding neediness. It also seems true that the human species is heading toward a planetary triumph as complete as that of corn in Iowa; the paved-over and wired-up earth will produce a single crop, people, plus what people eat, and there will be nothing left of nonhuman nature for contrast or enlivening metaphor. Monoculture of any sort is frightening, and an invitation to a sinister triumph of the microscopic; already, microbes are outbreeding our pesticides. But even in the dire eventuality foreshadowed by the growing, crushing spread of our poisonous cities, nature will live on, in our own anatomy and biochemistry, a fortress and a touchstone amid whatever further illusions and magnetic distractions technology breeds. The antediluvian angel-beast within us will hold true, and will continue to serve as the measure of all things.

JACQUES BARZUN

———⊰•⊱———

Wise Counsel

A historian's historian talks about something that never was

JACQUES BARZUN *has been a professor of history at Columbia University over the past 73 years. He has written more than 30 books, more recently the best-selling* From Dawn to Decadence.

A S A HISTORIAN, I am naturally, professionally, interested in truths—thousands of them—and this concern brings with it several kinds of puzzles.

The first is, of course, the disentangling of the muddled reports of the past. Another is how to describe faithfully what bygone ages took to be absolute truths, now disbelieved or forgotten. A third is what test of truth to apply in each case. The last and most baffling is to frame a clear idea of what truth actually is.

In any definition of truth, reality is mentioned or implied. What is said to be true must relate to something experienced and must state that experience accurately. Moreover, the whole vast store of recorded truths is supposed to hang together, and every new one must jibe with the rest of them as well.

These demands make up a tough assignment, and when one looks at any sizable portion of these claims to truth, one keeps finding a good many more to challenge than to adopt. An obvious sign of this truth is the amount of nonstop arguing and fighting in the world. Human beings, individually and in groups, are sure that they possess the truth about things here and hereafter, and when they see it doubted or attacked by their neighbors, such dissent is intolerable and must be put down.

There is, of course, an obvious exception to this chaos of thought and action. If one measures by the yardstick, then this piece of string is 28½ inches long. One can measure carelessly and make an error, but as soon as it is pointed out, one agrees with the correct answer. Other measures—the meter, the calendar, the clock, the number series, or any other system that rests on common agreement and fixed standards—yield statements that are not denied by anyone in his senses who is familiar with the terms.

These conventions are endlessly useful, both in science and in practical life. But there is a host of equally immediate and important concerns for which no system and no terms have been agreed upon. It is about these interests that the battle of ideas and the bloodshed take place. This in turn tempts one to think that these contested truths are the most important of all. They have to do with religion, art, morals, education, government, and the very definition of man and his nature, and his role in the universe.

A cultural historian's work brings him face to face with those passionately held ideas. At a certain time and place, millions of human beings felt absolutely sure that a divine revelation proved the existence of God, who dictated all men's beliefs and actions. The uniformity of that faith stamped it as unshakable truth.

After more than a thousand years, some of the descendants of those millions began to question the revelation and all it meant. Since then, there have been many different "truths" about it, each clung to with the same fervor and confidence as before. A like diversity runs through the rest of the culture—in morals, government, and the arts.

The only sure thing is that mankind is eager for truth, lives by it, will not let it go, and turns desperate in the teeth of contradiction. That may be a noble spectacle, but tragic too—and depressing. If, as required, all truths must hang together consistently, it would seem that in religion, art, and the rest, truth has never reigned. Human beings begin to look like incurably misguided seekers for something that never was.

At this point, a small but remarkable group of people put on a superior grin and say: "You forget the method that clears up all doubts and delivers truth on a platter. We scientists are busy taking care of your troubles. Look at what we have done: We have gotten rid of all the follies and superstitions dreamed up about the real world in the first 5,000 years of man's existence. Give us a little more time and we will mop up all the other nonsense still in your heads and give you cast-iron truth."

This sounds delightful, but even in those disciplines where exactness and agreement appear at their highest, there is a startling mobility of views. Every day—and this is no exaggeration—the truths of geology, cosmology, astrophysics, biology, and their sister sciences are upset. The earth is older than was thought; the dinosaurs are younger; the stars in huge galaxies have so much space they can't collide, yet they collide just the same; after being dry as dust, Mars has liquid water. The human bones in Central Africa do not mean what they were said to mean, and a new fossil shows the origin of birds to be entirely different from the view that was thought true yesterday. As for the speed of light, it can be exceeded. If only the latest is true, then all earlier ideas were hardly better than superstitions.

The condition is still worse in the semi-sciences of psychology and medicine, and confusion grows as we get to the social sciences, ethics, and theology. There are "schools" in each, the telltale sign of uncertainty. The boasts of an earlier day about finding "laws" governing society and predicting its future have been muted for some time. In history and philosophy, some wise heads have admitted that these laws are not exact transcripts but simply documented visions, respectively, of the past and of Being as a whole. None excludes other accounts of the same particular subject.

Practitioners of physical science rightly claim continual variation as a virtue. It avoids dogmatism and follows evidence. Everything is debated openly and widely. This is indeed very fine. But it also means that at any one moment there are "schools" in other kinds of research, and they form and re-form rapidly.

A number of scientists have taken time to ponder these puzzles of their own making and have offered two suggestions. One is that science is not description but metaphor. It seems a poor term. A metaphor needs four parts: in "the ship plows the ocean," the ship is likened to a plow and the ocean to a field. The facts and the language of science add up to two parts, not four. Perhaps the meaning is that science is not literal but poetic, its phrasings inspired by observation and calculation. That must be why we now come across the word *charm* and others like it in theoretical physics, a tacit recognition of its suggestive, poetical character.

If so, it also means that reality is beyond our grasp, and truth along with it. Such is, in fact, the other answer to the riddle, which is that there is no need for the idea of reality. From this negative it follows that we should stop being so solemnly intent on truth. Above all, we should stop fighting over tentative notions we believe in. Imagine instead that we are at a picnic, making up disposable fictions about what we see and feel. We then play with the jigsaw, but pieces are missing and others don't fit.

Where does that leave me as a historian who struggles to discover what happened in the past and to make of events and persons some intelligible patterns? First, I am not ready to throw reality into the trash can. I feel it ever present and call it by the more vivid term *experience.* It includes all my thoughts and feelings, the tabletop and the electrons, light as waves and as particles, the current truths and the past superstitions.

The common task, I conclude, is to place each of these within its sphere and on its level; they are incompatible only under a single-track system. One must, moreover, be ready to deal with new paradoxes and contradictions, because experience is neither fixed nor finished; it grows as we make it by our restless search for truth. Truth is a goal and a guide that cannot be dispensed with. The all-doubting skeptics only pretend to do without it.

But we must recognize that our work to attain truth succeeds only piecemeal. Where our hope of truth breaks down is at the stage of making great inferences from well-tested lesser truths. Still, we cannot help inferring. Our love of order impels us to make theories, systems, sets of principles. We need them both for comfort and for action. A society, however pluralist, needs some beliefs in common and will not trust them unless they are labeled truths. It is there that our efforts betray us. Sooner or later, experience jabs us with an event, a feeling, or a perception that shatters the truth-value of the great inferred idea. It is like actually going to the moon or prospecting the planets with a sensor and finding that the entirely logical and satisfying inference is dead wrong. As the historian knows, the breakup of old truths is painful, often bloody, but it does not condemn the search for truth and its recurrent bafflement, which are part of man's fate. It should only strengthen tolerance and make us lessen our pretensions. Just as in the past man was defined as the rational animal and later comers said, "No—only capable of reason," so man should not be called seeker and finder of truth but fallible maker and reviser of truths.

VIRGINIA POSTREL

⟶◆⟶

Mine Eyes Deceive Me

Is the Internet bringing the world into sharper focus?

VIRGINIA POSTREL *is the editor at large of* Reason *magazine and the author of* The Future and Its Enemies: The Growing Conflict Over Creativity, Enterprise, and Progress. *Her next book is on the growing importance of aesthetics.*

WE LIVE, writes a critic, in the "Age of Falsification," filled with surfaces we cannot trust. Some are digital creations. Others, from ad slogans to plastic surgery, are not. But the problem is pervasive: Our civilization's artifacts are deceptive, fake, inauthentic, a pack of lies. Today, the whole world is a theater.

No wonder Shakespeare is experiencing a revival. His plays—and his times—were so obsessed with appearance and reality that one of my professors used to refer to the theme as "your basic A&R." Boys pretending to be girls pretending to be boys. In Shakespeare's world, characters cannot trust their senses.

Is the ghost in *Hamlet* true and truthful, or is it a demon, tempting young Hamlet into murderous sin? Is Juliet dead or merely sleeping? Does Lear really stand at the edge of a great cliff? Or has the Fool deceived him to save his life?

The theater itself is a lie. Its deaths are mere special effects. Its tales never happened. Even the histories are distorted for dramatic effect. The theater is unnatural, a place of imagination. But the theater tells the audience something true: that the world requires judgments. You cannot believe everything you see or hear. *Othello* is the tragedy of a man who trusts the wrong source and thus misunderstands what he sees.

Nature alone, to some, seems true. But is it? Nature, too, must be interpreted. Imagination, declared Shakespeare's contemporary, Sir Philip Sidney, is a triumph, a creative act in emulation of man's Creator. The poet "goeth hand in hand with Nature, not enclosed within the narrow warrant of her gifts, but freely ranging within the zodiac of his own wit." This was, in Sidney's day, a controversial stance.

It is in ours as well. All that is different is the technological context. Today's cultural critics, heirs to Plato and the Puritans, don't attack poetry. They attack new media. But the attack and its targets are not new. Some eras are acutely aware that the truth is hard to discern. Others are complacent.

We got so used to the old technologies that we forgot their capacity for deception. We believed photography was "real," as though World War II literally happened in black and white. We forgot that selection creates its own biases. Despite evidence ranging from Soviet propaganda to the evening news, we believed that pictures—especially moving ones—never lied.

You can hear nostalgia for those good old days on almost any C-SPAN media panel, in which journalists from broadcast news and monopoly daily newspapers lament new media for degrading ethics. Ethics, in this context, means maintaining a uniform stance toward the audience and the issues—making judgments so the readers or viewers don't have to.

Like Galileo, born the same year as Shakespeare, we have new tools, and we see things we didn't see before. "In our time," wrote Galileo, "it has pleased God to concede to human ingenuity an invention so wonderful as to have the power of increasing vision four, six, 10, 20, 30, and 40 times, and an infinite number of objects which were invisible, either because of distance or extreme minuteness, have become visible by means of the telescope."

Appearance now suggests a more complex reality. The Internet exposes a diversity of opinion, experience, and taste we'd been led to believe didn't exist. If you were unusual in 1950 or 1980—and everyone is unusual in one way or another—you were an isolated anomaly. Now you're a Web ring, a Yahoo category. But that still doesn't mean we can trust what you say.

Like Shakespeare's art and Galileo's telescope, the Internet reminds us that the world is not only complicated and diverse but also requires more discernment. We cannot believe everything we see, hear, or read because what we see, hear, and read is contradictory and potentially false. Even our senses can deceive us.

We live, says author Kurt Andersen, in an era of "magic realism." Dinosaurs march through movie landscapes, and dead actors are morphed into TV commercials. These deceptions don't bother us anymore. We know they are part of an act, and we enjoy it.

But we are nonetheless anxious, fearful of manipulation, and the worry shows up in our art. Politicians saw only the movie's violence, but *The Matrix* was an artistically powerful meditation on your basic A&R. That's why it was so popular.

The movie's relevance to the Columbine shootings wasn't in the gun battles and the long black coats. It was in what the movie said about the difficulty of figuring out the truth when reality is mediated and manipulated. Were the Columbine killers members of a "Trench Coat Mafia"? Are every school's weird kids killers in the making?

The mass media told one simple story, in which all the answers were yes. The Net, with its telescopelike ability to see the minute and distant, to discern what was once invisible, found contradictions. The stories on Slashdot and Salon were more complex and ultimately more trustworthy than the nightly news. The newspapers eventually followed, mostly too late to change the first impressions. Journalists, too, must make judgments about which leads to chase, whom to trust, what makes a story. Their senses, and their prejudices, can mislead them.

"Free your mind," preached *The Matrix*. A start, but just a slogan, and not much of a guide. Look through your telescope yourself, but what do you see? The challenge is in interpretation, in judgment. Are sunspots "an illusion of the telescope," or perhaps undiscovered planets hovering around a pristine and perfect star? Nature, unadorned by reason and imagination, may be "true," but it is also incomprehensible. Galileo was a master not only of observation but also of imagination and argumentation. The truths he uncovered were not easy to discern.

Appearance and reality do not come with labels. Confronted with new tools, new cultures, new ways of telling stories, we are shaken from the complacent assumption that truth is simple and obvious. We grow anxious. We ask questions. The pursuit can make us as crazy as

Hamlet or as creative as Galileo. Either way, the search starts with a truth we forget at our own peril. There are indeed more things in heaven and earth than we once dreamed—and we must inspect every one of them through the lens of our imagination.

REYNOLDS PRICE

Dear Harper

A letter to a godchild about god

REYNOLDS PRICE, *a Rhodes scholar, is currently James B. Duke Professor of English at Duke University. His novel* A Long and Happy Life *won the William Faulkner Award in 1962.*

IT'LL BE SOME YEARS before you read this, if ever. But given the uncertainties of all our futures, I'll set it down here at the time of your baptism and will hope that—should you ever need it—it will be legible still. Since you're under the age of 2, chances are slim that you'll feel the need for well more than a decade. By then the 21st century will be thoroughly under way. Since it's likely to move as unforeseeably as the 20th, I'll make no effort to predict how the world will feel then about religious faith.

And I certainly won't guess at what your own relation to faith may be, though your parents and godparents have vowed to guide you toward it. Those adults have old ties to churches, though those ties vary. Above all, none of us who know you in the bright wonder of your laughing, open-armed childhood can begin to imagine who you'll be and where you'll want—or need—to go in your youth or your maturity. So here, by way of a gift, are some thoughts that may interest you in time.

As I write, in the spring of 2000, a large majority of the world's people say that they're religious. This year, for instance, 84% of the residents of the United States identified themselves as Christian, associates in the world's largest religion. What did they mean by their claim? The *Oxford English Dictionary* says that religion is:

Belief in, reverence for, and desire to please, a divine ruling power; the exercise or practice of rites or observances implying this.

Most Americans today would agree, and I'd suggest only one change. Instead of "divine ruling power," I'd substitute "supreme creative power." And I'd wonder if it mightn't be desirable to strip the definition to its bones—"religion is the belief in a supreme creative power." But perhaps those bones define the word *faith* more adequately than the word *religion.*

I hope you'll be interested to know that I—near the start of a new millennium and at the age of 67—am still able to believe, with no serious effort, that the entire universe was willed into being by an unsurpassed power whom most human beings call God. I believe that God remains conscious of his creation and interested in it. I believe that his interest may be described, intermittently at least, as love (and I say "his" with no strong suspicion that he shares qualities with the earthly male gender).

Whether he's attentive to every moment of every human's life, as some religions claim, I'm by no means sure. But I do believe that he has standards of action that he means us to observe. I believe that he has communicated those standards—and most of whatever else we know about his transcendent nature—through a few human messengers and through the mute spectacles of nature in all its manifestations, around and inside us (the human kidney is as impressive a masterwork as the Grand Canyon).

God created those spectacles many billion years ago and began to send those messengers, to this planet at least, as long ago as 4,000 years, maybe earlier. Those messengers are parents and teachers, prophets and poets (sacred and secular), painters and musicians, healers and lovers; the generous saints of Hinduism, Judaism, Buddhism, Christianity, Islam, and a few other faiths—all the deep feeders of our minds and bodies. One of the matchless gifts of our present life lies in the fact that those messengers continue to come, though the task of distinguishing valid messages from the false or merely confused is hard and often dangerous. At least one of those messengers, I believe, was in some mysterious sense an embodiment of God; and it's to him—Jesus of Nazareth—that you were recently dedicated.

Finally, I believe that some essential part of our nature is immortal. The core of each of us is immune to death and will survive forever.

Whether we'll experience that eternity as good or bad may depend upon the total record of our obedience to God's standards of action. Most of the long-enduring faiths say that we accumulate the weight of our wrongs—our sins, our karma—and will ultimately be confronted with that weight.

A wide lobe of my brain finds it difficult to believe that the maker of anything so immense as our universe—and of who knows what beyond it—is permanently concerned with how I behave in relation to my diet (so long as I'm not a cannibal), or my genitals (as long as they don't do willful damage to another creature), or my hair (so long as it doesn't propagate disease-bearing vermin), or a good deal else that concerns many religious people.

God likely cares how I treat the planet Earth, its atmosphere, and its nonhuman inhabitants (I think it's possible that he wants us not to kill or eat other conscious creatures, though I'm a restrained carnivore who feels no real guilt). Above all, the Creator intends that I honor my fellow human beings—whoever and from wherever—and that I do everything in my power never to harm them and to alleviate, as unintrusively as possible, any harm they suffer. God likely expects me to extend that honor to other forms of life, though how far down the scale that honor is to run, I don't know—surely I'm not meant to avoid killing, say, an anthrax bacillus.

Though I've mentioned that a preponderance of Americans presently share some version of my beliefs, it's fair to tell you that a possible majority of the social class I've occupied since my mid-20s— those who've experienced extensive years of academic training— don't share my beliefs nor hold any other beliefs that might be called religious. That characteristic of the intellectual classes of the Western world and China (at a minimum) is more than a century old and is the result largely of a few discoveries of the physical sciences and of the worldwide calamities of war and suffering that have convinced many witnesses that no just God exists.

My own educational credentials include 19 years of formal schooling. I've likewise read extensively in the literatures of many cultures that are not my own. How then can I explain my defection, in the matter of faith, from the doubts or flat rejection of so many in my social class? And am I suggesting that the reasons for my defection should have any weight with you, if you should face a crossroads of belief and rejection, at whatever point in your life?

In fact, I haven't defected. Put plainly, I have never held all the central dogmas of my caste. I received the rudiments of my faith long before I began to read or attend school. And while that faith has undergone assaults—from myself and others—it's never buckled. To be honest, I've sometimes been suspicious of that apparent strength. Shouldn't anyone who's lived as long as I, on two continents, and who's sustained more than one maiming catastrophe, have felt occasional very dark nights? Well, of course I have; but they've been dark nights of the sort described by the Spanish monk and poet St. John of the Cross—certain souls may feel God's absence as a form of near desperation, but that pain (which may last a very long while) never tumbles finally into disbelief.

Note that I said just above that I received the rudiments of faith. They came from the usual sources—my parents and other kin, the natural world around me (which tended to be rural or wooded suburban) and from God and his various messengers. To say that much, here and now, runs the severe risk of pomposity, an absurd degree of self-love, and a ludicrous elitism. Yet I know of no more accurate way to describe a situation that's far from uncommon.

My preparation for faith likely began with the gift of two Bible storybooks—one from my Grandmother Price when I was 2 or 3, the second a year or so later from my parents. They proved to be long-range endowments for the only child I then was (my brother was born just as I turned 8). Each of the books contained strikingly realistic illustrations; and with a small amount of guidance from my parents, I launched myself on an early fascination with the prime characters and stories from Hebrew and Christian sacred texts—Abraham, Isaac, and Sarah; Ruth and Naomi; David, Jonathan, and Saul; Samson and Delilah; Joseph, Mary, and Jesus; Jesus and the girl he raises from the dead; Jesus himself rising from the dead.

At about the same time I began occasionally to go to Sunday school with my father; and there I glimpsed the fact that those stories meant something important to other men, women, and children. I must likewise have begun to sense how vital this thing—whatever it was—was to my father. It would be years before I understood that he was, at just that time, withdrawing from years of alcoholism. And in the absence of Alcoholics Anonymous in our part of the world, help for him could only have come from my mother, his minister, and his own tenacious will to quit (he'd reached the age of 33 before beginning his battle).

When I was 6 years old, we lived on the edge of a small town. Within roaming distance for me were thickets of pine with plentiful birds, rabbits, foxes, possums, and raccoons; and there was a small stream filled with crawfish, toads, turtles, minnows, and snakes. I spent countless solitary and silent hours exploring that teeming world. And there I began to store up an invaluable sense of the endless inventiveness of life and the savage conditions of so much animal existence. In those same woods, I even found and saved my first flint arrowheads from long-vanished Indians. The simple endurance of those shaped stones helped me further onward with their intimations of the doggedness, and yet the frailty, of human life.

Then late one afternoon, still alone but blissful in that world, I was given my first visionary experience. I'm still convinced it came from some inhuman force outside my own mind and body. And though it would be years before I knew it, it was a vision of a kind experienced by more than a few lucky children. In brief, in a single full moment, I was allowed to see how intricately the vast contraption of nature all around me—and nature included me, my parents a few yards away in the house, and every other creature alive on Earth—was bound into a single huge ongoing wheel by one immense power that had willed us into being and intended our futures, wherever they led.

We were all, somehow, one vibrant thing; and even the rattlesnakes, the lethal microbes, and the plans of men like Adolf Hitler (whom I'd heard of from my father; it was 1939) were bound with the rest of us toward a final harmony. At the age of 6, of course, I couldn't have described it in such words; but memory tells me that the description is honest. And there that day, in the core of a much-loved but often unaccompanied childhood, it seemed a benign revelation.

While it didn't result in an immediate certainty that God exists and knows me and tends me, it left me watchful for further intimations. And in some way that I've only just realized six decades later, it became the first private knowledge of my life. I never mentioned what I'd suddenly learned, not to my parents nor to any child I knew and trusted. My life as a largely solitary mystic had begun.

I don't recall other such climactic moments in my childhood. But my interest in Bible stories continued; and because at the age of 9 I won a free New Testament for bringing a new member to Sunday school, I eventually began to read the Christian scriptures directly, not in someone else's version. Above all, the four Gospels interested me with their varying but complementary pictures of a man as mysterious and potent, yet credible, as Jesus. For reasons I can't explain, Jesus became one of the figures I often thought about and drew pictures of, along with Tarzan and King Arthur.

Since I was then hoping to become a painter in my adult life, I was also increasingly aware of the towering presence in Western art of Jesus at every stage of his short, and brilliantly depictable, life. In a way that it may be difficult for you to imagine years from now, the world around me—which was most of America from the 1930s onward—was as permeated with reverberations of the life of Jesus as the sea is with salt. For good or ill—and he's still outrageously invoked as the guarantor of hatred, violence, and endless fantasy—he was a constant component (even for those who entirely rejected him) of the air we breathed.

The fact that Jesus was also plainly a man who'd suffered and died for his acts made him more and more interesting to me as I entered adolescence and encountered the usual daunting amount of unhappiness. Mine, like so many others, came at the hands of a pair of school bullies. Like many boys who grew up in Christian cultures then, and perhaps even now, I spent a fair amount of secret time in prayer to Jesus. I'd ask for the meanness to stop and for kinder friends to materialize (my demons had once been my friends). It was my first acquaintance with unanswered, or partially answered, prayer. Other friends appeared but the bullies never relented till we moved from the town.

Somehow that partial success with prayer didn't stop me. I thought I'd heard the beginning of a dialogue. And life improved rapidly. Relations with my schoolmates in the new town were free of hostility, and I made a handful of friends who've lasted. But almost anyone's adolescence, as you may know by the time you read this, is subject to frequent attacks of self-doubt and melancholy, even bouts of hopelessness. Life sometimes seems too bleak to continue. Why should young people believe that things change—and often for the better? They've frequently had little experience of such improvements.

I don't recall ever plunging so low; but still I went on investing a fair amount of time in prayers to Jesus and his mother (a beautiful Catholic girl had taught me the rosary, and it became a part of my attempts at reaching and persuading the Creator and—what?—his household). And in the absence of the old tormentors who'd even made churchgoing difficult, I began attending church—my mother's Methodist and my father's Baptist. The Methodist minister took an interest in my developing curiosities about the historical Jesus and the origins of Christianity; and he readily agreed to what must have seemed peculiar requests from a boy—requests for private communion at times when I needed special help, like college scholarship competitions.

By age 17 I clearly had some sort of vocation for a life with regular attempts at persuading God's attention and cooperation. I don't think my daily behavior looked unusually "holy," and I don't recall that my parents or my minister ever mentioned the possibility. But toward the end of high school, one of my teachers suggested that I think of preparing for life as a pastor. Though by then I'd joined the Methodist church, I felt at once that the idea was wrong. My sexual energies and their direction seemed far too powerful and heretical for such a career. In any case I'd already decided on the parallel careers I've ultimately followed—life as a writer and a teacher—and as I moved on to college, I headed for those choices.

As I worked even more steadily at my undergraduate studies and my writing (especially poetry)—and as I began to express my sexual needs—I slowly began to feel less compelled toward the public worship I'd enjoyed for the past few years. I'd begun to suspect that a yen for display played a part in public worship, especially my own. Yet despite my involvement in a number of academic courses that questioned, and occasionally mocked, the foundations of religious thought, my withdrawal from church represented no loss of the faith that had grown as I grew.

My withdrawal was likewise a response to my increasing awareness of the hostility or indifference of all major American churches to the coming crises in racial justice and sexual tolerance. Most honestly, though, I was returning to a means of worship that was more natural for me: private prayer, reading, and meditation, and the beginnings of a comprehension that the chief aim of any mature religious life is union with the will of God, as opposed to one's own, and the finding of ways to assist other creatures.

My first year of graduate study in England, where study is largely self-monitored, marked also my launching on a near full-time dedication to my writing and on my first real delight in reciprocated love. In the chilly atmosphere of one of the oldest colleges at Oxford and the beautiful 13th century chapel whose emptiness echoed the rapid expiration of Protestant Anglicanism, it was easy enough not to seek out a congenial church, and my sense of the Creator—of the duties I might owe him and the means of communicating with him—continued on the solitary track to which they'd reverted. Yet in normal human fashion, I was now praying mainly when I needed quick help.

I felt mild guilt at my separation from a religious community, especially when my mother or my old minister inquired about my British churchgoing. But I told myself I'd made a necessary choice. I imagined I'd learn to locate—through my teaching and writing—communities where my own questions and whatever useful findings I might make could be best conveyed to others, potentially a wider community than I might have found in a dedicated building and a congregation.

In retrospect, I estimate that my subsequent years of work may have communicated to a few thousand readers and a few thousand students how one relatively lucid and respectably educated man, in the final two-thirds of the 20th century and somewhat thereafter, has managed to live at least six decades of a life that (while it's committed a heavy share of self-intoxicated incursions on others and has broken at least five of the Ten Commandments) has so far hurled no dead bodies to the roadside, abandoned no sworn partners or children, and has managed to turn up—shaved and sober—in a writing office, a teaching classroom, a kinsman's or lover's or friend's place in time of need on most promised occasions.

I've been especially chary of broaching discussions of my relations with God in the arenas of either of my careers, in books or in classrooms. That's partly because, by nature, I'm among the world's least evangelical souls but also because my own beliefs were acquired so gradually, and in response to such personal tides, as to be almost incommunicable if not incomprehensible. In recent years, however, I've relaxed a little in that reluctance.

I've spoken of my faith in two volumes of memoirs, a number of poems, and a published letter to a dying young man who asked for my views; and I'm writing this new letter to you. After more than 30 years of teaching Milton's *Paradise Lost,* I've begun, very lightly, to confess to my students that I'm a renegade Christian and that they might be at a certain advantage in studying a Christian poet with me. Wouldn't they like to study Homer with, say, an actual Zeusian?

So my life has gone through youth and middle age. It was normally subject, as I've said, to serious wrongdoing. And it was frequently challenged by disappointment and at least one bitter remorse. Throughout—despite several deep dives into self-blame and the sporadic lack of any clear view ahead—my faith has been the prime stabilizer. Like many other navigational aids, it's done most of its work when I had only the dimmest awareness of its service.

Then, when I was 51, I found myself having difficulties walking. After a few weeks of denial, I was discovered to have a large and intricately entangled cancer of the spinal cord. Despite surgery, with the best technology of the early 1980s, the tumor couldn't be removed; and no chemotherapy was available. The only medical hope was five weeks of searing radiation, directly to the fragile cord. I was warned that such a brutal therapy might leave me paraplegic or worse. The alternative, however, was to wait while the tumor paralyzed my legs, then my arms and hands, and finally my lungs. With no other imaginable choice, I agreed to the radiation.

A few mornings before the daily treatments were to start, I was propped wide awake in bed at home, when I experienced the second visionary moment of my life, some 46 years after my childhood glimpse of the unity of nature. I've written about this second moment in other places. Enough to say here that I was, suddenly and without apparent transport, in a different place—by the Sea of Galilee—and a man whom I knew to be Jesus was washing and healing the long wound from my failed surgery, the site of my coming radiation.

My conviction, since that second vision, is that the experience was in some crucial sense real. In that moment I was healed, and the fact that my legs were subsequently paralyzed by radiation two years before a new ultrasonic device made the removal of the tumor possible, the tumor was merely a complexity in the narrative that God intended. There does seem a possibility that, had I avoided the withering radiation, I might have been healed in any case. My doctors felt that, along with its damage, the radiation had stalled the tumor for a lucky while.

I'm aware that many of my contemporaries will read such a statement as groundless, if not howling crazy, and I can all but share their laughter. Yet 16 years after my initial diagnosis, I'm an energetic man working when virtually none of my therapists thought I had a serious chance (one of them told my brother that I had 18 months at best). And since I've mentioned my healing in print, I've had dozens of letters from patently sane strangers who confide similar transcendent experiences in a time of crisis.

They mostly describe an experience in which some entirely real figure, whether Jesus or some matter-of-fact plainclothes angel, comes and consoles or heals them. Such confidences almost always end with their telling me that they'd mentioned their experience to no one else for fear of ridicule. My correspondents also generally say that their experience, like mine, was singular—that is, never repeated, thereby eliminating the possibility that we'd all been merely cheering ourselves with pleasant dreams in the face of calamity.

My moment by the Sea of Galilee occurred 16 years ago and has not recurred in any form. Those years have brought me an unprecedented amount of work—21 books since the cancer—and an outpouring of affection and meticulous care of a sort I wouldn't have allowed myself to expect from kin, friends, and strangers. In addition to the books, I've continued my regular schedule of teaching. I've traveled for business and for pleasure more than in my able-bodied life. And those changes have only deepened my certainty that my illness—its devastations and its legacies of paralysis and chronic pain—was intended for me at that point in my life and perhaps ever after.

What the ultimate intention of such a blow may be, I barely guess at. Time, or beyond, will presumably uncover as much of that mystery as I'll ever need to know. I can say, however, that the drastic reversal led me to abandon certain choices that I'd always explored with both pleasure and uncertainty of purpose. I've made that simplification because I've slowly come to suspect that a curbing of past choices was intended. And while this new course has left me deprived of a few physical rewards, I've all but ceased to miss them. If nothing else, paraplegia either leads to a rapid refining of human focus and one's ex-

pectations from other creatures or it plunges its cripple into queru-
lous, or wailing, neurosis or worse.

Yet now I've outlived both my parents; and though I'm nearly 70,
I'm hopeful of as much more time as I have work to do, the resources
with which to do it, and the help I need in my straitened circumstances. My relations with God run a fairly normal course. They in-
tensify when I'm in trouble; and when things go smoothly, they tend
to resemble the domestic relations of family members—a good deal
of taking-for-granted on my part, with a dozen or so snatches of prayer
per day (mostly requests to understand God's intent, if any; to learn
patience, to bear what I can't change and then to incorporate it). I'm
aware of no substantial fears of age or death, though I won't say I welcome either prospect. And I have no doubt that the usual calm I live
in—and here I tap on the nearest wood—comes as a form of mercy
from whatever force created the world and knows of me in it.

Can I expect that spotty run through 60-some years of faith to be
of any weight for you, years from now, or for anyone else to whom religious belief is either a baffling phenomenon, an inviting curiosity, or
an intellectually impossible position? From a friend, I might hope for
the patience required to read these pages—something less than an
hour. But I can hardly expect it to be convincing or even comprehensible for unbelieving strangers. One of the characteristics of faith that
can seem so repellent is the apparent necessity that faith be given help
from God. The most sophisticated theologies of the Western past—
millennia of rabbinical debate, the treatises of Augustine, Aquinas,
Calvin, and Barth—deduce a similar necessity.

The leap of faith that believers so often recommend is preceded by
a serious hitch. It almost invariably requires God's presence, on the
far side of the abyss, saying, "Jump!" In Christianity, anyhow, Calvin-
ists agree. God calls certain creatures to believe in him and thus win
salvation; others he simply permits to live and die in preordained
damnation. It's another idea that looks absurd to anyone who has not
been inclined to faith by a propitious early atmosphere and training.
For me, as for more than a few writers of the early Christian documents comprised in the New Testament, that terrible prior choosing
by God seems at times the baldest deduction from attentive witness
of the world.

How can anyone reared in the desert air of contemporary science—physics seems the most relevant science—even begin to move in the murky direction of faith, especially when so many manifestations of religious faith lead to violence, disdain, if not outright hatred, and dithering or murderous nonsense? In any day's news, half the world's human wrongs are done in God's name. That one obstacle to faith, if no other, is all but impassably high. (Yet, again, the majority of human beings claim some form of faith.)

It's my seasoned instinct, then, that any slow scrutiny of contemporary science will demonstrate at many points its intellectual inadequacy as an ample chain of theories to explain the face and the actions of the world. Thus Isaac Newton, who in many ways invented modern science, was a fervently convinced believer; and physics, here at the beginning of the third millennium, is uncovering at a breathtaking rate subatomic phenomena that surpass the imaginings of the wildest hierophant scraping his sores with a cast-off potsherd.

That's not to claim that anyone should fling posthaste into the arms of an invisible God or any religious cult simply because science has proven so prissily bankrupt as a guide to what's here and what's there (here and there seem increasingly to be the same thing). Helium-filled New Age unfortunates are steadily chattering away on television to warn us about that. Yet if nothing else, an honest, well-informed creature must now acknowledge that the world—the universe of physical objects, forces, and actions above, within, or below the range of human or instrumental vision—far surpasses in extent and wonder what we can see and absorb.

But if anyone with a persistent curiosity about faith, anyone who has lacked a sane early grounding in one of the central faiths of his or her culture, were to ask me where to go to begin to understand the inevitability of belief and its mixed rewards (faith is more difficult than unbelief), I'd suggest two initial courses, each to be pursued with quiet steadiness. First, begin to read the sacred texts of your native culture. For the majority of Americans, those texts would include the Christian Bible (which includes the Hebrew scriptures).

Simultaneously, begin to read the thoughts of the great believing minds. For you, friend, those would include a concentration on the actual words of Jesus as preserved in the four Gospels of Matthew, Mark, Luke, and John and then an awareness of the lives and works of figures (among hundreds) such as Francis of Assisi, Søren Kierkegaard, Albert

Schweitzer, Simone Weil, W.H. Auden, Dorothy Day, and Flannery O'Connor.

Second, considering that your family will have reared you in a world deep in the knowledge and the resonance of the arts, I'd urge you and others to immerse yourself in the lives and works of the great believing musicians and painters—such witnesses as the preservers of Gregorian chant, Giotto and Michelangelo, Palestrina, Rembrandt, Bach and Handel, Mozart and Beethoven, Van Gogh and Rouault, Messiaen and Pärt. None of those believers was a fool nor a mere hired hand of the pope nor some prince with an idle and unadorned chapel.

On the contrary, the inspiration of their work, the craft it employs, the makers' surviving personal statements, show them to be intellectually and emotionally tough-minded and trustworthy—and I've omitted the whole world of poetry, which is, if anything, even more bountiful than music and painting. The same advice can be given for virtually all the world's religions, freighted as they are with glorifications of the mystery and presence and the dreaded absence of God, though the artists of Judaism and Islam (because of their prohibitions against the portrayal of living things) have brilliantly concentrated their findings in such nonvisual forms as prophecy, poetry, and music.

While you're reading and listening, you might want to try—if you never have—speaking short sentences to the air around you (be sure no one is watching; people have been carted off for less). Call the air God if you can, though it's not a god; and state as honestly as possible some immediate need, some hope for guidance. With luck and further effort, your sentences will grow less self-obsessed. They may even begin to express occasional thanks. For long months you may get no trace of notice or reply. In time, however, you may hear answers on the same scale as that on which we measure the masters I've just named. And if an answer comes, you can be almost sure it wasn't simply the air that answered.

There are numerous possible next steps. You might want to begin frequenting spaces that have a natural benignity for you—whether it's the lobby of Grand Central Station or a quiet corner church or a one-man fire-watch tower high above some primal forest. You might begin to talk about your findings with some friend whom you suspect of having similar curiosities. You might commit some part of your time to working with the wretched of your neighborhood or town—the homeless, hungry, abused, the unloved whom most religions insist that we comfort. You might want to try attending some regular religious ceremonies. If they fail you, go back to yourself and the ambient air.

Soon or late, you'll likely get some response from that space to which you first spoke. It may say what it's said to many good people: "There's nothing here but atoms of air. Get a life." It may also say what it's said persuasively to even more of the earth's human beings: "Keep talking. Learn how. You're listened to. One day you may hear me, should I need or want you."

You may, in short—and finally, my valued young friend—have begun to speak with and to hear from the truth, some form of the truth that wears many masks for its likely sole face.

Yours in hope,
Reynolds

INDEX